W9-CPE-420

ALSO BY PACO UNDERHILL

*Why We Buy: The Science of Shopping*

# PACO UNDERHILL

# *CALL OF*

# THE MALL

## *How we shop*

**P**

PROFILE BOOKS

First published in Great Britain in 2004 by
PROFILE BOOKS LTD
58A Hatton Garden
London EC1N 8LX
*www.profilebooks.co.uk*

First published in the United States in 2004 by
Simon & Schuster, Inc.

Copyright © YOBOW, Inc., 2004

1 3 5 7 9 10 8 6 4 2

Printed and bound in Great Britain by
Clays, Bungay, Suffolk

The moral right of the author has been asserted.

All rights reserved. Without limiting the rights under copyright reserved above, no part of this
publication may be reproduced, stored or introduced into a retrieval system, or transmitted, in any form
or by any means (electronic, mechanical, photocopying, recording or otherwise), without the prior
written permission of both the copyright owner and the publisher of this book.

A CIP catalogue record for this book is available from the British Library.

ISBN 1 86197 442 6

*Generation 3 at Envirosell has been a good one.*

Jenny Bonilla

Bob Bowman

Robyn Cushing

Diana Dawson

Kerry Elsasser

Gustavo Gomez

Dave Guerdette

Delise Dupont Jackson

Mark Pingol

Hillary Ross

Adrienne Sforza

Jennifer Vondrak

# Contents

# CALL OF THE MALL

# Prologue

**W**HY ARE we here?
We're here to buy stuff.
We're here because we're bored.
We're here because tomorrow's Mother's Day.
We're here for the new Avril Lavigne CD.
We're here for emancipation.
We're here for lip gloss.
We're here because our mom made us come.
We're looking for sheets and towels.
We're looking for sex and love.
We're looking for self-esteem.
We're looking for jeans that fit.
We're here for our first business suit.
We're here because our daughter made us come.
We're here for a nice afternoon with the grandkids.
We're here for the food court.
We're here for the video arcade.
We're here for the movies.
We're here because it's pouring.
We're here to buy sneakers.
We're here because tomorrow's our anniversary.
We're here because he needs underwear.

1

We're here because she needs underwear.
We're here because everybody needs underwear.
We're here because there's nothing on TV.
We're here because it's fun!
We're here because our wife made us come.
We're here for no reason whatsoever.
We're looking for boys.
We're looking for girls.
We're looking for work.
We're looking to shoplift.
We're here because we love the mall!
We're here because everybody else is.
We're here because Christmas is coming.
We're here because Hanukkah is coming.
We're here because Kwanzaa is coming.
We don't know *why* we're here.
We're here to find . . . something.
We're here because *we're here*.

# Introduction

ARE WE really going to spend an entire book inside a mall?

Yes, we are.

It's not as though studying people as they congregate to buy and sell things is a totally frivolous or small-minded endeavor. Consider the history of our species, a fair swath of which has been propelled by merchants or their emissaries traveling to the far reaches of the planet, sometimes at great risk, in order to bring back stuff to peddle to the rest of us. As any schoolchild can testify, the romance of the ancient world teems with spice routes and trade winds and trafficking in silks and precious metals, frankincense and myrrh, gunpowder and fur. Theoretically, we could all grow our own food and make our own clothes and build our own houses. But it would be boring. So let's agree that the saga of humankind can be told at least in part through the story of shopping.

Surely, then, you'll concur that the sites of so much significant social activity might be worth a look now and then? We tend to think of the mall as a recent, primarily American phenomenon, and a rather banal one at that, born of demographic convenience—we all bought cars and moved to the 'burbs—rather than any profound change in who or what we are. But the mall has been with us always, under other names and in somewhat different forms. Virtually since the dawn of civilization, we have organized our world in part around the function of shopping.

3

Even the simplest agrarian societies needed places to assemble to trade in goods, and from that basic impulse came everything else—marketplaces, villages, towns, cities. The mall is, at heart, just an ancient organizing principle that hasn't yet outlived its usefulness. Perhaps it never will.

But it's also easy to forget how recent the enclosed regional shopping mall is, maybe because it has so quickly become such a mainstay of American life. The first one popped up (in Edina, Minnesota) a mere seven decades ago, and now malls are the dominant arena of American shopping, which is itself an economic force the likes of which the world has never known. Without even meaning to, the mall has transformed our country, and not always for the good. For one thing, it drew shoppers away from vulnerable towns and big cities, and when that happened, decline usually set in. But there's no guarantee that malls will be with us forever. In fact, some evidence points to just the opposite outcome.

What's that, you say? You're okay with shopping but not with the mall? A common condition. Many otherwise fair-minded, intelligent people scorn and despise malls. Some still end up shopping in them on a regular basis. But they're not proud of it. You of this opinion may not be swayed by arguments of how the mall is a contemporary version of the souks, bazaars, arcades, bourses, and markets of olden days. But by studying the mall and what goes on there, we can learn quite a lot about ourselves—about the state of the nation and its inhabitants—from a variety of perspectives: economic, aesthetic, geographic, spiritual, emotional, psychological, sartorial.

I might agree with those who say that some of the adventure and romance associated with trading has been lost along the way. Somehow, the glorious history of commerce has culminated in a sanitized architectural clichè in which you typically find not exquisite treasures and exotic wares but rather eighty different styles of sneaker or sixteen varieties of chocolate chip cookie. No wonder we look at the mall—at the ambition of it, at the reality, at that already obese teenager stuffing her jaw with a drooling Cinnabon—and we can't help but wonder: Is this the best we could do?

It's no surprise that the mall is such an easy target for American self-loathing in particular. It's a lot like television in that way: another totally fake environment that attempts to pass itself off as a true reflection of who we are and what we want. We disdain it, and yet we can't stop watching. Or shopping. Once in a while, TV fulfills its highest calling—when a man first lands on the moon, say, or during the Watergate hearings. But most of the time it contents itself with reruns of *Three's Company* and infomercials for the home rotisserie.

It's the same with the mall. It *could* be much better—more vivid, intelligent, adventurous, entertaining, imaginative, alive with the human quest for art and beauty and truth. But it's not.

It's the mall.

# 1 *America Shops*

WE'RE DRIVING toward the mall.

I spend a lot of time in malls. Too much, I think. I daydream of life on a ranch out west where I'd go to Wal-Mart every two weeks for groceries, and that would be it for me and shopping.

It will never happen.

You are riding with a tall, bald, stuttering research wonk on the cusp of his fifty-third year. I am called a retail anthropologist, which makes me uncomfortable, especially around my colleagues still in academia who have many more degrees than I do. For whatever combination of reasons, I've spent my adult life studying people shopping. I watch how they move through stores and other commercial environments— restaurants, banks, fast-food joints, movie theaters, car dealerships, the post office, concert halls. Even in church, I study people. It is an odd skill, not one I would have sought. Yet I am good at it, and it pays the bills. I can't imagine not doing it.

I am definitely not a shopper. I don't own lots of stuff. When I do buy, in spite of whatever professional knowledge I have, I perform like an ordinary guy.

I own a research and consulting business called Envirosell. We work with merchants, marketers, and retail bankers around the world. Our specialty is looking at the interaction between people and products, and people and spaces. We look at all the ways in which retailers, product manufacturers, bankers, restaurateurs, and commercial and other public spaces either meet (or fail to meet) their customers' needs. It is a niche business, but it's our niche. We've been doing it for almost twenty years.

Our home office is in a funky landmark building, a former hotel, in New York City, in the middle of what was the department store district at the turn of the nineteenth century. We have an old-fashioned manual elevator run by a guy named Billy. The company occupies the hotel's second-floor lobby. I sit in the old manager's office, which has a gas fireplace I have never used. My south-facing windows look out onto what was once a Lord & Taylor store. It's now a shop that sells fancy dishes. We also have offices in Milan, São Paolo, Mexico City, Tokyo, Moscow, and Istanbul.

We have done hundreds of research jobs in mall stores. There are only six states of the fifty where we haven't worked a mall (the Dakotas, Alaska, Montana, Wyoming, and Louisiana). I average 130 days a year away from home, nearly all of which are spent in retail settings. I have been inside about three hundred North American malls, and some in other countries—Canada, Argentina, Brazil, Mexico, the United Arab Emirates, Italy, France, Spain, Holland, Germany, Sweden, Finland, Britain, Norway, Portugal, Turkey, Australia, Japan, Korea, Malaysia, Hong Kong; the list goes on and on. If someone mentions a mall somewhere in the United States—the Galleria in Houston, say, or the Del Amo in L.A.—I can picture the place, whether I want to or not. There are more than one hundred American malls to which I could give you accurate driving directions off the top of my head. I don't know whether to be proud or ashamed.

Okay, look around.

We're getting close to the mall, but you'd never know it. There are no directional signs anywhere on this highway, as there might be if we were headed toward Disney World or New York City or some other destination. The mall itself isn't a looming, dominating presence, even on this flat suburban landscape. We're just about to pass the only marker, a smallish road sign directing us to our exit, but beyond that there's nothing to steer us toward the mall, no attempt to inspire an impulse purchase, no billboard aimed at the road-weary traveler with an hour or two to kill. A mall is a huge commercial entity, but it tends to appeal strictly to the local shopper, the one who is already familiar with it and what it has to offer.

It's *our* mall. Maybe you have a mall, too.

You see a lot of a community's life in its mall. Families especially tend not to be on display in very many public spaces nowadays. You can find people in places of worship, but they tend to be on their best behavior, and they're mostly just standing or sitting. Increasingly, cities are becoming the province of the rich, the childless, or the poor. I love cities. But America hasn't lived there for a long time. The retail arena is still the best place I know for seeing what people wear and eat and look like, how they interact with their parents and friends and lovers and kids. If you really want to observe entire middle-class multigenerational American families, you have to go to the mall.

It's also not a bad place to shop.

A French historian I like named Daniel Roche wrote a book called *A History of Everyday Things.* In it, he examines and reconstructs the lives not of kings, queens, and generals but of ordinary French people in the seventeenth and eighteenth centuries—what they ate, what they wore, what they knew, and how they acquired what knowledge and possessions they had. In the spirit of Daniel Roche, this book is not about the official history of shopping malls and the tycoons who build and manage them. This is about malls, stores, and parking lots as experienced by us consumers.

Studying shopping provides the rhythm that governs my life—pack, leave home, fly somewhere, pick up a rental car, check into a hotel, then drive to a mall or store. For myself and my colleagues, it's a life of science and research, except instead of going to an excavation site in Peru, we end up at Tyson's Corner, a mall outside Washington, D.C. It's an unusual way to make a living, and an even odder way of experiencing and understanding a time and place.

On the other hand, I never run out of socks.

The job has become a habit. If I have two hours to kill before a flight out of Dallas, I'll visit the Irving Mall or Outdoor World on my way to the airport. I don't know what I expect to find; but like any research geek, I'm constantly on the lookout for something I haven't seen before—some innovation in digital signage, or a new sneaker style, or an interesting way to manage the line at the cash register. If I'm on vacation and get bored with the beach, I'll find the nearest mall and spend an afternoon there. It's not *such* a weird thing to do. If I said I enjoy a stroll along Madison Avenue in Manhattan, where Armani and Calvin and Donna Karan sit cheek by jowl, you'd understand. Doing it at the Beverly Center in Los Angeles or Bluewater outside London isn't so different.

I remember the first big research project my company landed, studying AT&T stores in two suburban Chicago malls. Back then it was just me and a few freelance researchers out in the field. Over a four-month period, we studied several incarnations of the same basic store, which meant I practically lived in those malls. I'd arrive at the telephone store and arrange the time-lapse cameras to watch how shoppers interacted with the merchandise and displays. The film cassettes had to be changed every two hours, so I couldn't stray too far, but unlike my researchers, I didn't have to remain inside the store. Moreover, I felt it was my responsibility not to appear in my own research footage. As a result, I spent many days roaming those malls— from ten A.M. to ten P.M. without a single productive thing to do except change film. I went into every store. I didn't buy much, but I saw a lot.

My fascination with stores is rooted in childhood. My father was a diplomat. As an offshore American raised in Third World nations and behind the Iron Curtain, my national identity was secondhand and based heavily on the Sears catalog. But to those around me, I was all-American. Sometimes I paid the price, like when I was beaten up on the street in Warsaw after the Bay of Pigs in 1961, or when rocks were thrown at our car in Seoul. When the kids in the British Army School I attended in Malaya chose sides for playground games, it often wound up as the few Americans against the rest of the world.

Still, to me America was always a far-off, mystical place, familiar yet completely exotic and fascinating. I wanted to feel connected to it, even long distance. When we'd return briefly to the States, I'd look at what the other kids were wearing, or playing with, or watching on TV, and realize how hopelessly out of it I was. It was painful to ask my grandmother to send me rock records, knowing that what she'd get would be awful, given her preference for Lawrence Welk. In Kuala Lumpur in 1963 there was no *American Bandstand* on TV, no T-shirts or lunch boxes. I was in cultural exile. My friend Steve was a little older than I and listened to a radio station he picked up from Bangkok. Thanks to him I knew that the Beatles existed, but that was about it.

Even today, that early cultural deprivation haunts my life. I am no good at the board game Trivial Pursuit, having missed too many cultural references from the 1960s and 1970s. I've had friends try to explain to me what was so hilarious about Rocky and Bullwinkle, or who the Waltons were, and why girls who favor Laura Ashley always liked *Little House on the Prairie.* I still don't get it.

Having gone from life abroad to living in downtown Manhattan, the shopping center was still an exotic locale, something I'd heard about but had little real exposure to. It's where, for the first time, I felt completely swallowed up inside white-bread middlebrow median-income America. It wasn't bad at all. I suddenly understood those 1980s émigrés from the Soviet Union who would come to this country and cry tears of joy over the splendor they found in the produce aisle of an average supermarket. At last I found what seemed to be the real America, and it was out shopping.

The morning of September 11, 2001, I was stranded in Dallas, unable to get home, which is a twenty-minute walk from what was the World Trade Center. On September 12 I spent the day wandering around the new mall in Plano, Texas. I just gravitated there. I needed to be around something familiar. It was the eeriest thing, though—a sparkling mall, in the middle of a beautiful September afternoon, with all the stores open and not a single shopper in the place. Around one-thirty I walked into a RadioShack and asked the clerk, "Am I the first person you've had in here today?"

"Yup," he said.

Strolling around got too lonely, so I decided to see a movie. I was just in time for *Tortilla Soup*. I was the only person in the theater. They screened it for me anyway. After the show I returned to my hotel, but I still had lots of time on my hands, so a few hours later I drove back to one of the mall's restaurants for dinner.

I was the only customer, but by the end of my meal the manager and the waiter had joined me at my table, and we three sat around drinking and talking, just the same as many people across the United States did that night. It felt all right to be doing it in a mall.

As I said before, I've devoted a lot of my life to malls, and in a few minutes we'll begin spending another Saturday in a typical one. We'll have lots of company.

Look up ahead—you *still* can't see it, but take my word, we're almost there.

# 2 *You Are Here*

ALMOST *where?*

We're going to spend today at a large regional enclosed mall, one of 1,175 in the United States at last count. Which specific mall we'll be visiting doesn't really matter, since the things we'll see and the lessons we'll learn apply to all. Therefore, I won't bother naming our destination, except to say it really does exist and it's a good one for our purposes.

But it's worth knowing a bit about the place and its history, since it *is* typical. This particular mall covers forty-six acres, including the parking lots. It is bordered and nourished by a six-lane state highway and a four-lane county road. We're in a suburb that's a twenty-minute drive (barring bad traffic) from a major metropolitan area. This is the largest mall in the immediate vicinity, although there is a slightly smaller one exactly four miles away. Both are owned by national commercial real estate development firms, companies with a history of aggressive competition with one another. So a certain degree of rivalry exists between the malls, although both thrive. Perhaps that's because each has its own personality. Ours is known for its high-end stores. The other is more solidly middle class. Not low-rent by any means, but not haughty, either.

Early in the twentieth century, the land under our mall was the estate of a wealthy local family. By the mid-twentieth century, the fortune and family were gone, and the plot was vacant. A developer bought it in the early 1950s and built a department store on the site. A decade or so later, some smaller stores were added around it, creating an ad hoc open-air shopping center. Three decades ago, a second department store was built on this parcel. Not long after, the developer announced plans to enclose the entire development under one roof—to turn it into a proper mall. It was an easy decision to make: In the early 1970s, *U.S. News & World Report* conducted a poll and found that adult Americans spent more time at malls than anywhere else except for home and work. This was in the feverish early stage of our love affair with malls, back when a few new ones opened every week and no suburb felt complete without at least one.

Turning the shopping center here into a mall involved a major construction project that went on while the existing stores remained open for business. Today, total gross leasable area in the complex is nearly 1.5 million square feet, which puts it among the top 2 or 3 percent of American malls—big, in other words, though still considerably smaller than the largest mall in North America (Canada's Edmonton Mall, over 5 million square feet) or the United States (Mall of America, in Bloomington, Minnesota, over 4 million square feet).

Our mall reeks of money—inside we'll see acres of marble, in tasteful shades of tan, brown, and white. The flooring is tile. There's a glassed-in elevator. There are 144 stores. Befitting its middle- to upper-middle-class market, there's a Versace and a Ralph Lauren, a Cartier and a Tiffany, a Nordstrom and a Saks. There's also a Gap, an Abercrombie & Fitch, a Victoria's Secret, but no Spencer Gifts. The biggest single category is women's apparel, which is also the mainstay of every other mall in the world. There's a record store, a toy store, a video game store and nine stores selling sneakers. There must be close to twenty places to buy cosmetics, if you include the department stores and the boutiques that sell it as a sideline. There's a beauty parlor with big, old-fashioned hair dryers that look like something out of a science-fiction movie.

There's also a fourteen-screen cinema at which, this weekend, two screens are devoted to the new Jackie Chan movie. (I can't wait.) There's a video arcade. There's a rock-climbing wall. There's an Aqua Massage, which requires more explanation than I can pause for here. (But maybe we'll give it a whirl later.) There are three national chain sit-down restaurants, all civilized affairs, serving food that's utterly acceptable. There's a food court, a vast, high-ceilinged arena offering no fewer than forty different outlets, mostly fast food. There's a funny little 1950s-style hamburger joint, Johnny Rockets, in which the waitstaff, a bunch of listless teenagers in dingy uniforms, are required to perform a line dance several times an hour. It's hilarious and distressing, and I recommend it highly. There's a Cinnabon stand, four cookie stands, three pretzel stands, three ice-cream stands, and no place wheresoever to buy an apple.

There's no bookstore, hardware store, home electronics store, computer store, sporting goods store, or office supply store. Perhaps not coincidentally, all these categories of retail typically attract a high proportion of adult male shoppers. There are not very many adult males here except for those in the company of women or children.

Usually, malls this size draw shoppers from between five and twenty-five miles away. According to one survey, 30 percent of the adults living in this county have been here at least once during the past three months. Just 2 percent of adults living in the two neighboring counties visited during the same span.

Today, malls account for around 14 percent of all U.S. retailing (not counting cars or gasoline), about $308 billion in annual sales. Our mall accounts for just over $600 million in sales a year. It's our duty as Americans to add to that. So let's get going.

# 3 A Mouse Hole

FEAST your eyes.

It's big and beige and boxy. Virtually featureless. What else could it be? We're here.

The first glimpse of any mall is usually also a look at what's wrong with mall architecture in general. From the outside, as a rule, malls give us no clear idea of what's inside. This is not a good thing.

Little consideration seems to have been given to how the building will appear to the shopper as he or she approaches from the highway. No one has bothered to create something that says *shopping*, let alone says it clearly or handsomely or interestingly. The ugliness of much of roadside America is discouraging, and malls are the largest buildings ever dedicated to the art of retailing in the history of the planet. So their ungainliness is of monumental stature and gargantuan scale.

It's no great mystery why this should be so.

For centuries, the people who built places to shop tended to be merchants. And so they took seriously their responsibility to attract shoppers. They created environments intended to present their wares, and to give shoppers a sense of moment, of event, of *place.* You can look back to the ancient Greek *storas* or the bazaars and souks in the days before Christ and find a merchant aesthetic already at work. A selling space didn't have to be fancy or pretty, and it didn't need to be built from luxurious materials. In many cases, just the opposite was true— an environment where goods are sold at rock-bottom prices *should* feel authentically no-frills. If you're interested in fresh vegetables and fruit, nothing is more promising than a rough-hewn roadside stand or rustic farmer's market. You wouldn't want your neighborhood newsstand to feel like a fancy jewelry shop, and you don't want a lumberyard to look like a florist. In each instance, the design of the store itself is a reflection of the main activity taking place within.

Look around any American city that still sports prewar architecture, and you may find at least a few grand emporiums of the past, the department store. In many places, New York included, some examples continue to stand: Bloomingdale's, Saks, Lord & Taylor. The principles of good retailing held sway everywhere, starting with the architecture. The buying experience began when you, the shopper, first caught sight of the edifice. It got the acquisitive juices flowing.

There was another force at work, too. The merchant princes were nineteenth century men, driven by ambition and muscle and determination to succeed in the brick-and-mortar vocabulary of the era. Their stores were their alter egos, and these titans of retailing all had serious edifice complexes. The great department stores of the day bore their owners' names—Gimbel, Macy, Wanamaker, Neiman Marcus, Marshall Field. These men were the contemporaries of figures like David Rockefeller and Andrew Carnegie, captains of industry who left their lasting marks on the world. Bank buildings were temples to one impulse, and city halls to another, and stores to yet another. Today, public architecture still expresses intentions and functions: sports arenas, libraries, hotels, universities—their design usually attempts to articulate something about what goes on inside. At the very least, they manage to look different from one another.

But then there are malls.

In part, their inglorious history is to blame. The mall was begat by the shopping center, which was begat by the humble little strip of stores facing a parking lot, which was the first form of shopping begat by suburbia. The earliest retail organization principle inspired by automotive life was that strip of shops—sometimes anchored by a supermarket—featuring maybe six or eight little establishments. There would be a row of parking spots out front, and easy zoom-in zoom-out access off the road. The shopping center's innovation was to turn things around, so that the stores faced not the road but one another—a circling of the suburban wagons, so to speak, now surrounded by (rather than facing) the parking spots. It was a small step from there to placing a roof over the whole thing. That history, and the fateful turning away from the eyes of the outside world, steered the mall to the state in which we find it.

Today's malls do a dismal job of signaling us as to what goes on inside. This is mainly because of the disconnect that exists at their very core. Malls house retailing, but they are not owned, developed, or built by retailers. Malls are made by real estate development companies. The men who direct these firms are not merchant princes. They are the ones who take the risk—who amass the parcel of land, line up the financing, secure all the governmental permits, and then hire the architects and contractors and so on. But they make money by putting space to work. Their tools of the trade are a spreadsheet and a good leasing agent. The mandate is to turn a hunk of suburban turf into a gold mine, something that generates profits by charging rents and a percentage of the take, not by peddling goods or services. It's very different from the financial model of their tenants, the stores. The mall exists to contain stores—it is, in fact, a store of stores. But it does not think of itself as a store. That is at the heart of what's lacking about malls, and, through the course of this book, it will come up over and over again.

Anyway, here we are. What do we see?

"A big wall with a little mouse hole" is how typical exterior mall architecture was described to me—and this was by the design director of one of America's biggest and most respected mall developers. If even his firm was willing to settle for that usual configuration of high blank walls punctuated by nondescript entrances, it's no wonder that most malls are eyesores, at least from the outside. Aesthetic value is the last thing on anyone's mind when imagining a mall.

That's a problem.

The fact that some malls are well designed just explains why most are not. Typically, city malls possess some design equity. They look good. I'm thinking of Faneuil Hall, in Boston, one of the handsomest landmarks in that city. It was made to look good in part because its developer knew that it would be a showpiece. Everybody who comes to Boston eventually visits. Another reason urban malls tend to be well designed is that city governments are adept at forcing real estate developers to build things with intrinsic value that enhance their surroundings. Municipal lawyers, planners, and community and design review boards are experienced at hammering out compromises that, in the end, benefit all parties. As a result, urban malls usually are made to fit harmoniously with their surroundings. This is true in cities all over the world. Lisbon, Portugal, is home to one of the world's most striking malls, the Vasco da Gama Center, which was built to look like a giant ship. Diagonal Mar, in Barcelona, Spain, also manages to make a mall a beautiful thing. Bluewater, in Great Britain, used to be a quarry; in Atlanta, a defunct steel mill and notorious brownsite is being turned into Atlantic Station, a New Urbanist development built to integrate housing, offices, and shopping. So it's possible for shopping centers even to improve on what they replace.

But imagine what typically happens when a big developer makes its intentions known to a suburban township. Most local governments have little experience at hammering out these deals, since most suburbs get only a few such projects in a lifetime. Even if the township wanted to play hardball and force the developer to spend money on a handsome design, or one with extra features such as parks or community centers, the mall owner holds all the cards. It's easy enough to move the mall a few miles away, within another town's boundaries. Now consider the extent to which a shopping center will contribute to a suburb's tax coffers—a big regional mall can easily cover most of what it takes to run a township school system. It's hard to say no over a question of architectural integrity.

Mall of America, the biggest in the United States and the most potent tourist attraction in all of Minnesota, may have looked good on the drawing board. But it has aged badly since it opened in August 1992. You can see stains on the outside of the building, and grass has begun to poke through the asphalt of the parking lots. It is huge and unsightly. You can't imagine Disney World or the Statue of Liberty being allowed to decay this way. Yet this mall has more visitors than Disney World, Graceland, and the Grand Canyon combined.

Next time you're at a mall, instead of going directly inside, stroll around the perimeter of the place. It will be one of the more joyless promenades you'll ever make. You'll be very alone out there, on a narrow strip of sidewalk, assuming it has a sidewalk—many malls don't—with maybe a security guard or two to keep you company. (They'll be watching you closely, since someone who walks around a mall is, by definition, an odd character.) There will almost certainly be shrubbery, neatly clipped, but it's greenery of the most generic kind. Nobody thought you'd ever look too closely at it. Its only job is to be green.

The building itself may be in good condition, depending on its age and the quality of materials used, but still the surface might be chipped, cracked, or discolored. Nobody takes this stuff too seriously, since nobody ever thought you'd be walking out here to notice. You'll no doubt come upon America's new pariah class, smokers. They'll be gathered by the entrances, close to the industrial-size ashtrays. There may be an occasional cell phone caller out there, too, in search of optimal reception.

Some malls feature display windows facing the parking lots, and some don't. Windows are problematic in a setting such as this because there's no real pedestrian approach to the building. You may drive up close to it while searching for a parking spot, but if you decide to examine the store windows you'll crash your car. Once you've parked, you dash to your destination: inside. Maybe it's raining or it's cold. It could easily be windy, given the lack of any neighboring structures. And anyway, you're here to walk around a mall, not a parking lot. A store may have the most spellbinding windows in the world, but nobody is going to pay much attention in a mall parking lot. All the action is on the inside.

Fashion Show, the ultra-glitzy mall in Las Vegas, exhibits a unique flair for architecture and visual presentation starting on the outside. It's one of the splendors of the Strip, which is saying something. Signage technology gets more spectacular every day—take a walk through Times Square in New York, a magnet for tourists from around the world, and you witness all manner of digital video, huge-screen TVs, vividly colored "ribbons" of news headlines slithering at high speed around curvilinear building facades. These same innovations exist at every sports stadium and rock concert hall—we're a nation of cutting-edge sophisticates where big visual communication technology is concerned. Our eyes are trained to watch for the next hot thing.

Of course, it's impossible to prove that more attention to architecture would make a bit of difference to a mall's bottom line. In the end, that argument carries the day—the marketplace doesn't require more beautiful shopping center design, so why spend more for it? That's the short view, at least. Today, when most American malls are over twenty years old, the question of what to do about aging centers will soon be upon us. If the buildings themselves had any intrinsic value, we'd be more likely to restore or salvage ones that need it. We restore and re-purpose many public structures, such as former post offices, hotels, libraries, even churches. But most malls are too ugly and banal to warrant such effort. They've been designed to be serviceable, nothing more, and once they no longer can serve they'll have to be razed, and replaced with . . . I don't know. Maybe something even worse.

We need to find a place to park.

# 4 Dude, Where's My Car?

Okay, NOW we're *really* here. Nearly really here, I should say. We still have to park.

Because America lives by the automobile, we live by the parking space, too. When ruminating over all the reasons that city dwellers embraced suburbia, we sometimes overlook the promise of painless parking. Imagine the daily ordeal of primitive man circa 1950, back when urban streets designed for horse and wagon traffic became home to two- and three-car baby boom families. The lure of knowing that you could retire from the nightly blood sport of parallel parking, never again to circle endlessly while waiting for another driver to budge, was part of what inspired urban flight. Not only racial unease or class aspirations. Pure convenience. Having a garage or just a driveway of one's own was bliss.

Try to imagine any suburban institution such as the mall without parking. Can't be done.

The entrance to the parking lot is where the mall really begins. As you approach, there's always that moment of anticipation when you see whether the lot is full, empty, or somewhere in between. It sets the tone for the day. Enjoy a smooth transition from the highway to the front door, and you feel blessed. Hit a snag, and you start your shopping trip under a black cloud.

Once in the lot, you could drive around and around the building without ever finding an entrance that announces itself as the "main" one. There may be several unprepossessing doorways at regular intervals, none of them marked with any kind of sign to alert you to what lies inside. Or, you may just take the easy way out and enter through one of the department stores. Even if there is one mall entrance that feels like a primary one, this may not be the one used by all or even most shoppers. We've studied many malls where there *is* one door used by people unfamiliar with the mall. We call it the "stranger" entrance. But it's usually not the portal of choice for those who know the mall well.

In fact, mall design reflects the same lack of hierarchy of which suburbs themselves are often guilty. Cities organize themselves into distinct zones—downtown, outskirts, central business district, rich-people housing, middle-class housing, poor-people housing, good part of town, bad part of town, and so on. This scheme has evolved over the course of centuries, and so we're all familiar with it the instant we come upon it.

Suburbs are to a large degree an escape from that urban structure— they are islands of homes with enough retail to serve most of the natives' needs, and then just enough institutional uses (schools, police stations, firehouses, churches, movie theaters) to get along. The mall reflects that lack of hierarchy. A single main entrance would run counter to the suburban automotive ideal, which dictates that you should always be able to park as close as possible to your own personal destination. So, instead of the most desirable parking spots being concentrated in one area, they form a ring around the building. Your parking priorities will almost certainly differ from mine. It permits a truly American freedom of choice, expressed in a form of architectural and spatial chaos.

When choosing a mall parking spot, you've got four priorities to juggle:

1. You want a spot that's easy and fast to reach when you arrive.

2. You want a spot close to the mall.

3. You want a spot near the entrance that will bring you closest to your first destination inside.

4. You want a spot that's fast and easy to reach when you leave.

Parking within fifty feet of your preferred entrance is probably the highest priority of the four, especially when it's cold, hot, or rainy, but even when it's nice outside. Nobody enjoys a springtime stroll through a mall parking lot. When you shop in a city, getting to your destination is an enjoyable part of the experience and may turn up some pleasant surprises along the way. All manner of information is gleaned, almost without noticing, when we walk down a city street. We see other store windows, of course, but also we get to study how people dress, how they wear their hair, what kind of dogs they walk. None of that exists in the parking lot of a mall.

I've spent plenty of time out here in the lot, and not just in my car. Often, when I start a consulting assignment for a retail chain or developer, I'll drag executives out here. They're usually puzzled: *Wait a sec—the stores are in there!* But I insist. For all their knowledge and experience, few merchants or managers understand how much of the customer experience takes place in the parking lot. Executives who would be appalled by a lack of regard for shopper comfort within the store don't give a moment's thought to what happens out here.

"Can't we just go into the security office and see the lot on the video monitor?" I've been asked.

"Not the same," I say.

So we all trudge out there. I march my captives to the farthest extreme of the lot, and then make them stand there a minute. Part of my mission is to get them to see the mall itself as the shopper first encounters it. I want them to witness how the signage and display windows play under normal conditions.

If the mall devoted much thought to how shoppers experience the place, they'd spend a little money and effort on the parking lot. As soon as you turned in off the road you'd come upon a car greeter—a traffic cop. He'd be the boss, and he would have two or three minimum-wage high school kids running around to inform drivers where all the spots are, would keep traffic moving smoothly, and would give shoppers the sense that fairness and order prevail.

Doesn't happen. I've been at this particular mall on the Saturday before Christmas when by ten A.M. traffic is at a standstill and tempers are flaring. Mall management remains uninvolved. Find your own spot, fight your own battles, it tells us, *then* come inside. Mall operators think they control parking lots by installing surveillance cameras. As any police officer will tell you, control is about being visible. Most of the time this isn't a huge issue, but there are about thirty shopping days a year when this lot will reach capacity. On those days, a little help would go a long way.

❀    ❀    ❀

We all have our own personal parking styles—it's just one more way we express who we are. Some philosophical types are content to park at the farthest reaches of the lot and trudge in from there; more competitive drivers will stalk the prime spots, even tailing shoppers as they exit the mall and head to their cars. I had an aunt who refused to park where she had to back out.

There's also the matter of how we will find our cars when it's time to leave. How many of us pay only half attention to the landmarks of the lot? Research has shown that people landmark the lot based on age and gender. Men like numbers and letters. Women like colors. Kids prefer symbols—animals or fruit. For every time I've memorized my landmarks, there have been more where I have wandered aimlessly looking for my chariot. On those days I walk row after row of cars pressing my keyless ignition, muttering, "Here, Greta [the name I've given my Audi], where *are* you?" At a mall outside Houston, after an hour of searching for my rental, I began to doubt my sanity. I missed my flight that day. There must be some kind of car homing device that Hertz could install. That little gizmo would win my loyalty forever.

❀    ❀    ❀

Malls treat parking lots as necessary evils. I wish developers would notice how we sometimes make great, creative use of these broad expanses of asphalt. The obvious example is something most sports fans are familiar with—tailgating parties and picnics in the stadium parking lot. Some of these efforts are downright lavish, with charcoal grills and Champagne coolers set up amid campers, minivans, and trailers. Ford now makes a truck with optional sink and gas grill.

That marriage of RV camping and parking lot has been handsomely exploited by Wal-Mart. To the horror of campground owners across the United States, the giant retailer now permits overnight camper parking in its lots. This is a genius move—the overnighters take advantage of the stores' bathrooms in the morning, but those folks also spend money on food, clothing, and supplies. The NASCAR circuit has reinvented another ancient retail tradition—the peddler's wagon. On race days, trailers park in the lot and turn into stores with varied product lines that put the old factory parking lot "roach coach" (my favorite term for lunch wagons) to shame.

The concept of the portable open-air store has merit. The best example I know is the tent sale that happens in the high-end carpet business. Bloomingdale's Home Store and others use it to good advantage. The huge tent goes up in a parking lot, carpets are piled inside, and for an intense week or two the store conducts what ends up being a huge percentage of its annual rug business. It shows that under the right conditions you can sell even a very fine and costly product in a parking lot.

Some supermarkets are great utilizers of the parking lot. In summer, you'll find a little convenience store set up out there, maybe under a tent to protect the cashier from sunstroke. They don't stock the usual C-store items such as milk, beer, and aspirin. Instead you'll find bags of charcoal briquettes, barbeque tools, lawn chairs, sun hats, water guns, bug spray, suntan lotion, and other trappings of suburban summer. This is the stuff you always remember only at the last minute, and the market saves you the trouble of running back through the entire store to pick up a few Saturday afternoon essentials. If you came to the market with no intention of buying any of that stuff, the ministore out front is a potent reminder.

What frustrates me as a researcher is that parking lot innovations are being tried, but on an ad hoc basis, with no attempt to measure what works and what does not. As small-town main streets have died, the biggest and most predictable public gathering in many communities is the big shopping center parking lot. That's a phenomenon to be taken advantage of, not ignored or discouraged.

A few years ago I was part of a small group hired to help the Phoenix Zoo imagine its future. The director picked us up at the hotel in the zoo's minivan, covered with airbrushed animals rendered in bright colors. As we pulled into the parking lot, he drove toward his spot, closest to the main entrance. I asked him to park instead in the middle of the empty lot. As we walked away, two cars screeched to a stop and a bunch of young boys ran to examine the van up close.

"If you have a billboard," I told the director, "use it."

A common problem in all suburban shopping used to be when employees arrived early and hogged all the best parking spots. By now, most stores recognize this and order staffers to park away from the front door. Rarely, the problem is just the opposite. Recently my firm studied something found only in rural America—the Farm & Fleet network. These regional chains run huge stores—a hundred thousand square feet and up—that serve farmers and rural businesses. They stock an enormous cross section of goods, from jeans and high-end cowboy boots to barbed wire and harnesses for your donkey. Out on the edges of nowhere, these stores sit in the middle of endless parking lots. Rural land is still cheap.

The problem is that the lots often look painfully empty. The store we studied required employees to park behind the store. As a result, when you drove by in the morning, the lot was deserted, and you couldn't be sure the store was open. Our advice was to move employee parking around to the front, midway through the lot—thereby leaving the prime spots for shoppers, but signaling to passing drivers that the store was open for business.

Hey! How's this spot? It's near a fairly nondescript entrance to the mall, a fine place through which to enter the belly of the beast. Help me remember where we are: E6, E6, E6, let's go, E6.

# 5 Why Malls Fear Freedom

WHAT HAVE we here? It looks to be three hundred or so six-year-olds assembled in an open space on the mall's ground floor, just inside the entrance, kicking at one another as hard as they can. Their mothers and fathers and siblings surround the squalling mob, smiling and waving. How wholesome can you get?

All over American malldom, similar scenes are playing out—here we see the local martial arts schools raising money for a worthy cause with what they call a "kick-a-thon." Somewhere else, it's the local ballet school, or the glee club, the marching band, the Boy Scouts, the art league, the roller hockey league, the Junior League, the spelling bee, the high school drama club performing highlights from *Brigadoon.* Or is that *Bye Bye Birdie*?

This is where the mall-as-community shows its shiny, peppy face. If we were a village society, or even an urban one, these activities might take place at the schoolhouse, or the community center, or in the village green on market day. But since we're a predominately suburban nation, and suburbs tend to be short on gathering places, it all happens at the mall.

For which the mall, of course, is mostly happy. It's not earning a profit on every kick these little tae kwon do apostles deliver, but this is a good way to ensure the presence of their moms and dads at ten-thirty on a Saturday morning. Once you've gone to all the effort of driving here and parking, it seems wasteful not to acquire something or other. Best of all, the little ones may be so exhausted by then that they'll behave themselves. The mall likes having the cute children of wage-earning parents around. It brightens up the place. It's cheaper than real entertainment. It's good for the image. There's a profit motive to being such a willing host and accommodator of various community-minded endeavors.

Some of the attempts by suburbanites to take seriously the mall as quasi-public space seemed innocuous enough. For example, an entirely new form of mass exercise was born of the mall. No sooner had America's first enclosed shopping center opened, in 1956, in the Minneapolis suburb of Edina, than did area doctors begin advising older patients to get their cardiovascular exercise inside the mall, where they could stride without fear of slipping on snow or ice. Mall walking quickly caught on. If you've ever gone into a mall before the stores open (as I have), you know the sound—the silence is broken only by the squeak of senior citizen mall walkers in their sneakers. Many malls decided to extend a special welcome to these elders in sweat suits and began allowing them inside before normal business hours. (There was always the chance that they'd stick around and buy something.) Some shopping centers began special programs for senior citizens—mall-walker clubs, free coffee, discount coupons, holiday parties.

And then, inevitably, came the backlash. Malls began to feel taken advantage of by the walkers, some of whom began to feel entitled to the amenities and special favors they had been granted. There was always some question as to whether the discounts and programs actually made any economic sense. Eventually, some developers tried curtailing mall walking altogether. Mall of America attempted to force mall walkers to use a parking lot so far from the building that shuttle buses were required. The walkers retaliated with an informational campaign, reminding the stores of how much money they spent there. Before long the mall caved in and allowed normal parking for all.

More recently, Evergreen Plaza, near Chicago, attempted similar measures. Management aired its grievances in the local press, complaining about senior citizen sneakers muddying newly polished floors, and mall walkers hogging all the good parking spots and demanding Christmas gifts. "It got out of control from a standpoint of entitlement," a mall executive told a reporter. "Predominately they are seniors, okay, and seniors are not great spenders, are they?" Perhaps not, but they excel at gaining public sympathy in battles such as this one. A torrent of bad publicity ensued, reaching all the way to page one of the *New York Times*. Competing malls even began making a play for the banished senior citizens, at which point Evergreen Plaza management turned tail and invited the walkers back.

"Mall walking is pretty much a given and something that is hard for malls to avoid," a spokesperson for a mall developer trade group said in an article. "On the whole, our industry embraces the walkers as viable customers. The rub some retailers might have is that they tend to get there early and take the best parking spots. And they are not really that dynamic as shoppers."

Sneaker-scuffed floors are the least of the inconveniences that come with being suburban functional Main Streets, malls have learned. The various free speech–related activities that go with American democracy soon followed everyone else to the mall—the activists realized there was no other way to be encountered in a suburban milieu where no one walks. These were the moments that tried a mall's commitment to a vision of itself as some kind of quasi-public space, the town center for towns where no true center exists. This got at the heart of the question of whether a mall is the suburban Main Street or a tightly controlled fortress devoted to a single activity: retailing. Or is it somewhere in between?

Political candidates collecting signatures, activists protesting, sympathizers leafleting for causes popular and otherwise, even Klansmen, all descended upon American malls. In 1968, the U.S. Supreme Court began getting involved in the matter. In that year, it ruled that malls cannot interfere with the exercise of First Amendment rights. Score one for the people. Then, four years later, it reversed itself and said the First Amendment did not require shopping centers to permit the distribution of antiwar leaflets on the premises. Score one for the mall. That ruling seemed to settle the argument by establishing shopping centers as private property, the same as an individual store might be.

Then, in 1980, in a unanimous decision involving a California mall, the court said that individual states' laws could require malls to allow greater free-speech rights than the First Amendment does. Since then, courts in six states (California, Colorado, Massachusetts, New Jersey, Oregon, and Washington) have deemed malls to be at least quasi-public spaces, where at least some forms of expressions must be allowed. Eleven more—Arizona, Connecticut, Georgia, Michigan, Minnesota, New York, North Carolina, Ohio, Pennsylvania, South Carolina, and Wisconsin—have decided not to require malls to behave like public places.

❊   ❊   ❊

Developers are technically correct when they point out that the mall is private property, not the village square. According to one survey, nearly three-quarters of shoppers believe the mall *should* keep out political activists—which is consistent with what we know of the average person's tolerance for commotion (especially when it interferes with shopping). And yet, the fact is that the mall phenomenon came along and took the place of the town square, the public zone.

The mall is a monument to the moment when Americans turned their back on the city. To many of us, cities are civilization's greatest achievement—they are vast, complicated, marvelous machines created by our collective energies and dreams, a way for us to come together to live, work, play, love, learn, create, protest, worship, and die, all in one glorious place. Cities, going back to Athens, managed to bring together every imaginable worthwhile human activity (and some not so worthwhile ones) in harmonious fashion. A good city—hell, a good city block—is a treasure forever. I've gotten myself in trouble for saying that America's villains of the twentieth century were Frank Lloyd Wright for romanticizing the suburbs and Henry Ford for making the suburban dream accessible. To be fair, many of the cities people fled were dangerous, dirty, and unhealthy. The trade-off in quality-of-life terms was probably a good one. This book is about one consequence of that flight: a big air-conditioned vanilla box with all the action on the inside.

If you need proof of suburban malls' smug, insular nature, consider this: They can almost never be easily reached by public transportation. If you can't drive here, the mall seems to say, you can't come. This is in marked contrast to European and Japanese malls, which are often built near train stations for the convenience of shoppers. In Japan, malls even feature bicycle racks, something I've never seen in the United States, although a great many people live within bike distance of malls and might like the chance to get a little fresh air and exercise in with their shopping.

America's postwar suburbs are for the most part inhospitable to *any* form of transportation that isn't an automobile. So the mall isn't remarkable in this regard. But sometimes the consequences are tragic. In 1995, an African American teenager was killed while trying to cross a busy seven-lane highway on her way to a mall near Buffalo, New York. She was forced to walk across the road because the mall prohibited city buses from stopping on the property. Local civil rights activists accused the developer of doing so in order to keep out minorities, since the buses carried residents from a mostly black part of town. The mall denied any racial motive, saying it wanted only to keep rowdy young people away. The bus ban was lifted after the activists threatened a boycott. The dead girl's family sued the mall, which settled the case for $2 million.

Are malls racist? It's not such an outlandish question. It seems clear that malls hope by limiting public transportation they can control who may enter and who may not. The fact that you need to drive doesn't completely ensure that a mall will get only the law-abiding middle class, since in America people of extremely modest means still manage to own cars. Still, city dwellers and teenagers most often are the ones without wheels. So keeping the mall unattainable by public transportation goes a long way toward segregating it from anything even potentially scary.

Malls might argue that, from a business point of view, keeping low-income urban teenagers out is a smart goal. In one survey, 50 percent of malls claimed they had problems with gangbangers, and 90 percent said they had attracted troublesome teenage loiterers. After all, the mall is meant to be a refuge from the bad city streets, from cold and wind and rain but also from panhandlers and vagrants and teenagers with bad attitudes.

In truth, it's easy to stroll these tranquil pathways and forget that crime exists anywhere, let alone that shopping districts are sometimes magnets for pickpockets, shoplifters, and muggers. That's the lulling effect of the mall—you are surrounded only by fellow shoppers, all drawn together in a communion of consumption. There are no out-skirts here, no dark recesses or easy getaway routes (not even for the law-abiding), which makes crimes such as purse snatching an unlikely occurrence.

Suburban subdivisions segregate people based on how much they can spend on real estate. Everybody knows that wealth and poverty exist, but many suburbanites get no closer to either end of the spec-trum than their television screen. We humans seem to find comfort in economic homogeneity, and the mall does its best to preserve that con-dition.

We are living in a time when, nationally, crime is down, especially the personal, violent offenses that worry us most—murder, robbery, rape, and assault. The danger of urban streets, whether real or pre-sumed, is part of what drove us to the suburbs and then to the mall in the first place.

I know a mall in a posh suburb of New York that was a target for or-ganized urban criminals. A few years ago, police reported that a modern-day Fagin was actively recruiting city teenagers to plunder the place as shoplifters and pickpockets. In one day more than forty youths were arrested while shoplifting there. In all, more than one hundred arrests were made, including children as young as eleven. Some were discovered with printed manuals telling them which bus routes would get them to the mall, and then which stores to hit once they got there. The guides instructed them in the art of hiding their loot, evading guards, and exiting the mall swiftly; the kids knew which designers' clothes could be most easily fenced once they got it home. At the Mall of America there have been a few shootings and some assaults, all attributed to gangs. There has been one murder (of a seventeen-year-old woman, by her estranged boyfriend). There were also a few rapes, including one of a teenage girl, in a service corridor, by a man she had met at the mall that day.

Malls probably don't need to make much special effort to keep dangerous elements out. There's already a remarkably efficient self-regulating mechanism that maintains orderliness in the world of shopping. It uses symbolism and nuance to attract certain people while repelling certain others. Say what you will about the snootiest shopping districts of any city in America—you can get there by public transportation, or even on foot, no matter where you live. In New York, for instance, it takes only subway fare to go from some of the poorest, toughest neighborhoods in the city—indeed, the country—to some of the poshest, most exclusive boutiques in the world. There's no obvious police or private security presence stopping armed thugs or mobs of marauding adolescents from descending upon Madison Avenue and making waste of it. And yet, it doesn't happen.

People of modest means may dream of someday indulging a taste for Armani, but they tend not to try for it until they can afford it, and no armed guard is required to turn them away in the meantime. People enjoy shopping in places where they feel wanted and needed and loved, even people without much money. They have their own favorite stores where they shop, not necessarily out of need but because it's fun. Even muggers and stick-up men take their ill-gotten gains and go shopping like everybody else.

We think of malls as being wholesome and all-American, but they are not uniformly so. Some are also snobbish, xenophobic, elitist. Hateful. But we're *still* going to spend the day here.

# **6** *I Brake for Meanderthals*

SPEAKING of mall walking, how are you holding up? Strolling around in here is quite a bit easier than doing it in a city. For one thing, there's no weather to worry about. For another, the pace is quite a bit slower. This is one of the areas in which, almost undetected, the mall has had a huge effect on American life: it has actually taught us to walk differently than we once did, as we'll see. Huge deal, right? That's especially so for me, since in my line of work the way people walk has major implications for how they shop. We now have several generations of Americans who have never walked for any length of time in cities or even towns. They ride everywhere and walk only here, at the mall. Which is quite a bit different from walking anywhere else.

For safety's sake, you maintain your gaze at eye level and under when walking city streets. In New York City, a pedestrian walking briskly covers about three hundred feet per minute. As you move, your eyes do, too, shifting slightly from side to side covering almost a full

180-degree semicircle. As human eyes age, depth perception deterio-
rates, and we put less trust in our peripheral vision. An older person is
much more conscious of where her feet are. Children tend to move
their heads more than adults do; in our research work, eight-year-olds
are the ones who spot our cameras, never teens or adults. Head position while walking in a city is also a matter of preference; people would
rather look at other people than just about anything else.

Nevertheless, you're also on the lookout for the usual pedestrian
hazards, such as curbs, potholes, and homeless people lying in nooks
and crannies. But with the advent of traffic lights and good paving,
urban eyes are usually earthbound. From the retailer perspective, this
is good—it keeps our eyes more or less in the zone of store window displays.

These conditions do not allow city walkers to see much that's out of
that zone, however. New Yorkers in particular are always stunned when
by some odd chance they look up and notice what's on the second and
third floors of the buildings they pass every day. There's an entire level
of business windows in crowded midtown Manhattan that are like an
open secret. The job of seducing people up or down a flight of stairs is
not an American strength. In New York, there is a long tradition of mar-
ginal businesses trying to cling to the upper and sometimes lower registers of our vision. Those attempts usually contain some kind of display,
or signage at the very least. However, they're hidden in plain sight.

But when visitors come to town, they walk and look according to
rules and habits acquired elsewhere—like at the mall. In cities they do
that little gee-whiz-ma-lookit-how-tall-*that*-one-is dance when seeing
a real skyscraper up close. Native walkers will sometimes come upon a
group of people standing stock-still, looking at some fixed point high on
a building's facade, and be briefly misled into thinking there's something of genuine interest up there—like a jumper, or maybe King
Kong. Then we look a little closer and realize we've been fooled by a
bunch of bedazzled tourists, or an effete architectural walking tour. Do
we care about what the Municipal Art Society thinks is significant on
that facade? That's when we sneer and shoulder our way past, irritated
at being had by a bunch of rubes.

There's something so innocent, so childlike and trusting, about how tourists walk in a city. They lack pedestrian radar, that combination of peripheral vision, hard-won experience, and ESP that alerts you to the taxi that's about to occupy the space where you're standing, or the bike messenger who's speeding into your intended path. Neither do visiting walkers anticipate the usual urban decision points. For instance, veteran city walkers will usually begin to plot a turn well before they reach the corner, whereas visiting pedestrians stroll as though they'll be continuing in that direction indefinitely; when they do hit an intersection they halt, convene, swivel in all directions, and only *then* begin to figure out where they'll go and by what path they'll go there. Urbanites use a special body vocabulary, from a dropped shoulder to a shifted briefcase, that tells fellow travelers our intentions.

In the city, and especially in the hectic districts where stores and shopping predominate, people move with a great sense of purpose. No matter where you're headed, you tend to go as though you're on some mission of high importance. Partly it's because no self-respecting urban dweller wants to admit, even by the implication of a leisurely gait, that he or she is not urgently needed somewhere else. But it's also the way that we internalize the rhythms and the velocity of the city. The late William H. Whyte, the distinguished American Urbanist and my friend, used to say that the pace and character of New Yorkers was set by the traffic lights. They trained us to walk as fast as possible, so that we can make it through the next intersection without stopping for a red light. He discovered that the stoplight cycles form us into what he called pedestrian platoons—a crowd builds at a crosswalk, waiting for the green light, at which point we all hurry forward in a cluster until we are stopped by the next red light. If you're watching from above, you see that while the groups spread out slightly as they move forward, the pattern is densely packed sidewalk followed by long, mostly empty stretches. Twenty years ago, Lexington Avenue at lunchtime was the most crowded stretch of pavement in Manhattan, with some four thousand people moving in an hour through a twelve-and-a-half-foot space. I'd argue that in 2003, sections of Canal Street on Saturday rival the density of Hong Kong and Shanghai, or the entrance to the Spice Market in Istanbul.

I spent hours at Tokyo's Shibuya Station watching the train and subway stations push out shoppers as if from a fire hose, spraying them across a broad square and into a fan of arterial streets. The plaza outside the station is a dense staging area combining all the classic elements of great urban public space—a little shade, places to lean or sit, formal and informal selling from stores and kiosks, and music. There is enough of a cross section of humanity to make everyone feel comfortable, while at the same time providing everyone with someone to gawk at. The sea of hairstyles and costumes makes New York's East Village look tame. It is a great show.

Like many commercial districts in Japan, the electronic signage is overwhelming. Beyond the huge screens playing rock videos, electronic advertising is shotgunned across every facade. Appearing on those video screens in Shibuya Square is the dream of every aspiring Japanese rapper. Doe-eyed high school girls cluster in pods, staring at the screens, thumbs flying across the keypads on their oversize cell phones as they punch out instant messages. At seemingly regular intervals sound trucks blaring political messages roll through the square, their distorted voices careening across the high-rise windows and plate-glass department store facades. The background noise is constant; music, taxis, announcements from the station all carried on the smell of salty food and burnt diesel.

The square's main intersection is a series of five converging streets. At the crosswalks, the crowd surges ten to twelve people deep. The patience of the Tokyo pedestrian is rooted alternatively in Zen and fast food. Cars pull slowly through the intersection, and people are careful not to look at one another, but the mounting sense of impatient energy is palpable. As the light changes, the octagonal street transforms into a surreal barn dance as thousands of people charge around oblique corners in ordered chaos. The pace of the dance is a steady, manic cadence—however driven or desperate you might be, you can't move any faster. Bodies pass close enough to give second-hand hits of tobacco and the faux-fruit fragrance of the month. Especially in summer, the ripples of body heat are a triumph of human radar and coordination as everyone brushes but no one touches. They watch their feet and feel their polite insignificance because in a shopping district all pedestrians carry the same residual weight.

urban vs mall

shibuya

Shibuya is one of the world's busiest commercial corners; the shopping extends two levels below the street in some places and six to ten levels above. The entire coming and going is funneled through sidewalks only three to four yards wide. The compression is palpable, which is part of the attraction, while at the same time exhausting. It is a mosh pit that predates punk.

The experience of a city, whether New York or Tokyo, is in great contrast to how walking is performed in malls. There, for starters, the surface is reliability itself—usually some smooth petrochemical product, either linoleum or vinyl or acrylic. In the swankier districts, such as the one we're in today, you may find tiles made of ceramic or stone, but these are no less dedicated to the safety and comfort of the walker. There will be no obstacles or surprises of any kind down there on the floor itself—the rules of the mall guarantee this much, and the store leases, the legal contracts that define the environment, require it. As a result, looking down while walking in a mall is utterly pointless. There's nothing down there to see. This is a matter of trust. Only the most crabbed and paranoid pedestrian looks at the floor in a mall.

Similarly, in a mall you walk safe in the knowledge that everyone is there to do the exact same thing you're doing, however we define the complex set of missions you've undertaken. There are no bicycle messengers, careening taxis, distracted truck drivers, no hell-bent young career women storming past, shouldering you out of the way, no office drones racing through a lunch hour's worth of errands, no mobs of high school kids out frolicking, pretending they own the sidewalk. Nobody here but us shoppers. The corridors are unipurpose. We are all in agreement about why we are here. With that homogeneity of intention comes safety.

Safety is also defined here by the lack of any of the menaces we routinely face when we're out in the wild. As we've said, there's no crime here, at least none where anyone can see it. No bad weather, either, no wind, no rain. No spitters, even, or cigarette-butt flickers. No litterbugs. No dogs. Life under that big mall roof is safe and warm and slow. (Doesn't sound so bad that way, does it?) And the walking pace in here is a reflection of the wider lassitude. Interestingly, on a city street men walk faster than women; in a mall the positions are reversed, since men tend to wander malls like semi-lost children, whereas women are the ones who inhabit the place with a true shopper's sense of purpose.

There's even a term for it—poky pedestrians are known as *meanderthals.* But the use of *mall walker* as a term of derision has been around for some time. That refers to the speed but also to the practice of strolling three, four, or more abreast. In the city, "if we try and go three across, it slows us down," confessed a mall walker from Birmingham, Alabama, to a *New York Times* reporter writing about the tense life of a Manhattan pedestrian. Most people drive a lot and walk little, so they forget how it's done. Will future generations have to take walker's ed in high school?

In a city store, speed overall is much more important to shoppers than it is in a mall. A company we've studied routinely deploys twice as many cashiers at its store near Wall Street than it does in a branch of roughly the same size located in a mall. Mall shoppers are willing to wait a little longer. City shoppers are not. City shoppers have bigger fish to fry, while mall shoppers don't—even when they're the exact same people. The mall makes them more patient. Conversion rate is higher in a mall, too—in a city store, shoppers race in, look around for what they need, become frustrated when they can't find it immediately, and split. In a mall, you'll take a little longer, consult a sales associate, and in the end find what you're looking for.

✻　✻　✻

In cities we have systems that help us figure out where we are. Fixed landmarks (tall buildings, subway entrances) combined with dynamic references (streets, sun position, shadow lines) keep us oriented. It's also socially acceptable to ask for directions in a city. Being lost is stressful, and the stress is exacerbated in a mall. Because it is a planned environment, there is no such thing as being deliciously lost in the mall.

In malls, way-finding requires maps, and when malls meet cartography, the result is not magic. To be fair, cartography often relies on some generally understood basic reference points: North is *that way,* or Fifth Avenue is *over there.* Having stepped from the featureless parking lot through a mouse-hole entrance, is there any surprise that we are disoriented? Some malls attempt to name interior corridors as though they were streets, but such efforts generally fail. At best, the quadrants of the mall are recognized by the anchors—oh, that's the Sears side, or the Bloomingdale's end.

Stopping to ask for directions in a mall is often an exercise in frustration. There is no tradition of talking to, much less helping, strangers in a mall. This is not to say that people aren't friendly—they just seem surprised that someone is talking to them. Some people know only one small section of a mall. Even some sales associates know only their immediate surroundings. Security guards are surprised even to be noticed, much less stopped and solicited for help.

A map at the entrance seems like a good idea, until you actually come across one. Do all mall maps stink? In our studies of people in shopping centers, we've timed how long they spend staring at those big, lighted board mall directories. In one study the average was twenty-two seconds. That's a *very* long time to study a map. Too long. It indicates that a fair number of people never find what they're looking for—shoppers struggle to decipher the map and then just give up. They walk away in frustration. Malls are too huge and, unlike when driving, you move at will throughout a mall. And it may exist on two or three levels, adding to the complexity. The directories in most malls look like they were designed for electricians—like wiring guides. They don't look like malls. Shoppers negotiate spaces better if they have fixed points to guide them, like "Shoes over here" or "Escalator there."

Department stores might also benefit by placing maps instead of directories right inside the doorway. Without them, you stand in the entrance and look out over the floor of the store with absolutely no idea of what you're looking at. It's just a huge expanse of undifferentiated space. There's a sea of merchandise.

Here's what a good store map would look like. It would be horizontal, like a tabletop, instead of vertical like most mall maps. You could look down on it, at waist-level, find what you need—say, the shoe department, and then look up to locate it for real. You can't do that standing behind an eight-foot-tall board.

My perfect store map would use symbols. If, for example, the ladies' shoe department was on the left-hand side of this floor, halfway back, there would be a big shoe on the left side of the map, halfway back. Maybe I'd even have a huge shoe hanging from the ceiling over the shoe department, so you could see it from the entrance.

Maps in department stores and malls are important because, when properly designed, they can help avert shopper frustration. You could argue that a shopper who is temporarily lost may wander deeper into a store and discover sections she or he might otherwise have missed. But it's more likely that the shopper will grow exasperated and impatient, leading to walkouts, lost sales, and ill will.

In the course of our research we watch thousands upon thousands of people shop every year. In some instances, they spend time in a store because they're enjoying it, or they're accomplishing things. That's good. But in other cases, they're spending time in the store because it's so badly designed and stocked that it takes forever to find things. That's not good. We draw the paths that people follow—we call them "tracks"—on paper maps of a store's floor plan. You should see the track for a lost shopper—it goes a little ways in this direction, stops, goes off over there, stops again, retraces itself back to the starting point, then goes off on a totally different path. You can look at it and feel the shopper seething. Before long, the track goes right back out the door.

Men dart in, look around, refuse to ask for help, try two or three directions, give up, and split. Boom. All a store can do is accommodate male nature by putting the goods men buy near the entrances and making the signs big and clear.

Not long ago I toured a mall with a female executive I know. We had never been there before and tried to make use of the mall map, which was the typical vertical affair.

"Where's the little YOU ARE HERE symbol?" she asked. "Even that's tough to find."

"That's true," said an elderly man trying to study the map over our shoulders.

"Is this helpful?" I asked.

"I've only been here one time before. I don't live around here, my daughter does. And the first time I tried using this map it took me two minutes just to find the YOU ARE HERE thingy. And look at it—it's just a little sticker somebody stuck on here. It even covers a whole store!"

An entire business wiped out by an instrument meant to help shoppers to find stores.

"The other day I saw an interesting mall map—it was a Coke machine with the map on its side," my friend said.

"How was the map?"

"Same as this. Same as all the rest."

"But you could buy a Coke from it?"

"Yeah. Considering how long people end up staring at these maps, it was a pretty awesome product placement. What would improve these maps, really?"

"Voice-recognition software maybe. You could ask the map, 'Where's the Banana Republic for women?' and a trail of tiny lightbulbs on the map would guide you from where you're standing to where the store is located. Or even better, they could install tiny lightbulbs in the actual floor of the mall, and when you ask for a store the floor itself would light up. You could just follow the bulbs to your destination."

"That's not a map, that's a guide."

In theory, there *is* something meant to perform that function: the mall's customer service desk. Every mall has one of these. They're intended to fulfill a narrow range of tasks: pointing lost shoppers in the right direction; selling mall gift certificates, reuniting lost kiddies with their keepers, and so on. Some malls use these desks to gather names for mailing lists—they give you a bogus gift or mall membership card, and in exchange they get your name on their database, free of charge. It's a lot cheaper than buying mailing lists from direct marketers.

These desks might clear up a certain amount of shopper confusion, except that many malls defeat the purpose by placing them in a less-than-prominent location. Often, you need assistance just to find the assistance desk.

The key to a sense of place is often a human face. Management in malls is passive as far as the customer is concerned. While the premise of the mall is that we customers should wander, and that the longer they hold us the more we'll spend, many of us are making our shopping choices based on an understanding of how the layout works. For both male-hunter and female-gatherer, whether at the mall or in the woods, our use of shortcuts demonstrates our expertise. Teaching us to use the right mouse hole is also ensuring that we return. No expert shopper looks at a map, or visits the customer service desk, unless they must.

# 7 Nose and Toes

AT LAST, a store. The shopping begins.

You might think that retailers would fight to be nearest the entrances. But take a look at what's here, just inside the doorway. A hair salon on one side and a store that sells exercise equipment on the other. The beauty parlor is nearly full, although you can bet these are regular customers, not mall shoppers who have decided on impulse to get a cut and color. The exercise store is empty, which makes sense—how many treadmills does the average consumer buy? If the shop sells one or two it's a good day. You'll sometimes find banks in these locations, another low-profile tenant. Post offices. Video game arcades. Why is it that the least attractive tenants get these high-traffic positions?

Call it the mall's decompression zone. The fact is that when we enter any building, we need a series of steps just to make the adjustment between out there and in here. You need to slow your walk a little, allow your eyes to adjust to the change in lighting, give your senses a chance to detect changes in temperature and so on. You walk through any door and suddenly your brain has to take in a load of new information and process it so you'll feel oriented. You're not really ready to make any buying decisions for the first ten or fifteen feet. This transition stage is one of the most critical things we've learned in two decades of studying how shoppers move through retail environments. Nothing too close to the door really registers. If there's a sign, you probably won't read it. If there's a display of merchandise, you'll barely notice it. Some stores have the bad habit of stacking shopping baskets just inside the doorway. People zoom right past them.

Because of this transition zone, the best stores in the mall are never near the entrance. The reasoning is simple—the mall owner charges every tenant a flat rent based on space plus a percentage of sales. So it's in the mall's own interest to have the hottest stores in the prime locations, inside. Because this particular doorway feels like a secondary entrance, only a small portion of all shoppers will even see these shops. Fewer eyeballs equals fewer bucks. That equation is the basis for all mall math. And that's why underachievers go nearest the door. When entering a mall, your eye is immediately drawn way up ahead, to the heart of the place. That's where you want to be. So let's join everybody else speeding past the ladies under the hair dryers. We've got a date.

❈   ❈   ❈

My friend Carol understands a thing or two about shopping and malls. She's a fortyish woman who has spent plenty of her own time in stores. But she's also an executive with a major corporation that specializes in selling things to women shoppers. Carol's expertise is visual merchandising, meaning she's responsible for everything her company puts on the floor of a store—the product, the displays, the signs, the whole thing, from sea to shining sea. So she knows her stuff.

She's also fun to shop with.

Carol had requested that we rendezvous near a little-used doorway in one of the mall's department stores. It's a smart move for at least one reason—the parking lot right outside here is never crowded.

"This is the entrance for somebody who really *knows* the mall," says Carol as she breezes through the door.

"Good call," I say.

This entrance takes us into Filene's, the famous Boston-based retailer, but not to the heart of the store. It takes us right into men's underwear.

Men's underwear is the bottom of the barrel where Filene's is concerned, no doubt about it. This stuff sells twice a year, when it goes on sale. No man has ever come here to buy underwear. Their wives and girlfriends shop for them. Otherwise, it's the dead zone.

"Being a single woman, I don't need to pay *any* attention to men's stuff," Carol says. "But this door gets me right to cosmetics. And there's something else that makes this a great entrance."

"Which is?"

"The bathrooms are right over there."

"And the elevators and escalators."

"It's interesting," Carol says, "how this out-of-the-way entrance puts us right into cosmetics and ladies' shoes, two of the most heavily trafficked areas of the store. People in the company probably thought it was crazy to put shoes and cosmetics across the aisle from each other because they couldn't see the connection. All they saw was why take two successful departments and put them close together? Where, in reality, being together like this makes each department even stronger."

"Because?"

"Because think about it: You're standing in the shoe department, you've told the salesperson which styles you want to see in your size, and now you're waiting for her to get back. You're not going to keep looking at shoes, because you've already done that—you did it *before* you sent the clerk away to get your size. Most logical thing in the world. So now where do you look? You look across the aisle at the cosmetics counters. You see all these things you want to try. And especially if you don't find anything to buy in the shoe department. You can walk right across the aisle and find something there."

"How did the executives miss that connection?"

"Because the connection is all in the heads of the women shoppers, and it was probably men making the decisions about what would go where. What do shoes and lipstick have in common? Nothing. But because men don't shop for shoes like women do, they don't know what it's like to be a woman standing around for five minutes waiting for your size to arrive."

"Wait a sec—sure they do."

"Well, then maybe men just don't behave like women do. Women want to look at something while they wait. They want to *shop*. I bet some woman had to point out to the store-planning executives that placing shoes and cosmetics close together was a good idea."

This is the kind of thing that comes up every day in my line of work watching people in stores. Any time a shopper is standing or sitting around with nothing to do, the retailer has got something to deal with. Problem or opportunity? It can go either way. Boredom makes time crawl. Interest makes it race. If a woman is bored waiting for the clerk to return with her shoes, the wait feels longer than it really is. The problem becomes an opportunity when, in instances such as this one, the retailer fills the empty moments in a potentially productive fashion. If there were something for that shopper to browse—some other category of goods, like bags, or even something totally unrelated—I don't know, laptop computers—it could work. "While you're waiting for your shoes, take a look at the slim new Apple notebooks we just got in. . . ."

If jamming the shoe department with unrelated merchandise feels like a bad idea, the retailer could try a message of some kind or other. Maybe a video catalog of what's new in the sportswear department. Maybe a sign explaining the store's made-to-measure suits. A good, long sign with lots of words would be sensible here—you've got a captive audience for at least two minutes, and they'd be grateful for something absorbing.

Or, as Filene's has done, you could put cosmetics adjacent to shoes. It's a smart move—the makeup counters and shelves are big and graphic enough to see from this distance. Makeovers are also an activity and one of the reasons we go to the mall to get some action. Smart cosmetics companies vie to be near shoe departments in stores such as this. Of course, only one side of the cosmetics section can be facing the shoe department. So *really* smart cosmetics companies insist on being on the side that faces the shoes instead of, say, the side facing the handbag department. Smart stores have learned to treat anything that faces ladies' shoes as prime real estate.

"But there *is* a potential downside to this," I point out.

"Which is?"

"Shallow loop."

"Oh, right."

Let's say there's a woman out there who needs shoes and cosmetics. Two staples of malls and of women's lives. A smart shopper, one who really knows this mall, can park in our little-used lot, run in, get the shoes, get the cosmetics, and run back out to continue her busy day. That's a good thing, right? Maybe that woman would get her shoes and cosmetics elsewhere if she didn't know how easy Filene's makes it for her. The juxtaposition of these two departments here creates a third department—the shoe/mascara section—and drives sales.

But I could just as easily argue that putting two strong departments together like this squanders the power of each, individually, to attract shoppers. Carol alluded to that—why put two magnets side by side when you can separate them and have each one draw women to their respective parts of the store? It's an old dilemma in retailing. Supermarket layouts always used to put the dairy case in the rearmost corner of the store, on the theory that everybody had to buy milk, meaning they'd all traipse through the rest of the store to get it. A sound practice, except that it gave rise to the convenience store as the supermarket's prime competitor. Instead of making it hard to buy milk, the C-store made it easy—you park, run inside, grab the milk (which was probably within thirty feet of the door), pay, and are on your way. In response, some supermarkets created little C-stores within the store, just inside the entrance. If all you really needed was milk, you could get it and go. That's the shallow loop—instead of going from the front door to the rear and back to the front again, you barely penetrate the store.

Which layout makes more sense? Each approach sacrifices something. The old-fashioned strategy for luring shoppers through the store works. But it makes getting what you want and getting out a little less convenient. Once shoppers caught on, they began to feel manipulated. Which is not a good thing.

"If you know this mall well, you know you can get in and out in twenty minutes. Today, speed is everything for most women," Carol says. "This is good for the shopper."

"Though it could be bad for the retailer," I add.

"Well, I guess the retailer is going to have to figure something out."

                              ❁    ❁    ❁

Shopping with Carol is always productive for me because we tend to focus on what the process is like for women, and women are the primary actors in the world of shopping. Especially mall shopping.

The big theory of stores once held that women liked spending time in them because it was their main method of interacting with the world of grown-ups—of business and finance and money. They were home all day with the kids, and then home all night, too. Their husbands were completely exhausted by their involvement in the world of commerce, and seeking a little bit of respite from it. Whereas she hungered for a life of adult concerns and activities.

The midcentury shift to the suburbs only increased female isolation. Now there was no such thing as a stroll down the street to the cleaners or the appliance store or the dress shop, since no place could be easily reached by walking, and in suburbia, even if you did walk, you didn't enjoy any of the happenstance meetings a city stroll afforded. Step outside your city door, and there was the world, filled with activity and purpose and hustle. Step outside your suburban door and there was . . . another homemaker, stepping outside her door, looking back at you.

You can see how shopping at the mall came to seem like an appealing activity. It wasn't everything a woman could wish for, true, but it was quite a bit better than anything else available.

The mall rose up in response to the suburban existence, but it actually came along on the cusp of yet another major demographic shift, one that would throw shopping centers for a loop. By the 1980s, a great many of those suburban homemakers had begun working outside the home, either full- or part-time. Roughly two-thirds of adult American women today work outside the home. Their infusion into the world of work is what made the past two decades of middle-class life so materially splendid, even extravagant. And it left women with a lot less time for the mall. Their lives became crunched, and the world of retailing— stores, restaurants, and banking—had to respond. Women became the most avid users of ATMs, for instance, contrary to what the banking gurus expected. Women weren't scared off by the new technology; in fact, in the workplace, they were the ones required to master innovations in hardware and software. Women were also caught most severely between competing responsibilities at work and at home (and in the commute between the two, which, again, affected suburban women most direly).

The restaurant and retail food industries have been utterly transformed by the needs of women who work. "Meal replacement" has become the hottest growth area in the food industry. Supermarkets are forever increasing the space devoted to making and selling of prepared foods—you can't find a market today that doesn't include a bakery, charcuterie, soup station, salad bar, sushi chef. And what the supermarket doesn't do, the fast-food and family-restaurant chains do. We can complain all we like about the quality and nutritional value of the food these businesses provide—and we might start by wondering if there's any connection between the boom in prepared meals and the obesity epidemic—but we must give them their due when it comes to identifying and meeting a need.

How have the malls done in that regard? If women are at work, they're not at the shopping center. The very nature of the relationship between the woman shopper and the mall has been jeopardized. She no longer has the time to spend hours there, moving from shop to shop at a leisurely pace. She may now have to run in, grab what's necessary, then run out. Unless, of course, the mall can respond to the changes in her life with changes of its own.

Which brings us around to cosmetics. The beauty business is hardball, and yet it's full of voodoo, just as you might expect. It represents the triumph of hope over greed. There are many labels, each with its own niche and devotees, but for the most part the firms all buy their products from the same small group of factories. The cost of a lipstick and its packaging is around a dollar or so. The rest is marketing, distribution, and a whole lot of profit.

The world of beauty used to be divided into two classes—the stuff sold at mass-market retailers (drugstores, supermarkets, discounters) and what went to the fancy cosmetics salons in department stores. Think Revlon, Cover Girl, and Maybelline at the former, versus Lancôme and Estée Lauder at the latter. It was a tidy little world, until competition came along and opened up some exciting new channels. Suddenly there were boutique brands sold directly through their own stores, such as Bobbi Brown, MAC, and Aveda. The French retailer Sephora came along with its sophisticated European stores and suddenly the world of beauty retailing became a lot less orderly and a lot more interesting, at least for the customers.

Let's look at just one product—hair color. When she's sixteen, hair color is a girl's fashion accessory. My goddaughter spent her teenage years changing the color of her hair every ten minutes. It was fun and easy. By twenty-three she had made peace with the color God gave her, which didn't stop her from coloring it for special events or to annoy her mother. It was still a fashion statement.

For most women, hair color starts to get serious at around age thirty-five. The search for her proper hue gets narrower, and the range of experimentation becomes focused and purposeful. By her mid-forties, hair coloring is a staple. She renews the coloring on a fixed schedule, whether at the salon or at home.

Cosmetics moves in the same arc, from play to necessity. For the young customer it is dress up. It's entertainment, and the range of options is governed by price and brand appeal. Most middle-class, middle-aged American women started buying cosmetics at the drugstore. Gen-X and Gen-Y got their start at Kmart, Target, or Wal-Mart, or at the supermarket, as the distribution of cosmetics fanned out. Historically, the department store sold to well-off middle-aged women. The price difference between a drugstore lipstick at $6 and the fancy department store brand at $22 is a big jump, even though the difference in quality is slight.

Like hair color, makeup started out as fun and became a serious aspect of a woman's presentation to the world. As it traversed that span, it moved from the drugstore to the department store and went up in price. The ritual of putting on one's face in the morning and using restorative products at night was set.

The difference between mass and class (the industry term for the drugstore/Kmart/Wal-Mart and Filene's/Bloomingdale's/Burdines) was well defined until about ten years ago, when the lines started to blur. Today, the orderly world of cosmetics is gone. Some women shop both ends. They buy Revlon nail polish at the drugstore and Clinique face products at the department store. Women whose economic situations improved no longer reliably traded up from L'Oréal to Lancôme. Those women didn't like the way goods were being sold to them; they especially resented the peculiar industry practice of not putting price tags on the goods. Many women were too intimidated to demand to know what they were spending, and walked away from the department store counter having shelled out a lot more than they were expecting to pay.

Sephora opened up a new world by introducing "open sell." Traditionally, the salesperson at the department store was necessary to the transaction—she was the go-between linking you the shopper to the cosmetics manufacturer. Letting women examine and try the products changed the nature of the relationship. It put the customer in charge and turned the sales associate into her makeup pal.

Department stores' hold on the high-end cosmetics market has weakened, but makeup counters still occupy the prime real estate at the front of the store. That's due to the universal appeal of makeup, but equally to the fact that it is a high-margin category.

"They're willing to make less profit on apparel," Carol explains, "so long as they can make more on mascara. A mascara dollar is worth more than a dress dollar."

We stop walking a second and look around at the spectacle before us. There's something Felliniesque about a department store cosmetics section. You stand here on a Saturday morning, dressed in the standard mall-casual suburban wardrobe, gazing at a chamber glittering with chandeliers, populated by saleswomen wearing makeup and hair dramatic enough for opening night at La Scala. Their faces are like masks of pale, poreless skin, ruby-red lips, smoldering eye treatments—positively kabuki-like. They're almost intimidating.

The purchase of cosmetics is as public as a private art form gets. It isn't quite a massage, but it is an intimate act between two consenting adults. The beauty adviser will perform a makeover and offer advice, at the end of which you may simply walk away without making a purchase. So a good beauty adviser needs to build a following among her customers. Some cosmetic lines, such as Trish McEvoy, drive their business by staging mass makeover events where teams of "expert stylists," including Trish herself, run marathon sessions. It's quite a show—it sells a lot of cosmetics and builds a devoted following.

I've always been fascinated by how selling cosmetics resembles fishing. The sales associate needs to get involved, but she can't rush things. If she offers help too soon, the shopper can easily demur and walk away. In fact, we learned that if the clerk approaches the shopper within the first thirty seconds, it scares her away. The trick is to let the customer browse unaided, then watch her carefully for the first time she raises her head, even for a second. That means she's found something she might want but needs a little information. It's the equivalent of a jerk on a fishing line—that's the moment the sales associate needs to start reeling her in.

Cosmetics seem to be everywhere in this mall. In addition to department stores, you also have at least three or four cosmetics boutiques—the specialty shops like MAC and Sephora and so on. And some of the stores that sell women's clothing also sell cosmetics. Victoria's Secret now does an entire companion store for cosmetics and bath and so on. And there's a drugstore, if not actually in the mall then very close by.

Women will shop for cosmetics just about anywhere. If a store can get a woman to look into a mirror, it can sell her lipstick or blusher. One hot new line of cosmetics is sold only through plastic surgeons' offices. The thing that male researchers misunderstand is *how* most women buy cosmetics. Overwhelmingly, they purchase cosmetics on impulse—a woman approaches the counter, looks into the mirror, realizes that her lips could stand some color. So she begins to shop to meet that immediate need. She may also buy because she's low on mascara or she lost her favorite eyebrow pencil. But by and large it's for right now.

Here's another bit of voodoo in the world of high-end cosmetics. They never go on sale. *Ever.* Because women, it is thought, will not buy discounted cosmetics. It feels wrong. They'll buy anything else marked down as low as possible. The other day I came upon a huddle of sophisticated young Manhattan women, shivering outside on the coldest day of the year, waiting in line at the Manolo Blahnik sale. Women will risk hypothermia to save money on stiletto heels, but cut-rate cosmetics feels like you're putting something ratty on your face.

So instead of sales, the manufacturers offer something known as gift-with-purchase. Spend this much today, and you get this free gift package containing blah, blah, blah—a $25 value. The point is to give you the sensation of having saved $25 without having to discount the cosmetics. That system has been in place for probably thirty years now. The gift is intended to introduce eager shoppers to new products. But the industry has found that if there are three free things, maybe the customer will use two and come back to buy one. Cosmetics executives rue the day the gift-with-purchase policy began, but it's now a habit neither they nor their customers can break.

"There's a final issue playing out in cosmetics," I say.

"Which is?"

"The level of importance of anything women put on either nose or toes."

For most women, those are the areas that matter most. The extremes—the face and hair and the feet. When choosing a jacket or a skirt, there's some leeway for color and style and fit. Even in underwear. Most women are not expecting absolute perfection. But when you're talking about makeup or shoes, the standards suddenly go way up. No woman is going to settle.

"And women *always* shop those two departments, don't they?" I ask.

"Yes," says Carol, "it's something I notice when I shop with my sister or my friends. No matter what else we look at, we always go through cosmetics and shoes. You just do. If we're shopping a high-end store or a discounter, no difference. It's like you can't *not* go. Even if it means you're just sort of walking through and browsing because you're looking for something that gets you excited."

"I want you to give me a little guided tour of the counters here."

"Okay. Well, the first thing you may have noticed here is that there's almost no real selling space. Look at this counter."

It's a typical cosmetics counter.

"On the counter you have your visual here—the sign that announces they're giving away a free gift. Next to that is your tester unit, with a small sign giving some price information. But where do you do your selling? Where's a little bit of empty counter where you and the shopper can talk and put a few possible purchases down?"

"Come over into this area—you've got a major tester unit showing all the different shades of lipstick, then you've got a smaller color thing, and now we finally find maybe six inches of horizontal space. And a mirror, too, at last. So it's four or five feet of solid merchandise without a single mirror. I don't care where you go or which cosmetics counter you visit, nobody understands the mirror, which should be the simplest thing here. It's what cosmetics counters should be built around. How can you buy cosmetics without a mirror?"

This is a major problem in the cosmetics department. Insufficient mirrors. Not only too few, but also too small, and not well positioned, and not properly illuminated. This is true despite the fact that the mirror is the one thing that every woman shopping here really *wants* to see. She wants to see what's in the mirror. That's what she's buying. Not the poster. Not the lighting. If cosmetics departments were designed for the way women really use them, there would be plenty of mirrors, all at the right height. A shopper would be able to see her face from twenty paces away. It's what would draw her in. And all the expensive, flattering lighting would be trained on the shoppers' faces, not on Elizabeth Hurley's.

However, you can quickly scan the department and figure out which furnishings were thought to be most critical by the retailer. The graphics—the big, expensive posters, replicas of the big, expensive ads that ran in *Vanity Fair* and *Vogue*—are beautifully realized and prominently displayed and advantageously illuminated by spotlights. Somebody believes in these ads. The merchandise comes second.

You might think that given enough time and money, somebody would solve the problem of cosmetic tester units. But it hasn't happened yet. The challenge is to come up with a display that shows all the various shades of lipstick or powder or eye shadow and so forth, and allows the woman to try a few herself. This hunk of plastic (which is what it usually is) is the keystone of the open-sell method of cosmetics retailing. Without it—without giving women a way to see what that shade looks like on her skin—it all comes to naught. Women are always looking for something new in cosmetics. Even if they love the shade of lipstick they're using now, they're keen to find something newer, or better.

Each of these testers starts life looking attractive and inviting, brimming with shades and textures and so on. Then it hits the store, and all hell breaks loose. Women start using them! And that's where the illusion begins to disintegrate. In order to touch one pot of lip gloss, it is almost impossible to avoid dragging your cuff through three others. Or as soon as you pick up one pencil, all the rest go rolling onto the floor.

"They're struggling with pencils, too," Carol says. "*Everybody* has a problem with pencils. Nobody has figured out how to sell the pencil piece in an open-sell environment. And the lipstick presentation leaves a lot to be desired. The cleanliness problem is *the* number-one issue. Cleanliness is critical. Your lips are a very personal area."

"Don't you think the mirrors should be magnified?" I ask. "You know, as we get older, our eyes get worse. And the older shoppers are the ones who really need makeup, more than the kids do."

"Absolutely. But the companies don't design these departments to make the shopper the star. To them, the star of this counter is the supermodel or the celebrity who's in the ad campaign. After all, they paid her a ton of money—she *must* be the star. After her, the secondary star is the lady who is selling the product. Then, in last place, comes the customer. It's totally wrong."

"And the lights here are *horrible. . . .*"

That wasn't Carol or me—it was the sales associate, a very pleasant-seeming lady who has been quietly eavesdropping but now has her own two cents to contribute.

"They really are, aren't they?" Carol sympathizes. "Fluorescent lights give everything a yellow cast. It makes it hard to know what a color really will look like."

"Well, that's why I suggest that they go over to that full-length mirror there, near the window."

"You see?" Carol says. "That's what a good salesperson does. How long have you been here?"

"Two years in November. Are you people with the main office?" the saleslady asks us. "Because if you are, we have no product here on the floor."

"Yeah, I can see that," Carol says.

"The shelves are empty. I have nothing to offer. I am absolutely down on everything. And I won't sell my customers something that's wrong for them."

"That's great."

"Because then she'll never come back to me. I don't make customers, I make friends."

"As it should be," Carol says.

"Well, have a lovely day. It's a shame you have to spend it in here like I do."

"Oh, no," Carol says. "We're shopping. This is fun."

# 8 *Sex and the Mall*

NOW WE'RE leaving cosmetics behind and strolling the rest of the mall. We've gone a few paces before we come upon a window display that stops us, which is what they're supposed to do.

We're looking into the window of H&M, the giant Swedish apparel chain. They've done an outstanding job of cornering the market for what I call disposable clothes—garments that look really trendy and stylish but cost around $25 or less. Teenagers worship H&M. The window is populated by sylphlike mannequins, reed-thin representations of your average postadolescent girl-woman. Not one of them is dressed in anything you'd expect to see worn at Sunday school.

"My niece will *make* my sister take her to H&M every time they visit me in New York," Carol says. "My sister likes the prices but hates the styles."

"Some of it's like hooker wear, isn't it?"

"Teenage hooker wear."

"Older people look at how girls dress, with the belly exposed and hipbones exposed and the tight, flimsy tops and skin-tight pants, and it alarms them. But young girls have no idea what a hooker looks like or even what a hooker *is*. To her, it's just how glamorous young women look today."

"The other thing to keep in mind is that grandmothers today also dress less conservatively than ever before. When the line moves, it moves for everybody."

We move a few stores along, until the window with the number-one "capture rate" in any mall in America stops us again.

"Here's where mall sex really started," Carol says.

"Is that what Victoria's Secret is selling?"

"I think it's selling sex *appeal*. Inexpensive sex appeal. Women visit this store to get in touch with their feminine side. The company has taken underwear from being a staple to being something where there's a personal connection. This is especially true for women thirty-five and younger. Though I always wonder what the woman who's over thirty-five is supposed to do about getting in touch with *her* feminine side."

"Another example of how the mall reflects real life—because when women hit a certain age, society stops thinking of them as sexy. The stores are an example of that. Compare the H&M window with a window aimed at the fifty-year-old woman."

"Susan Sarandon must be pushing fifty-five."

"Sophia Loren passed sixty many moons ago. Where do you think she shops?"

"The funny part is that while Victoria's Secret sells modestly priced goods, older women could and absolutely *would* pay a good deal more for lingerie," I point out. "They're the ones who have the higher disposable income, and their tastes are more sophisticated. They're ready to splurge a little on themselves, to go along with the pedicures, facials, body waxings, spa treatments, and botox. They'd pay big bucks for gorgeous, high-quality underwear. If only somebody would sell it to them."

"There *are* fancier brands of lingerie, but sold either in department stores or in boutiques. Victoria's Secret has a special label for older shoppers, but I think the company is missing a bet by not opening a separate chain of stores for them. They could call it Victoria's Mother's Secret."

"They're also not aggressively serving the plus-size woman of *any* age," I say. "Now, maybe they don't want older or bigger women because they're afraid it would drive away the young, thin shopper. But it seems there must be a way for them to go after those other markets, too."

"Especially when you consider that a substantial percentage of the population of American women is overweight," says Carol. "And they're not even all old. I see a lot of fat teenagers and women in their twenties."

"Well, there *is* a high fashion chain now for young chubbies."

"I've seen it. There's a chain of stores called Torrid. And the clothes they sell are *sexy.*"

"Yes indeed. Big young girls tend to get big in the right places."

"And they're not bashful, either. As long as they're fat and curvy, they can make it work. Major cleavage. Narrow at the waist and tight on the butt."

"This is one of those weird gulfs between media imagery and real life," I say. "Judging by the fashion magazines you'd think that women would be ashamed to be overweight. Judging by how the weight of the average American girl has gone up, though, you get the opposite impression. But even if Victoria's Secret carried big sizes, could big girls get away with wearing this stuff?"

"Like thongs, you mean?"

"Well, yeah."

"Big girls wear thongs, believe me," Carol says. "And they buy them here, too. You won't see plus-size mannequins, but thong sizes absolutely go up to extra-large, you'll notice."

"Victoria's Secret really *did* make it okay for the average young woman to wear racy underwear."

"Yes," says Carol, "and the advantage of the low prices is that you can wear the stuff as long as it's fun, then replace it. This is where girls go when they first begin buying their own underwear. This is how they announce, 'My mom doesn't buy my underwear anymore.' Victoria's Secret sells hottie underwear for Catholic girls. It's not sleazy or even too sophisticated. They steered clear of the Frederick's of Hollywood image of a lingerie store. They got rid of the red and made it all pink."

"So, they do a good job, right?" I ask.

"They could do better," Carol says. "One problem I have with *all* lingerie stores is that—look, here you have a section of bras. And nowadays, every bra does something a little different. It's gotten to be like cosmetics in that regard. But there's no way to know which bra does what unless you've had personal experience with it. There's no information here to explain that this bra does blah, blah, and blah. This one pushes them together, and this one shoves them up, and here's one for strapless dresses. Now, partly that is intentional. They don't want you to get too much information on your own. They'd rather even confuse you a little so that you'll take a whole bunch of bras into the dressing room, because the more you take in, they know, the better the chance that you'll buy multiple items. They've measured this, and they're right. But at the same time, it frustrates consumers."

Carol is right about that: There's no communication here, no sign that says, for example, "If you've always loved this kind of bra, you'll probably love this new style, too." Maybe there could even be an informational display telling a young woman how to build a proper lingerie wardrobe. Like, you'll need one of these and two of those and here's how to choose these little thingies.

"Women pick up their knowledge of cosmetics and lingerie in a totally ad hoc way," Carol says. "You see something about push-up bras in a magazine, or your older sister lends you her new lip gloss, and you kind of piece your information together like that."

"It's like locker room conversation."

"Right. You see somebody else try it, and you ask a few questions . . ."

"The same way adolescents learn about sex. You read three issues of *Cosmo,* and then a fifteen-year-old tells you the rest."

We've made it all the way up to the second level of the mall. We've broken out of that little cluster of stores serving young female sexuality. But we're now looking into a den of older female sexuality—the threshold of a fancy department store's fragrance section. Department stores always put the fragrance section at the entrance.

"Is this positioning a good idea or bad, do you think?" I ask.

"Bad. The thing about fine fragrance is that people buy it twice a year."

"Christmas . . ."

". . . and Mother's Day. Maybe Valentine's Day, too, although men are much less confident buying perfume than women are."

"Tell me what you think of that," I say, nodding toward the huge poster above the counter. It shows a brooding, sulky-lipped hunk, a stud of maybe twenty-one or so, with hairless, highly sculpted pectoral muscles on prominent display.

"It doesn't do anything for me," Carol says. "He's the son of the consumer, not the man she's going to bed with. I bet he's a good fifteen years younger than the average shopper in this section. I mean, put Harrison Ford up there, not this twenty-year-old. He's a *boy.* This is the Madison Avenue mentality at work. Some creatives and executives in an ad agency dream this up and cast it and style it and shoot it without bothering to understand the consumer—the person who will have to look at it. They imagine how the picture will look in the ad in *Vanity Fair* or on TV, without considering how it will play in the store. They may want to target a younger consumer. They feel that the way to do this is with a new men's fragrance geared toward this beautiful young man. They hope they'll bring a younger woman to the counter to buy this new fragrance for her young man, and then she'll shop the cosmetics, too."

"Won't that work?"

"Look around."

Ouch. Department stores' core shoppers *are* getting old, and no young women are taking their place.

"Also, men anywhere near fragrance or cosmetics is a nonstarter."

"Same for lingerie?" I ask.

"Nearly as bad."

"Apparel?"

"About the same."

"If a man is uncomfortable hanging around in the perfume aisle or shopping the racks of undergarments, is he likely to buy there?" I ask.

"I don't see how he could."

"I wonder what would happen if, say, Victoria's Secret were to open a ministore just for male shoppers at Christmas or Valentine's Day. It might look a lot like the store now does. But it would work differently," I say. "It would have to actually address size and function, and in a completely new way. Women know their sizes, and so it's no great trick to handle that when they're shopping for themselves."

"A woman knows her man's sizes, but men don't know women's, do they?"

"Men don't even know their *own* sizes," I say. "Remember, we saw men's underwear being sold to women in Filene's. Can you imagine finding women's underwear for sale in a men's clothing store? Years ago, one of our video cameras caught a guy shopping the underwear rack when he suddenly twisted around, pulled out his waistband in back and attempted to read the size on the label. It's conceivable that in his entire life he had never before bought his own underwear—first his mother bought it, then his girlfriends, now his wife."

"Can you imagine a woman not knowing what size panties she wears?" Carol says.

"Unimaginable."

"Anyway, you can see how men might feel ill at ease buying lingerie for women. For starters, he doesn't know her size. I guess if he was really intent on buying her something intimate, he could always snoop around in her dresser drawer and read a few labels."

"True," I say, "but that requires some forethought. Plus, it sounds perverted. If he gets caught, she may think he's looking for something lacy to wear under his Dockers. How would you handle ladies' lingerie for the impulse gift buy? It's February 13, and he's in a panic. He's already been to the jewelry store and didn't find anything he liked in his price range. He's prowling the mall like a desperate animal. Time is running out. Suddenly he notices a display window filled with lingerie. The lightbulb goes on—for what a modest piece of jewelry costs, he can get something truly extravagant in the fancy underwear department."

"If only he knew her size," Carol says. "It's tragic."

"What do you suggest?"

"He can say to the saleswoman, 'She's around your height . . .' "

"Or, 'Gee, I think her breasts are a little bigger than yours.' "

"Or, 'Hmm, let me hold your butt a second so I can figure out if she's a medium or a large.' "

"That might be beyond what most salesclerks are willing to abide, even those working on commission," I say.

"How about if they had mannequins of various sizes?"

"And a bunch of male customers lined up, fondling them? I don't see that, either. Maybe a gift certificate works best here."

"Or maybe at gift time the window display is dominated by garments where size is easiest—robes instead of bras."

"Anything sheer," I say.

"Or black leather," Carol says.

"The point is that it's possible to make women's merchandise easier for men to buy. And that doing so around the romance-friendly holidays might not be a bad idea. I think if men walked by Victoria's Secret and saw that some of the signs and posters and photographs were directed specifically at them, they'd feel more welcome. Just something that says, 'Sir, we'd love to show you a few perfect gifts for her.' Because right now that entire store announces, 'Hey, buddy, stay the hell out of here.' "

"It's true," she says. "You don't see many men in there, do you?"

"Sure don't. And the few who are here are all just tagging along with wives or girlfriends, with their eyes cast downward in case they accidentally see something. They're ashamed! Look at that one pathetic little chair in front of the pillar, up by the register. That's the entire accommodation for men who end up inside the store. It looks like a punishment—like the dunce chair. Merely by sitting there, a man announces, 'I am an emasculated husband waiting uncomfortably for my wife to find a thong in her size.' Especially in a mall store, where you know the woman is likely to be with her family, you've got to plan for the nonshopper as much as the shopper. A Victoria's Secret on a city street, where the typical customer is a woman on her lunch break, can get away with neglecting the needs of men and children. A mall store cannot."

"But this mall does have areas where people who aren't shopping can just sit and wait or read the paper or watch everybody else, doesn't it?" Carol says.

"Sure it does. But think about the way it works in real life. The couple is walking along when suddenly it hits her that she needs underwear. Here are her choices. She can ask him to come inside the store with her. Or, she can run in alone and leave him standing out here cooling his heels in front of a window populated by panties and bras, which means that every window shopper who passes will be staring straight at him, too. He'll love that. Or, he can find another store to go and browse, assuming there's anything he finds remotely interesting in the immediate vicinity. Maybe there is a record store or bookstore or the new Apple computer store or something like that. But most malls now group merchandise categories, meaning the women's clothing store is probably surrounded by other shops of interest to women. So he's screwed. He could go all the way down the corridor and around the corner to the public seating area. But he may not even know it's there, and secondly, she's assured him she'll just be two minutes, and so he's got to ask himself if it's worth his while to go so far to kill a hundred and twenty seconds. If there was a small waiting area just outside the store, he'd probably go there. But then you run the risk that you'll have a gaggle of guys loitering outside the lingerie store, which isn't the most agreeable setting for female push-up bra shoppers. I think that lingerie stores should do more to make males feel at ease."

"I disagree completely," Carol says. "No woman in her right mind wants to come into this store with her husband and children. This is not the kind of thing you want to be shopping for where your guy or, even worse, your eight-year-old son, can watch. You're in here to create a little romantic fantasy starring yourself, and it doesn't involve somebody's lumpy husband or bratty kids whining to go to the food court. I think it's smart of them to make it difficult for men to loiter in here, and I bet they did it as a conscious decision."

That's a good point. It runs completely counter to all that we've learned about the science of shopping, and yet I am convinced that maybe she's on to something. We once studied a store that sold dishes and tabletops and so on. We saw that many women came in with their husbands, but the men got bored tagging along, and, as a result, the women seemed pressured. The store tried adding products men might browse—bar items like cocktail shakers, shot glasses, and so on. When that happened, the men went off on their own, and total shopping time for couples rose. Sales rose, too.

But perhaps what's right for dishes is totally *wrong* for lingerie. Maybe the woman wants to tell her husband and kids to get lost for fifteen minutes, and going into Victoria's Secret is a good way to do so.

A recent study of how men and women differ when it comes to the mall turned up this fact: Men, once you get them in the door, are much more interested in the social aspect of malls than the shopping part, whereas women say the social aspect is important but shopping comes first. Men enjoy the mall as a form of recreation—they like watching people and browsing around in stores more than shopping. Maybe they'll spend fifteen minutes in a bookstore or a stereo store and leave without buying a thing. They treat it like an information-gathering trip. Men also like the nonretail parts—the rock-climbing walls, the food courts, anything that doesn't actually require them to enter stores and look at, try on, or buy merchandise. Women, of course, are there for *exactly* those things. The only females who truly love the nonshopping aspects of the mall are teenage girls. They love shopping, of course, but they also love the food courts and video arcades and all that stuff, too. And that's probably because the mall is the only nonhome, nonschool environment they have. But they outgrow that by the time they're in college. From then on, they're at malls to shop.

"Let's get back to where to put fragrance if we want men to buy it," I say.

"In Sears near the power tools?"

"I bet more men would buy it there than in the cosmetics department."

"Where else?"

"Closer to jewelry might work," I say. "In fact, you could group all the traditional gifts that men give women and see how that works. That's one of the few remaining advantages this department store has over a specialty shop or boutique—that wide range of merchandise. They can get a little creative with their juxtapositions."

"So you'd have fragrance, jewelry, and lingerie all together, in a way that feels male-accessible," Carol says.

"Yeah. You'd put up graphics showing a man making a purchase of something gift-wrapped with a pink bow. With that big hint, at least some men might be psychologically able to enter the area and shop it. Put a salesclerk at the entrance to guide men across the threshold—a good-looking woman to take him by the arm and gently drag him inside. And I think women would be willing to buy things there, too."

"The Extravagance Shop."

"Right. I'd give it a name to appeal to guys. It would give them permission to shop there, something men really don't have now in women's departments. And I'd make sure it was marketed to male shoppers, especially around the usual gift times like Christmas, Valentine's Day. . . ."

"Yes," says Carol. "Because fragrance only gets shopped twice a year, having it at the entrance gives the impression that the store is empty."

"It is less crowded there than anywhere else, but is that a bad thing?"

"Sure, who wants to shop at a store where nobody goes? It's like going into an empty restaurant. It doesn't inspire great confidence."

"Do you know why fragrance is traditionally right inside the entrance in department stores?" I say. "Because, back in the days before cars, the perfume section was a bulwark against the stench of horse manure coming in from the street."

"Fascinating," says Carol.

Sounds like Carol's had her fill of the mall, considering that today's her day off and she spends plenty of work time in shopping centers anyway. It's an occupational hazard, mall-sickness, one even I've experienced. Time to move on.

# 9 *The Charmin Challenge*

I NEED TO use the bathroom, and you're coming with me.

From the developers' point of view, this particular amenity is a necessary evil. If you're going to invite people to your mall, not to mention your food court, you've got to give them toilets. You don't have a choice. This may sound like a callous attitude—and it is—but it's also easy to understand. It's a real cost and effort to keep public bathrooms presentable.

Bathrooms are nothing but trouble. Years ago, some mall men's rooms were notorious as gay trysting stations, particularly ones located within department stores. It's less of an issue today. One wise developer I know always locates the manager's office near the johns, on the theory that employees will therefore be more likely to check in on the facility from time to time. I can't say whether it makes a bit of difference.

You can just imagine the insurance and legal liability issues that arise. To the extent that muggings do occur in malls, they may take place in rest rooms, which are usually hidden down some lonesome corridor away from the main thoroughfare. In fact, that's the best way to find the bathroom in an unfamiliar mall—look around for the least inviting hallway, the narrow one where the lighting is dimmest.

See? Here's just such a passage radiating off the promenade. It's gloomy and unwelcoming—if the mall were an urban setting, this would be an alley. Come on, let's go inside.

This is the typical mall bathroom—institutional tile and porcelain in neutral shades. At least it's clean, and it appears there are paper towels in the dispensers.

It's always striking how planners of big public places such as malls, sports arenas, concert halls, and so on mishandle the gender differential in bathrooms. Just stand out in the corridor and count the number of people walking in the rest room doors. You'll learn an important fact that architects seem never to realize.

Women use the bathroom more than men. They spend more time in them, too. These must be little-understood truths; otherwise, there would be twice as many ladies' bathrooms as men's, or the former would be double the size of the latter. But they're not. Planners are rigidly symmetrical where bathrooms are concerned. It's why, for instance, you often see a line outside the ladies' room but rarely at the gents'.

When you consider how much the mall depends on the goodwill of its female market base in particular, you can see how the number and condition of bathrooms might be somewhat important. As we've seen elsewhere, the critical issue for mall owners is finding ways to extend the average visit. Talk to any woman and you quickly learn how pleasant bathrooms make prolonged visits possible, while nasty toilets encourage the quick in-and-out.

❖   ❖   ❖

Not only do women use rest rooms more often than men do, but they require more once there. Is it any surprise that male mall executives might not always provide for the most pleasant breast-feeding experience? It isn't, but that's one of the added functions I'm talking about, and an important one considering how happy many mothers of young children are to take advantage of a mall's distractions.

I admire any mall, department store, or other retailer that pays attention to the lowly toilet, for that is a company building goodwill. There are so few good public facilities in America that firms which provide them will stand out. If you walk the streets of New York today, there are only a few reliable bathroom stops you can make: most hotel lobbies, and, for some reason, any Barnes & Noble. Even their men's rooms feature baby changing tables, which exhibits a sure knowledge of customer habits, since so many urbane dads take the little ones out for a stroll to the nearest bookstore. The bathrooms designed by Philippe Starck for the Delano and Paramount Hotels are so distinctive that they've become required stops for tourists. Still, most public places—malls included—go on treating this most necessary and human place as something shameful.

But at least the mall can be counted on to provide a bathroom of some sort. Retailers and even fast-food restaurants have seen fit to phase out this particular amenity, which strikes me as a heartless disregard for their customers' humanity and dignity. But they save a lot of dough and aggravation. The other day I was in a Starbucks in New York when a customer asked for the rest room. She had a French accent, and so, I assume, she had grown up under the misguided notion that businesses selling beverages make some accommodation for nature's call.

"We don't have bathrooms," the *barista* said, then added helpfully: "Try the diner on the corner—*they* have bathrooms."

Maybe it's just in the United States that we're so weird about washing and changing and going to the bathroom? In some Japanese stores and malls, you'll find freestanding sinks located outside of the bathrooms, permitting shoppers who need only to wash their hands a way to do so without crowding the johns. It is also a public statement about hygiene as an important issue. That's a smart move, but not surprising in a culture where bathing has an exalted role in the average person's life. (Some Japanese public toilets are equipped with bidets.)

What always amazes me as I stand in this spot is that the mall, which is a temple to blandishment and consumption, can't think of a single interesting thing to do with a bathroom. Here you've got a captive audience, one that will probably spend at least sixty seconds or so with nothing much to see or hear. And the mall does zero to fill those empty moments.

What would a more enterprising mind do? Well, the simplest solution would be to sell some advertising positions—maybe a few poster spots over the urinals, or on the inside of stall doors, or above the sinks. That's the obvious answer.

The rest room could be turned over to one of the several shops in the mall selling bath-related products, such as soap, skin cream, fragrance, hair care. Your average mall bathroom's ambience would be dramatically improved if, say, Aveda or The Body Shop furnished the sinks with samples of various sweet-smelling goods. Even cosmetics would work here—women love trying the newest lipstick or fragrance. A woman could test some new soap or moisturizer, want more, and be directed to the store to find it. A guy could discover some new hair gel or virile cologne and do likewise. Or there could be monitors showing promotional fashion videos or new DVD releases from the music store. The acoustics in here would be awesome with a decent sound system.

Not long ago I toured a new prototype store for Lowe's, the home improvement chain, with maybe ten members of the senior marketing team. At some point I asked to see the ladies' room, which caused a certain amount of unease among my all-male companions, but we found a woman to enter first to check if the coast was clear, and in we went. The first shock came when a quick poll of the group revealed that not one of these men had ever been in a ladies' room, despite their high position and years of service at a company that depends on female customer satisfaction practically above all else. The second revelation was that the bathroom, while clean and odorless, was also the most generic, no-frills facility imaginable—kind of weird, I pointed out, in a store that tries hard to convince people to buy modern, luxurious bathrooms.

"Has no one ever considered using this as a kind of showroom for the things you sell out there on the floor of the store, twenty-five feet away?" I asked. "What if you turned each bathroom over to a different manufacturer?" I asked. "This could be the American Standard rest room, and they would install all their coolest sinks and toilets here, and maybe Kohler could redo the men's room, and so on like that."

I've suggested to the marketing people at Proctor & Gamble that they sponsor ladies' rooms in major airports—hire an attendant with a mop and a bucket to keep the place clean, and stock the joint with all their newest products. They could, in each stall, offer some no-frills brand of toilet paper alongside the latest, plushest innovation from Charmin—a comparison test at least as compelling as the Pepsi challenge. It isn't an outlandish proposal—if the magic bullet in twenty-first-century marketing is creating buzz, the bathroom at the airport has the right demographics, enough anxiety to ensure that most people's personal radar systems are up and running, and the assurance that whatever the impression—it's going somewhere.

The fact that no bathroom to my knowledge does any of this—and I make a point of visiting the rest rooms on every mall trip—is but one more example of the usual disconnect between the real estate–minded management and the building's function as one great big retailing machine. An entrepreneurial approach to the well-appointed rest room could turn even this place into a profit center.

# 10 *Status Anxiety and Back Pockets*

**W**E'RE about to plunge into another shopping expedition. We have a seemingly straightforward task before us—finding jeans for Michelle. But as is usually the case in the mall, nothing is as simple as it seems.

We're going to meet Michelle near the Ralph Lauren store, which is as good a landmark as any. She is a twenty-year-old who hails from Staten Island. She has an Irish father and Palestinian mother, giving her a lovely olive complexion and a wit more mature than her years. She has a very precise style, no unusual piercings, no visible tattoos. Her eyebrows are neatly manicured, and occasionally the makeup gets a little dramatic.

Staten Island is a New York City borough separated from the rest of the world by three bridges and a ferry. It has a short subway, a small greenbelt, and a Tibetan art museum that more outsiders than locals know about. Staten Island weddings are famous for the pastel colors of the dresses and dinner jackets of the bridesmaids and ushers. Parts of it are grimy and industrial, but the side that faces New York Harbor has some of the most spectacular views on the eastern seaboard. The Verrazano Narrows Bridge linking Staten Island with Brooklyn has a $9 toll, making it an expensive trip to the mainland. It is home to mobsters and hardworking immigrants making the transition from urban to suburban life. Historically, the only reason to leave is to work or to visit Yankee Stadium, and now that Staten Island has its own minor league baseball club, there is even less reason to wander.

Michelle gets up before dawn to make the ninety-minute commute to her job in Manhattan. Twice a month she'll go clubbing there on a weekend night. Through her job and her excursions, she's seen the world beyond her island. As the product of a blue-collar family in a pink-collar job, she is growing in white-collar directions. Her aspirations and appetites are as boundless as her pocketbook is limited. She lives at home, and a big piece of her paycheck is devoted to car payments. She has definitely outgrown her teenage years. She knows the names of some famous English DJs, giggles at *Cosmo,* and can spot (or thinks she can) a fake Hermès bag at twenty-five paces. She knows about classic good looks and works hard to present herself.

To Michelle, our mall is nirvana. To get there she has to drive past at least three other major shopping centers, but she'll make this trip two or three times a year.

And here she is, right on time.

"Michelle, how far are we from your home?"

"Hmm, maybe twenty-five minutes if there's no traffic."

"So it's not really far. But this isn't your usual mall, is it?"

"No, there are two other malls where we'd normally go."

" 'We' meaning?"

"Me and my girlfriends."

She's here alone today.

"Why *do* you come here?" I ask.

"It's got some nicer stores that the other malls don't have. There's a Diesel and an Armani Exchange here. This is where you come when you know what you're looking for. This isn't a browsing mall for us."

"What does that mean? Why wouldn't you come here to browse?"

"Because everything here is more expensive than at the other malls. And it's farther away."

"Got it. If you were here with your friends, would you all drive separately?"

"No, together."

We're walking past a department store when we see a sign announcing the presence of Georg Jensen silver.

"What do you think of this sign here?" I ask.

"I have no idea what it means."

"Do you know the name Georg Jensen?"

"I wish I did, because it makes me feel a little ignorant to see a sign like that and have no clue what it's about."

"It's a Scandinavian silver maker. Just a brand name, like Ralph Lauren."

"Actually," she says, "I went into the Ralph Lauren store while I was waiting for you."

"Did you look at jeans?"

"No, I felt invisible there."

"What?"

"Because nobody seemed to notice me, not even the salesclerks."

"So you left."

"Of course."

"Is there something intimidating to you about this mall?"

"Sort of."

"Can you describe it?"

"Well, you walk in, I don't know . . . if I go into Saks, I don't feel like anyone thinks I'm going to be a big spender, so they don't care enough to ask me how I'm doing, or if I found my size or anything like that. I even get the same feeling about the people who shop in the mall. That they're all kind of snooty, and so the people who work in the stores are, too. Or they want to be snooty."

We enter a fashionable young women's apparel retailer.

"Have you been in this store before?"

"Yeah."

"Ever bought anything?"

"No."

The slender and attractive sales associate comes over.

"Hi, how are you?"

"Good," says Michelle.

"Fine," say I.

Michelle has barely begun examining jeans when she has a question.

"Do you have any with back pockets?"

"No, we don't."

"None?"

"No."

Michelle turns to go.

"What's the deal with the pockets?"

"I only wear jeans with back pockets."

"Only?"

"Yeah."

"Why?"

"Because the ones without pockets don't look right on me."

"You like the pockets?"

"I like how they look."

"Would you ever put anything in them?"

"It's not about what you put in them."

"So you *wouldn't* put anything in them?"

"Oh, maybe if I was going out and I didn't wear a jacket and didn't want to carry around a bag, I'd put some cash and my license in the back pocket. . . ."

"Not a wallet?"

"No!"

"A cell phone?"

"Very funny."

"So what's the point of the pockets, then?"

"Pockets makes the difference in how they're made. And usually jeans without pockets are stretch, and I don't like how stretch jeans look on me."

"It has something to do with how they look in back, I'm getting that sense, am I right?"

"Yes," she says patiently. "If you're really skinny, then it doesn't matter, but I'm not skinny back there. So it matters."

How did I know it was headed back there? Somehow, when shopping for women's clothes, it invariably comes down to the butt. No wonder there's such dizzying variety in the world of jeans, meant as they are to display (to good or ill) that part of their wearer, male or female. Jeans are also the uniform of the mall, regardless of the age of the wearer. I've made the point that we come to the mall to satisfy our need to watch people, but I'd wager that, after faces, the most popular focus for our looking is the butt. Most of those butts being watched are female, because women scrutinize them as avidly as men do, albeit for different reasons.

"How often do you sell a pair of jeans to someone over thirty?" I ask the associate.

"Every day."

"How about over forty?"

"I sold a pair this morning to a woman around seventy-five."

"They were for her granddaughter, though."

"No, they were for her."

"Did she look good in them?"

"They looked nice."

Next we come upon Diesel, the weirdly named, high-style Italian sportswear store.

There are plenty of jeans inside, displayed in a prominent and extremely confusing exhibit front and center in the store. You can't even tell which are women's and which are men's. In addition, the variations are dizzying—the fit, the shape of the leg, the coloration, on and on.

"Do you think these jeans are for guys or girls?"

"I think these are guys'."

An employee has ambled over to listen in.

"What makes you say that?" I ask.

"These look a little feminine. But those definitely look masculine."

"You're probably right. But do you notice how often this kind of confusion happens in clothing stores today?"

"It happens to me all the time. At the Gap especially, but anyplace where they sell men's and women's clothes next to each other. It happens at the sneaker store even, until you begin to pick out the pink trim."

This is a real issue for retailers, finding a way to signal gender to shoppers. You'd think that knowing which garments are for which sex would be the easiest thing in the world. I'll bet that back in the 1950s no one ever anticipated a world where clothing for adults of both sexes was sold side by side, and you'd have trouble telling one from the other. This is where graphics, especially big photographs, come in handy. It's an obvious solution, but fairly foolproof.

"Can I help you?" the associate asks at last.

"Yeah," I say, "what are we looking at?"

"Well, uh, these up this side are for men, and these down here are for women."

"Are you conscious that this is deliberately confusing?" I am referring to the fact that Diesel executives freely admit that they design confusing displays on purpose, based on the principle that a shopper who requires sales assistance is more likely to buy than one who shops solo. This is a truism in the world of shopping, by the way, and so quite possibly this decision was a clever one. Smart retailers are always trying to figure out ways to get shoppers to talk to their employees. The most obvious means, the no-brainer method, is what's known as "the six-second greeting" (or, in slower environments, "the ten-second greeting"), which simply dictate that a clerk will address a shopper within six (or ten) seconds of entering the store. The question then is what happens after that hearty, "Hi, howyadointoday!" In too many stores, the answer is "nothing"—nobody's bothered to figure it out all the way.

"But that's frustrating," Michelle says. "What if you want to buy jeans, but all the help is busy with other customers? And you just want to pick out a pair of jeans and go?"

"Well, the company doesn't believe that most shoppers will self-buy a pair of $150 jeans. So they make it all but impossible to pick anything without help from a clerk," I say. "They make it confusing—"

"Well," interjects the clerk, "it's not actually confusing, but—"

"No, I've read interviews with Diesel executives," I interrupt her right back. "They say it's confusing."

"Okay, I guess it is. But only the first few times you shop here."

This just deepens the sensation that you have to become a Diesel person—that you go through stages, from being ignorant to being somewhat knowledgeable to being a member of the club, which imparts a cultlike status. Which, again, is not a bad thing.

"Okay, can you take us through this?"

"Sure," the associate says, now turning her gaze on Michelle. "What you do is look at the picture and tell me what you like, and I can locate the style for you on the wall over here," she says, gesturing toward the built-in shelving that goes from floor to ceiling. "Do you know if you're looking for a low rise, a high rise?"

"Not too low. But not too high."

"A medium rise. Do you like boot cut? You're wearing boot-cut jeans."

"Yes. What color do they come in?"

"That style comes in the mocha, the copper, the green wash, that dark wash down there. . . ."

"Do they have a back pocket?"

"Uh . . . no. Do you like this color?"

"Not without a back pocket, I don't."

We head for another store.

"Michelle, let's check for back pockets first, okay?"

She rummages through the first denim display we hit.

"Pockets!"

We can relax a little now. The trail's getting warm.

"Hi, can I help you?"

"Do you have these in my size?" Michelle asks. The sales associate leads us over to a rack of jeans, all of which have back pockets, only now there's another issue to be considered.

"Michelle," I say, "whiskers or no?"

"Huh?"

"Whiskers. Those lines that make jeans look worn-in."

"Right. Whiskers, yes."

"Yes?"

"Why would they be a no?"

"No, I'm just wondering why they're a yes."

"They're cute. They look broken in. It's like new vintage jeans."

"True. But what's interesting about whiskers is where they bring the eye. We used to think jeans were only about the butt—how they fit back there. That still counts, only now *this* is the focus, too—the front. Whiskers draw your eye to the front."

"I guess they do!"

"Would you feel comfortable wearing jeans with whiskers if you were a guy?"

"You know," Michelle says, "until you mentioned it, I never thought about it."

"Or, if you see a guy wearing jeans with whiskers, do your eyes immediately go there?"

"I'll have to start paying attention."

"What is this guy talking about?" the associate asks her.

"Oh, nothing," Michelle says.

"My name is Melissa," she says directly to Michelle. "If you need any help, feel free to ask."

Michelle turns and waves to me. "Thanks, I'll take it from here."

# 11 *Fun*

I'M BORED.

Luckily, this mall offers quite a few things that have nothing to do with shopping. There must be a lot of people bored with shopping, since the nonstore portion of malls—what is sometimes optimistically referred to as the "entertainment"—keeps becoming a bigger part of the mix. Once upon a time, a dank little video game arcade was considered sufficient. Today malls have taken on a lot of the burden of keeping suburban America diverted.

In truth, the nonstore aspects are the only things that give a mall its character, since the stores are essentially identical from one mall to another. So far today here's what we've encountered:

A rock-climbing wall.

An ice rink. (For some reason, there was a spell when it seemed as if every mall in Texas was getting an ice rink. Do so many Texans really care to skate, or is it just that big Texas personality expressing itself by bringing rinks to areas where the temperature often tops a hundred degrees?)

A food court, of course. And that doesn't even take into account all the other shops and stands here where you can buy something to eat. All this food is meant for immediate gratification, too. Unlike malls abroad, ours rarely feature much in the way of real prepared food meant to be taken home and consumed. And malls here rarely include supermarkets. Mall eats are invariably low-fiber, high-sugar, high-fat, tasty, and fast. And there's food in your face every time you turn around.

A movie theater. But a movie feels like a treat after a day's shopping, not something you do in the middle of the afternoon. (Although just knowing that Jackie Chan movie is playing right now makes me a little antsy.)

And still awaiting us is the uppermost level of the mall. Reportedly, it is vast and given over to the amusement of adolescents and the young at heart (meaning middle-aged men who get as antsy as teenagers elsewhere in the mall).

The fact that malls keep increasing the amount of space they devote to nonshopping functions would indicate that there must be some economic sense to it. The thinking is simply that these various amusements extend the amount of time people will spend here. They do so in two ways. First, by supplying more than just a place to shop. This is a sound thought. If you've managed to attract people here for one purpose, you ought to see if there are other desires you can fulfill. It's fine if they come to shop, even better if they shop and eat, better than that if they shop, eat, play, socialize, and so on. This principle extends throughout retailing, not just here. If a convenience store can get you inside to buy milk, will you also stay to microwave a burrito?

It's been proven that the more time someone spends in a mall, the more stores they visit and the more things they buy. Again, there's an inescapable logic to that formula. Every mall owner in the world knows all this. It's just that they respond differently to it. Some like the idea of putting in a big, glitzy, raucous entertainment sector. It's the expensive way to go, but it's easy, too—you just install it and turn on the lights.

Entertainment also prolongs the stay by solving the central problem of group shopping: What do we do with the nonshopper? If an adult has to drag two sullen adolescents along for every step of a shopping expedition, you can be sure that the trip will end prematurely. Whereas if those adolescents can be given some enjoyable outlet for their energies, they'll let you shop for as long as you want. The mere promise of a reward may keep them quiet. (Of course, when you're ready to go you may have to drag them *out* of the mall.) This is the mall as suburban baby-sitter. You can force small children to go where you want, but once they wise up they present challenges. Taking them to the mall may seem safer than leaving them home, and sending them with a few bucks off to the arcade, food court, or movie is saner than keeping them by your side.

But the connection between such amusements and increased spending isn't ironclad. People may now come to the mall without intending to buy a single thing. In a recent study, slightly more than half of what people did in malls was unrelated to actual shopping—eating, movies, games, hanging out, socializing, and so on. Those who said the primary reason they came to the mall was "to have fun" spent less money than those who said they came to visit a department store—to *shop.* The survey also found that the overall perceived entertainment value of a mall is unrelated to the amount of time people devote to shopping or the number of items they buy. So shoppers can be exceedingly fond of their mall and still not spend much money or time in stores. It's a risk.

Malls sometimes err by placing the entertainment functions too far away from everything else. There's a certain logic to keeping the video game fans away from the devoted shoppers. But it's awfully easy to reach the entertainment cluster of this mall without having to pass many store windows. Perhaps the landlord should disrupt that smooth traffic pattern and force people to work their way through the mall before reaching this level. It might even make sense to put stores that appeal to teenagers—music, certain apparel stores, Spencer Gifts—either up here or at the base of the escalator leading here.

Teenage girls love malls best, I think—and here, according to a survey, is what they say they want in malls: a hangout-type Internet café–coffee shop (the kind of slacker paradise you find in cities, usually peopled with unemployed dot-commers); movie theaters; big seat-ing/socializing areas; places that boys might like; amusements, such as Ferris wheels and so on; and sports, including bowling alleys, batting cages, miniature golf, tennis. It's a long list.

One teenage girl tried to describe what would be in her perfect mall.

"I don't know if you've even been to Washington Square in New York," she began, "but it's this park, and they have these tables with like built-in checkerboards on top?"

These kids crave cities—they want to be a part of the human spec-tacle that exists whenever people come together. Sadly, what we've given them instead is malls. So the mall should attempt to provide some of the things that make adolescent society possible and enjoy-able.

Even stores can serve as forms of entertainment. Here's one cate-gory that's vanishing from malls overall, but can still occasionally be found: pet shops. Selling critters in the mall looks like a labor-intensive, somehow seedy undertaking. Still, go to any mall pet store, and you'll find children gathered around the front windows or the cages inside. It's like a zoo for small domestic animals—puppies, kittens, bunnies, the occasional piglet, all romping inside their too-small cages. It's one of those places parents dread. But five or ten minutes in such a store can restore the spirits of a cranky seven-year-old, thereby making it possible for parents to shop a little longer. Thanks to Animal Planet and the Discovery Channel, we get visually close to animals, but we can't smell or touch them. Even the modern zoo is discovering that close-ness to simple domesticated critters like goats, sheep, and ponies is a major draw.

Okay, here we are—the top level of the mall. It's crowded and bustling with high adolescent spirits and good energy as the teenagers bop from one video game to the next. There's a noticeable absence of shopping bags in their hands—these are not your prime shoppers. But that's not why they're here. The music is techno and loud. Over on one side is the food court, which faces the Ferris wheel. That's a good idea, considering how most food courts give you nothing to look at. It's also interesting to note that the only window in the food court is way up at the top of the Ferris wheel, meaning riders get a pretty cool view of the surrounding countryside. That's better than the celebrated new Ferris wheel inside Toys "R" Us's Times Square store, which affords only a view of the ceiling.

There's something that looks like the NASCAR wing of the mall up here—lots of driving video games and racing paraphernalia for sale. And it's mobbed, of course. Back behind that is the ice rink, and there's some kind of restaurant up here, it's a hybrid, part eating place, part playground. It actually has an old-fashioned tabletop shuffleboard set up, with sawdust and hanging lamp and everything.

And in back of the restaurant, maybe the purest entertainment chamber in the entire mall—a deafening, throbbing, clanging, whistling hall filled with every type of video game imaginable, including one in which you slam drums along to karaoke-style music. At some of the games you can win prizes, and under one teenage girl's seat is a long snake of tickets—there must be hundreds of them. This room feels like hell on earth to anyone over twenty-five, which means it's like Mecca for your average adolescent.

A few steps farther down the hallway, there's a large space that must have been devoted to something or other, once upon a time. Right now it's being used by two little guys for a Frisbee match. As garish and crazed as it feels up here, it makes a kind of sense. They've taken an entire level of the mall and essentially created a place where most adults wouldn't want to go. If they do come up here, believe me, they're not staying long. But it reinforces the concept of the mall as a destination with many purposes—like a city, in that regard. It goes from being a place for shoppers to one where the entire family can enjoy some of its leisure. Parents can shop and eat down there, and the kids can play, eat, ride the Ferris wheel, and so on up here. Having the kids' level up top makes perfect sense—parents can relax a little knowing that their children are upstairs, farther from the outside world.

# 12 *Hands-Free Shopping*

**M**Y HANDS are full.

If you've been paying attention, you know that I haven't actually purchased anything, and so my hands are as free as they were when I entered. But if I were a normal mall shopper, chances are by now I'd have bought *something.*

Depending on the weather outside and how far I parked from the entrance, I might also be carrying around my coat. If I had children along, I'd probably end up carrying their coats, too.

As part of the Envirosell playbook, what shoppers do with their hands is a critical issue. Whether you're stroking cashmere sweaters, hefting portable CD players or opening doors, your hands are key.

Some stores try to accommodate this fact of human physiology by providing handbaskets or shopping carts, which makes life quite a bit easier, especially if you're serious about buying something. We've done quite a few studies that bear this out, one way or another. Stores that offer baskets sell more than those that don't. And when stores increase the size of the baskets, they often find that shoppers purchase more items.

Many urban stores, as a security measure, ask shoppers to leave bags and briefcases with a guard just inside the entrance. This does decrease shoplifting as intended, but there's also an unintended benefit—it frees up the shoppers' hands, thus allowing them to scoop up more merchandise on their way to the checkout line.

If keeping a shopper's hands as free as possible makes a difference in a single store, you can imagine the impact in a mall, where the average person might enter a dozen shops in the course of a single expedition.

What do malls do to allow for this? Almost nothing. Once again, I believe this can be attributed to the disconnect between the real estate–driven developer and the retail-driven shopper. In a mall, space is money, and so management wants to dedicate as little space as possible to uses that don't generate profits. To be fair, you do find, in a few malls, coin-operated storage, like historically you found in bus stations and train stations. Even those were tucked away, often in the long corridor leading to the rest rooms. With the security concerns post September 11, that storage has largely disappeared.

I'm talking about coat check areas near every entrance.

I'm talking about will-call desks so that purchases can be held aside until you're ready to leave the mall.

Shopping carts to roll from store to store.

Baby strollers.

Hands-free shopping.

There are malls that offer coat checks. Typically, this service is provided by some local organization, such as the Kiwanis, who will charge a small fee and in that way raise money to fund good works. It may be admirable citizenship, but these setups always feel like amateur hour. They're usually tucked away in some underperforming corner of the mall, rather than where they should be—front and center, welcoming to every person who enters. Also, they usually handle coats and umbrellas only, which is part of the battle but far from all of it. And they don't inspire great confidence that your possessions will be competently guarded.

Ideally, every time you bought anything in the mall, the cashier would offer to run it down to the will-call desk for you, where you could retrieve it on your way out the door. In a perfect world, you might even be able to get your car first, then drive it up to the will-call exit, where a nice high school student would help you load whatever you bought into your trunk. It works at supermarkets, where some nice kid wheels your stuff out to your vehicle.

Never having to carry a purchase from one store to another (to another) and then to the bathroom and the food court and then up the rock-climbing wall would be a vast improvement over the current method, whereby you're stuck carting around whatever you bought, in whichever sequence you bought it. Even if you shop a small fraction of the 144 stores here, your burdens add up. The worst thing, from the mall's perspective, is the shopper who decides to run his or her bags out to the car. There's a chance that person will get out there and decide to go on home.

But maybe you're the kind of person who dreads coat checks and will-call desks because you fear a logjam just at the moment you want to leave. Plenty of people have an aversion to valet parking for the same reason.

In your case, the mall could offer shopping carts. Some shopping centers have experimented with them, but they have yet to catch on. Shopping carts are redolent of supermarkets, which feels a little low-rent to some mall operators and retailers. They're uncomfortable with the thought of tossing your brand new DKNY skirt into something better suited to carrying Cheerios. By contrast, many European malls have successfully and stylishly integrated supermarkets into the mall and thus shopping carts as well.

There *are* elegant shopping carts to be had—baskets riding atop silent rubber tires, with maybe a hanging rack for garments. Given the overall casual style of the mall itself, it doesn't seem as though carts would automatically be an aesthetic violation. Malls are now courting twenty-first century anchor tenants like the giant discounter Target. One of their criteria is whether shopping carts are welcomed, not just in the mall but in the parking garage or lot, too. More than one Target deal has been kiboshed by shopping cart–garage conflicts.

There's never a shortage of baby strollers in the mall, because parents feel free to bring them along. Still, it can be a hassle—you've got to unload the kids and the stroller and get the whole procession inside from the lot or garage. If an elevator trip is involved, it becomes even more cumbersome, especially on weekends when the mall is crowded. It's a temptation to leave the stroller in the minivan, except then the adult shoppers will be constrained by the endurance of small children, who can become tired and cranky without warning.

All this sounds like common sense, and yet malls make little accommodation for it. Some do provide strollers—but they, too, are usually hidden away in some corner, and almost always cost a few bucks to rent for the day. This seems about as sensible as charging people to use a shopping cart—making pennies off what, if offered free, would generate dollars.

# 13 *Pushcarts Rule*

Hey, WHAT'S this up ahead? Hold on a second.

I don't really need automatic gutter cleaners. I live on the first floor of an apartment building. And yet I am slightly fascinated by this little booth here—a pushcart, almost—right in the middle of the corridor, the one with the slightly bored-looking woman demonstrating for anyone who cares to watch (just me) how a gizmo can clear all the wet leaves and dead birds and whatever out of your gutters, thereby sparing you a climb up a rickety ladder.

It's not the kind of thing you'd expect anybody to buy on impulse while walking through the mall. And yet it's here, and paying a handsome rent no doubt, so somebody must be willing.

"How much does this thing go for?"

"Depends on your house," she says. "It starts at around $3,000."

"And do you sell any?"

"Enough," she says warily.

Maybe she thinks I'm a competitor? I'm standing here transfixed as a three-foot-long section of simulated roof gutter is swept clear by the gadget she's selling. The mall doesn't provide many guy moments, but this little demonstration has to rank among the most fascinating.

Right next to this is a more lighthearted pushcart—the bungee ball man, who spends the day showing off the coolness of his toy. It is an old pushcart profession that takes many forms. Someone takes a toy where some simple skill is involved—a ball tied to a paddle by a thick rubber band, a plastic airplane that returns to sender like a boomerang, a remote-control car—and demonstrates it. It always looks easier to master than it really is, as many customers can attest. The purchase is often as much a payment for the pleasure of watching the demonstration.

Judging by the audience he's gathered, this little vignette is a godsend. There are mostly dads and kids gathered around, no doubt happy to find something even mildly entertaining while mom goes about the serious business of acquisitioning.

It's a testament to the constantly evolving nature of the mall that most now include these freestanding kiosks. They tend to be locally owned and operated. Small-time retail, in other words, in marked contrast to the huge, slick chains that predominate in here. You may find some goods in kiosks that are sold elsewhere in the mall—costume jewelry, toys. But it's mostly the kind of merchandise that feels at home on a wooden cart plunked down right in the pedestrian path—cheap sunglasses, human-hair wigs, extravagant christening outfits, cell phones and pagers, put-your-photo-on-a-sweatshirt, celebrity posters. The "As-Seen-on-TV" shop thrives here, meaning you can buy a Hairdini braid twister even if you can never manage to jot down the 800 number before the commercial ends. Tupperware lives here, too—you can't really imagine an entire mall store devoted to plastic containers for leftovers, but it makes for a high-profile, crowd-pleasing kiosk.

When these things first began to show up in malls, tenants were outraged. The complaint was that the carts cheapened the ambience; they also were competitors who got away with paying less than the full mall rents, which didn't help their image among fellow tenants. So there was a trade-off, and even the danger that the kiosks would hurt the stores' sales, which would in turn cut into the mall developer's revenues. Still, the malls were willing to run a few risks if doing so allowed them to squeeze a few more leasable square feet out of the premises. Heretofore, the space occupied by kiosks was being used by shoppers to walk. Maybe they had more space than they needed?

At its inception, the pushcart was a brilliant retail concept. A small, efficient, mobile store, operated by one person, specializing in a few (or just one) product categories, and ideally suited to being examined by the shopper, since it is all surface and is approachable from all sides. No wonder pushcarts have been around so long, probably as long as we've had wheels.

Pushcarts were part of our retail memory, until they made their mall-related comeback. It started as a brilliant innovation at Faneuil Hall in Boston. At the time, the mall was about to open with less than a full roster of tenants. Somebody had the idea to fill in the gaps with pushcarts. They made things seem a little more bustling. The mall's developer, the Rouse Company, charged a nominal rent at first, unaware of what a dependable source of healthy income the carts would become. Since then, the classy peddler has become a signature of Rouse malls.

But then, as usually happens, the greedheads got hold of the concept and rode it for all it's worth. If you divide the mall into the smallest real estate parcels possible, you can charge a lot more money for them. Today, most malls have dedicated some portion of formerly open space to what are usually termed kiosks, in acknowledgment of the fact that rarely does anyone actually *push* these things.

From the mall's view, kiosks are wonderful for one main reason— the rents they kick in. Annual leases can hit $50,000 for a forty-five-square-foot kiosk, which is a lot more than Neiman Marcus pays, foot for foot. As much as 2 to 3 percent of a mall's total rental revenue can come from the carts. "It's real money, let's put it that way," said an executive from a developer that owns more than 150 malls. One estimate says that over 150,000 kiosks currently exist in American malls and shopping centers. They've become such a staple of retailing that now they proliferate in airports and office buildings, too.

The kiosks throw off so much easy rent (since they require no maintenance by the mall), that it's easy to overdose on them. Bring in too many and they begin to overwhelm the passageways. We use the terms "laudable crowding" and "impenetrable crowding." In the former, you're strolling through the mall and look up ahead to see an area that's bustling with genial hubbub. It makes you want to go there and see what everybody else is looking at. "Impenetrable crowding" is when you're strolling and look ahead to see a traffic jam of shoppers struggling to move. Kiosks placed too close together or jammed into inappropriate spots cause bad bustle. One look at the crowd of exasperated shoppers trying to get past and you decide to take a detour. In doing so, of course, you bypass every store in that area.

Good kiosks add something fun and even a little exotic to a mall's mix. Really good kiosks will surprise you—one of the best I ever saw was one selling microwavable heating pads. It's not that the pads themselves were so amazing, but I loved the lady who was selling them. She'd throw a few into her microwave while describing to the small crowd that invariably gathered how they worked. Once one was ready, she'd take it out and apply it to the aching neck or back of some volunteer shopper. It was a little bit of theater along with your shopping, and it harkened back to another vestige of ancient retailing—the barker.

Pushcarts are pure retailing. If you go to any store in this mall, you'll find some $40,000-a-year manager running the show, but only in the narrowest sense. In stores owned by national chains, all the big decisions about what will be sold and how, and at what price, and the way in which things will be displayed—the stuff that makes retailing an art—are made elsewhere. The kids running these shops aren't merchants by any stretch of the imagination. Whereas successful kiosk owners are working their retail magic—figuring out what works, succeeding or failing on the strength of their wit, ability, and energy.

They remind me of a produce stand I saw in a market in Istanbul. It was owned and run by an ancient man who'd probably been at it all his working life. I watched him for half an hour early one morning as he carefully positioned every apple and pear and eggplant, turning each piece in his hands to find the most perfect side, then placing it all just so on his cart. It was a work of art by the time he was through. He was no retailing titan or merchandising wizard. It was just a produce stand. But he was a merchant, top to bottom, intimately involved in every aspect of retailing, from purchasing the goods to displaying them for maximum appeal. I'm sure that his grasp of why we buy exceeds that of most mall store managers, simply because he understands and controls the process in its entirety. I don't mean to pick on mall store managers—it's not their fault that their employers expect so little of them. That's the nature of large, centralized corporations today, where all the meaningful decisions are made in a single office, by men and women who spend as little time as possible on the selling floor.

I love the Tupperware kiosk—the colorful plastic containers make for great displays, and they're just the kind of impulse purchase that does well in such a tiny space, in the midst of foot traffic. You don't need to deliberate for hours, just pick out what you need, pay, and go. I once saw a kiosk that sold only purple-colored merchandise, again, a brilliant idea from the display point of view.

Lots of kiosks specialize in goods meant for ethnic shoppers— human-hair wigs that are popular for African American women, or extravagant christening costumes that seem intended for Spanish-speaking customers, if the signage and staffing are any indication. You can't imagine these categories being able to support an entire store, at least not at these rents. But the kiosk is a perfect venue. This is another way that suburbia gets multicultural—most of the mall's shoppers will never even see one of these miniature tuxedos (complete with bow tie and waistcoat) that some Hispanic babies will wear to the baptismal font unless they see them here.

Most often, however, the pushcart world is populated with sunglasses, cell phones, costume jewelry, and the "As Seen on TV" shop. At first the malls thought the kiosks would be like an incubator—that today's pushcart would grow into tomorrow's store tenant. But that hasn't been the case. More common is the kiosk entrepreneur who expands numerically, growing from one cart to several (in separate malls) to many.

On a Saturday afternoon you may have thirty-three hundred people an hour passing a kiosk in a good spot. In our research we've found that more than half of the people in a mall will at least look at a pushcart and maybe 6 percent will actually shop one. They're especially popular among women twenty-five to thirty-four, who are most avidly seeking out the novel and the new.

Kiosks aren't the only things sticking out in the middle of the mall.

Car dealers are fond of sticking their new models in mall thoroughfares. It's a good idea, especially because there's precious little intended for men and boys here as it is. You can easily kill a few minutes checking out the latest Mini or Maserati. I don't know that a Saturn or Subaru or anything else that's already abundant in suburbia would make as much sense. And since women now either buy or influence the purchase of half of all cars sold in this country, the dealers are wise to reach them here in the mall. It's a great way to experience a car up close without having to talk to a car salesman or enter a dealership, which is an automatic plus in my book.

We're coming up on something now that's a cross between a kiosk and a resting place—a display of massaging easy chairs set right out in the main thoroughfare. You become part of the display the second you sit, which doesn't seem to bother those shoppers who are in the mood for an electric rubdown.

"Hey, how's it going?" I greet the chair's minder as I sit.

"Hi," the Asian man responds.

You see these chairs everywhere in Japan—they sell them in electronics stores. Usually they're set up in front of the TVs, so you can watch and try the chair, allowing you to sample it in a naturalistic setting.

"What's the wattage to run this chair?" I ask.

"Two-ten watts."

"Two lightbulbs."

"Yes. Like TV or refrigerator."

"Okay, and is this the price, $3,500?"

Not cheap by a long shot. A lot more than you'd expect to pay for a piece of furniture that's being sold right off the mall floor, without even a store to lend it an air of authority.

"Yes, plus shipping."

"Where is it made?"

"In Japan."

This display will be here for maybe a month, tops, and then they'll move on to another mall. It will get the most attention and trial use on the weekend, but I bet they don't sell a single chair from Friday to Sunday. These are commonplace in Asian homes, and they sell here mostly to Asian families. And there are now a lot of Koreans and Chinese and Taiwanese around here, as there are in and around most big cities. The serious buyers will come in during the week, when the mall is quieter, and buy then. For us curious browsers, it's a nice little stop.

Nice unless you're working inside the fancy healthy-back furniture store, I mean, where they also sell expensive electronic massage chairs.

"Come on, try the chair!" the saleslady coaxes when she notices me eyeing it. "What are you waiting for?"

"Have you seen the massage chairs out there in the mall?" I ask as I take a seat.

"Well, they're two different things," she says, smiling a little less. "What we sell here and what they sell there. We try to emphasize . . . that chair is too small for you."

She's referring to my height, in case you leapt to some erroneous conclusion.

"To answer your question," she says, "the same people who check out their chairs then come in here to compare them with what we have."

"And . . . ?"

"And so far we've had quite good responses to our chairs. You can adjust ours. You can select the spots you want massaged. In their chair, the spots are already set up. And we have two models. The one you're in is pretty much the same as theirs. It sells for $3,500."

"Same as theirs."

"Yes. But our *other* model sells for just $1,800. And the parts for our chairs are made by the same company that makes theirs. It's a little bit bad for us that they're allowed to be in our part of the mall, because they can be out there in the mall itself, and they can have more than one chair. But our store puts more of an emphasis on the ergonomics."

"Right."

"And on your back."

"Like with that $8,000 mattress?"

"Yes! Have you tried it yet?"

So far as I know, there's no mall that allows shoppers to try mattresses out in the main thoroughfare. So while the kiosks have their place, there's still something to be said for a store.

# 14 Mall Cuisine

I'M HUNGRY.

Personally, I am no fan of the mall's signature dining experience—the food court. I find them painfully noisy. Food courts are all hard surfaces, which are both durable and easy to clean. Tile, linoleum, Formica, stainless steel, and glass are all practical materials, except they turn the typically cavernous space into a giant echo chamber. The clamor of hungry shoppers creates quite a din. It's interesting to note that many of the most stylish restaurants and bars in Manhattan have this trait in common with the humble mall food court.

The noise makes it impossible for me to discern normal conversation. This means I'd normally stay far away from the food court, except as a place to study an important part of mall life. Feeding time.

We need food at the mall because, it seems, we need food everywhere. It's hard to think of a public space in America that doesn't offer up at least a few opportunities to eat. Each has its signature dish, too—

hot dogs at the ballpark (along with peanuts and Cracker Jack), pop-corn at the movies, and any number of delicacies on city streets. (I'm a traditionalist, and so I wait eagerly for roasted chestnut season on the streets of New York.) At the mall, you've usually got your pick of freshly baked chocolate chip cookie outlets, and by now we associate the pow-erful, Proustian aroma of Cinnabon with indoor shopping.

But the food court is the big act. Forget for a moment the quality of the food itself and focus on how it assembles dishes from every corner of the planet. Is there another place where the quasi-foodstuffs of Mexico, China, Italy, Thailand, Greece, Japan, and South Philadelphia come together like this?

From the mall's perspective, the food court has an important role—to prolong the shopper's stay. Without some kind of food you're good for two, maybe three hours before exhaustion overtakes you and sends you running for sustenance. Thanks to the food court, you can shop to the verge of starvation, fuel up, and maybe get in another hour or two. There's nothing inherently brilliant about food courts—the street ven-dors of hot dogs and ice cream and pretzels found in most downtowns serve the same function of feeding you quickly while holding you within the grasp of retail's visual come-ons. Depending on which city you're in, urban street eats are probably more adventurous than what you'll find at the chains, which predominate the food courts. Within two blocks of my office I can grab (depending on the time of year) some street vendor shish kebob, souvlakia, curry, hot dogs, a cross sec-tion of gourmet sausages, soft pretzels, sugar-coated nuts or coconut, bagels, falafel, knishes, Italian ices, pizza or calzones (from a pizzeria with a street side window).

Is food court food any good? It's good enough, I guess. If I were a suburban fifteen-year-old who had never experienced any delicacy more subtle than a Double Whopper, I wouldn't sneer at what I found here or wish for the barbequed eel roll from my favorite sushi joint. Nobody goes to the mall expecting anything more than a plastic tray full of edible nourishment and a clean table on which to enjoy it. Who are we to sneer?

The food court serves as the mall's Via Veneto, its main concourse for sitting and supping and sipping and people watching. I keep hoping to find one that takes this responsibility seriously—an ambitious food court that imagines itself as a huge sidewalk café, where tables all have a view not just of one another (clearly taken from the court's fast-food restaurant ancestry) but of the mall's main thoroughfares, with tables even spilling out a little into the corridors. I haven't found one yet.

The typical per person food court expenditure comes to around $6 or so, making it hard to complain too loudly. In fact, you'd find yourself hard-pressed to spend much more than that, which could be seen as a shortcoming of the operation. There may be shoppers willing to spend twice that $6 figure in the food court, but nobody to my knowledge has begun to find out. Where's the food court wine bar? The French bistro? If somebody knows, please send up a flare.

Let's move on and find one of the sit-down restaurants, which, luckily, this mall has in sufficient supply. Usually you'll find at least one or two, depending on the overall tenor of the mall. They're usually chains, which nowadays doesn't necessarily mean the food will be bland and inferior and the service awkward but chipper. Of course, neither are most mall restaurants the site of memorable dining. Wolfgang Puck has a few boîtes in malls, but by and large we end up with generic chain-restaurant fare.

In Japan, by way of contrast, restaurants and prepared-food shops at malls are of such high quality that many people stop there daily, on the way home, to pick up dinner. In any city there are plenty of good restaurants and takeout places that serve that purpose. Suburbanites, however, find limited choices in the prepared-foods department. Pizza, fast food, maybe a Boston Chicken, and whatever the local supermarket dishes up, and that's about it. If you're lucky you live near an ambitious diner, or a locally owned restaurant that takes itself seriously (and does takeout). In New York, there's a grocer/prepared-food shop in Grand Central Station that's always jammed at evening rush hour with suburban commuters picking up that night's dinner. If American malls' food operations took themselves more seriously as providers of meals, some of those people would no doubt grab something closer to home.

Interestingly, in one big mall we studied, one out of four people in the common area (*not* in the food court or a restaurant) were eating something. Some of these were having coffee or a chocolate chip cookie while walking, sitting on a bench, or leaning against a wall. Some had brought snacks from home. So it's clear that even food courts aren't capacious enough to house all the eating that goes on in a mall. Also, some food bought in the court migrates into the corridors of the mall itself. That, no doubt, is how some people express their dislike of the food court—they eat on the hoof, or while perched on the edge of the fountain. Given how often and how much we Americans eat, we must be willing to do it pretty much anywhere and everywhere, and certainly the mall lends itself to that—the surfaces are easy to clean, and everybody else is eating anyway.

At two points in my twenties I asked women to marry me. I got turned down on both occasions. Those two low points in my life were handed to me by ladies from Louisiana. More times than I'd like to admit, I wander into the Cajun joint in a mall food court, indulge in some Bourbon Chicken and Dirty Rice, and daydream over what might have been. Today is no exception.

# 15 Breakfast at Cartier

"OKAY," I SAY, "pay attention to that woman window shopping."

We're standing at an interesting spot in the mall, able to see both Cartier, the ultra-luxury French jewerly retailer, and its next-door neighbor, a discount jewelry chain.

"What's she going to do?"

"Hard to say. That's why we're paying attention."

I'm with Albert, a normal middle-aged guy, meaning there are a dozen places he'd rather be right now than here. He's shopping for jewelry for his wife. We've already scanned the Cartier window, which at this moment has that lady shopper's attention, and so we know it contains what's called a tennis bracelet—so named because Chris Evert, at the 1987 U.S. Open, dropped a diamond bracelet during a match and stopped play until she found it—a costly bauble in which a dozen or so round diamonds have been set in a straight row.

This is an interesting juxtaposition of stores, one engineered by the mall leasing office, which closely controls who goes where. The think-ing is that if you create a little cluster of stores that will attract like-minded shoppers, you increase sales for everybody (especially for the mall itself, which takes a piece of every dollar spent). It allows today's time-pressed shopper to hit one part of a mall, visit several stores that carry what he or she has in mind, and get the job done efficiently. But it's certainly not a new-fangled idea—for centuries at least, stores have organized into districts based on what they sell.

Jewelry especially lends itself to districts. Since buying it isn't an everyday experience, there's a degree of comfort in being able to shop more than one store. It also has historic roots. For example, however different in character, London has Old Bond Street, New York City has Forty-seventh Street, Istanbul has its Grand Bazaar, where jewelry dealers congregate. Another purchase that historically has gained syn-ergy from concentration is the art gallery. All are designed to help the underexperienced gain the courage to say "I'll take it." There is an-other reason, too.

At the mall, clustering by category gives the shopper a chance to make the circuit. In some cases, the stores are clustered into a good-better-best arrangement, though for the novice buyer it may be hard to discern the difference. That good-better-best setup usually involves a degree of overlap in prices and products. In some cases, the same com-pany may own more than one of the stores in the cluster.

Back in my urban-planner life, we studied pedestrian traffic along Forty-second Street in Manhattan in the "bad old days" of Times Square. Many New Yorkers cheered when former mayor Rudolph W. Giuliani rid the district of its pornographic sleaze and overall decay and Disney-fied it for family consumption. The fetid live peepshows were replaced by *The Lion King* and Madame Tussaud's Wax Museum, mak-ing the area safe for tourists, who now flock there to enjoy a dazzling variety of wholesome fare. It really was an ugly, seamy part of town back then, and yet there was something admirably authentic about it— it was one district among many in this city, a kind of partitioning that gave New York a great deal of its flavor. The porn zone served a pur-pose, and just because it's moved doesn't mean we're all nicer creatures where sex is concerned.

We urban-planner types would stand on the roofs of buildings and watch how pedestrians made their way down the street. We saw countless male strollers approach the strip of porn shops. Typically, they'd reach the first one and slow down a little. You could tell by that and how they'd turn their heads that the storefronts had gotten their attention. But they almost never entered the first store they reached. They'd gradually cruise to a stop by the second or third shop on the block, and that's the one they'd enter (after doing a quick head swivel to make sure no office colleagues were watching).

That's the effect of clustering on retailers. Shoppers who are intent on visiting a particular store will find it without any help. But the cluster slows the walking speed of the casual pedestrian, the one who may have had no intention of stopping. The first store causes you to hit the brakes, and by the second or third you've slowed down enough to pay attention. Once inside a store you may fail to find exactly what you want, but then you're close to other shops offering the same kind of goods, and, before you know it, you're shopping. That's one way in which the dynamic of the mall serves both the business and the customer at the same time.

In this particular cluster we've got Cartier, and just down the corridor a little way there's Tiffany & Co., and across from that there's Ralph Lauren, and one or two other high-end shops, too. It's a mini-mall here of fancy stores, something to make life a little more convenient for the shopper with money to spend.

What scares the Cartiers and Tiffanys of the world is the number of people who will walk past their stores without ever thinking about stopping. That's why these swanky retailers find themselves in the improbable setting of the mall. The flagship stores retain all the cachet of their fancy Fifth Avenue locations. But the business has to go where the shoppers are, and that means suburbia, especially affluent suburbs such as the ones that ring this mall. How often does the average suburban shopper make her or his way into town for the total Tiffany experience? Can you blame them? You're talking about devoting most of a day to such a venture. Who has that kind of time?

Albert's office isn't so far from the Tiffany store on Fifth Avenue, but he's busy working all day, and lunch hour ends up being the most crowded time. So even being two blocks away from *the* Tiffany's, a worldwide landmark, doesn't make it easier to shop the store. Whereas on a Saturday like today, without Christmas or Valentine's Day looming, the mall store is tranquil. And so what if Cartier and Tiffany have to go a little mass-market and mingle with the hoi polloi? They'll find a way to exist more or less at ease in the mall, even right next door to a discount jeweler.

It's interesting to see how the translation of luxury to the mall plays out. The issues begin at the lease line with decisions about the stores' facades. Everywhere else in the mall, as we've seen, design decisions make access to the stores as effortless as possible—yawning entrances, lots of plate glass, as little facade as possible, in keeping with the ideals of transparency and lack of pretense or anything else that might discourage a shopper from entering.

Here, however, you've got some competing values. The last thing Cartier wants is to seem as approachable and affordable as, say, the Gap. No matter where it exists, Cartier has to uphold its defining values, and a significant part of that is how it looks. There's something about fancy jewelry that requires an air of exclusivity, solidity—it wants to evoke a bit of the fortress in its very choice of home. Again, stroll Fifth Avenue and see how Harry Winston, Bvlgari, Tiffany, and Cartier do it up. How then do you say Cartier in the vocabulary of a mall?

You start by defying the mall's characteristic transparency, judging by how these stores do it. The equation seems sensible enough: the cheaper the goods, the more visible they are. Or, the more precious the merchandise, the less glass to show it off. Someone decided to clad the entire facade of the store in a black stone that appears to be slate. It makes a statement in the context of the mall—no other store comes close to creating such a definite distinction between *out there* and *in here.* The windows are small squares of light set in those black walls, which succeeds in focusing the passing shoppers' gaze. It *feels* expensive.

"So that's the question," I tell Albert. "How does Cartier dress for the suburbs?"

"How about a really nice track suit?" he says.

"Well, it needs to do something along those lines. It has to say

Cartier. But it has to do so in a way that is appropriate to the setting. It can't feel exactly like Fifth Avenue. There, a store can be understated in its presentation. There are enough other signals reaching the passerby. You know it's a high-end store, whereas here even Cartier needs to tell its story."

"Do the black walls say it?"

"I'm not sure. Do they seem a little forbidding?"

"Isn't that the point?"

"Well, to some degree, yes. They don't want every passerby to think he or she belongs inside the store."

"That's an unusual message for a store, isn't it? 'Dear shopper, stay out!' "

"Not really. Every store has to deliver that message. Just that some stores want lots of people inside, and other ones—like this one—don't. Cartier would suffer if tomorrow every hayseed walking down the mall corridor got the impression that he was welcome inside. Cartier's genuine customers wouldn't stand for it."

Our company has done studies for Bvlgari, the exclusive Italian jeweler. At their stores, they informed me, they don't want good visibility from outside to inside. They say it's because if Mrs. Rossi walks by and sees Mr. Bianco inside, buying something costly, she might go to Mrs. Bianco and say, "Oh, I saw your husband in Bvlgari the other day buying you a beautiful emerald necklace," and then Mrs. Bianco waits and waits for the gift before realizing that it must have gone to another woman. Maybe that's more of a concern in Europe than it is here. But it becomes part of the store's culture, that discretion, that sophistication. Even for shoppers in the Americas or Asia, it helps impart that European flavor. That's why at most jewelers, the really expensive diamonds and so on are kept in a small, secluded room in the very rear of the store.

"I thought that was so nobody would steal them," Albert says.

He's right, in part—a jewelry store puts the costliest goods at some distance from the front door for security reasons. But thieves still get away with the old grab and run. We did a research job for a luxury jeweler in L.A., and one problem with the store was its lousy lighting. The designer clearly had never spent much time around jewelry, and as a result shoppers wanted to bring merchandise close to the front windows, so they could see it in natural light. But the store got stung a couple times. The jewelry kept going all the way out the door.

Just last year, at a fancy store in New York, something like that happened when a well-dressed man asked to see a ruby and diamond ring. The clerk handed it over, and the customer turned to face the window, to see it in daylight. At that moment a young woman entered the store, at which point the man tossed her the ring. She caught it like a major leaguer and dashed back outside into a waiting car, which sped away. It happened so fast that all the security guard could do was watch. And as he watched the man just melted away. A smart little caper.

"I like it," Albert says. "Has somebody ever tried it in a mall?"

"How would you make your escape from up here on the second level to your getaway car?"

"And then what if you forget where you parked?"

This is one reason retailers like malls over streets—security is a breeze in here compared to out there. Yet, jewelry store symbolism remains the same in either locale. You sell the really good gems way in back. It's like the innermost sanctum—the vault, as it were. You shouldn't be able to see the best diamonds from outside the store, otherwise where's the mystery and drama? In this fashion, store design functions as a narrative device, drawing you deeper into the story. But that kind of thinking is totally contrary to how most mall stores operate. This is an issue because this store has to make itself accessible to other stores' shoppers. That's the whole point of being in a mall. Malls put somebody else's customers in your store.

Of course, city streets do the same thing. And yet, it's different. On Fifth Avenue, for instance, there are many pedestrians walking by the store on any given day, many more than in this mall. Even though most of those people don't go into Cartier. In fact, a great many of the people walking Fifth Avenue aren't even on shopping trips. They work in the area, or they're on their way to a hotel or a restaurant or to the park. But Cartier's customers know where to find the store. And Fifth Avenue itself draws people from around the world who know it as one of the planet's premiere shopping districts.

As a result, there will be Tiffany customers, or Gucci customers, who will make their way to Cartier. But this corridor is not Fifth Avenue, and, from where I'm standing, I can see the sneaker store and the store that specializes in overpriced, trendy T-shirts for teenage girls, and the dress shop for overweight women buying midpriced frocks. The Cartier name doesn't usually find itself in such company. And so it needs to figure out how to attract shoppers—certain shoppers—while discouraging others. It needs to take advantage of being in a mall that draws large numbers of people without the means to buy anything in Cartier, or even any intention of entering a luxury goods store with a haughty reputation.

So Cartier and stores like it must somehow select the shoppers who will walk in the door. There are three categories of people in this mall, at least where this store is concerned. One group is Cartier customers. Another is people who could be Cartier customers, but haven't ever gone inside. And the third is people who will never be customers. The store needs to attract everybody in category one. That seems easy enough, but that's the smallest category. It also wants to get some from category two. Finally, it wants to attract the attention of those in the third group, give them a bit of an education, but make sure they just look at the windows and are too intimidated to pass over the threshold. The store wants to pick certain people out of the crowd. It wants to send a message—"You, yes, and you, but not you."

The store must take care not to undercut that ambience with shoddy materials or workmanship, even around the edge of a facade in a mall that's thousands of miles away from Paris. After all, the most expensive piece in the whole place is probably smaller than a nickel. People who come in here have their eyes focused on tiny items—the scale by the very nature of the merchandise is small. You can't tell shoppers to examine this little diamond but ignore that smudged window, or the gray plastic trash can in the corner.

"Hey, where's the lady who was looking at the tennis bracelet?"

"She bounced off the Cartier storefront and went into the discount jeweler next door."

The relationship between Cartier and the discount joint next door is intriguing. It's easy to see how the cut-rate neighbor benefits from having such luxury so close at hand. Your appetite is whetted by Cartier's window. You covet what's in there. But you can't afford it, most likely. So you go next door, which you *can* afford, and buy there.

"How could it help the fancy store?" Albert asks.

"Well, once in a while, it might. Maybe you'll walk out of the discount place thinking it's beneath you, you'll feel brave enough to see what life is like in the big leagues. Or maybe a window-shopping couple will check out the discounter first, and then one will gently lead the other to the fine jeweler."

"But isn't the discounter likely to reap more benefits from being next to Cartier?"

"Possibly. That's partly because Cartier is not meant to capture a high percentage of the people walking this mall. But it also has a lot to do with the changing nature of jewelry purchases. Traditionally, jewelry has been purchased by men for women, in three basic arrangements. The first is as keys to the front door—call it engagement, anniversary, birthday—all public statements of affection and intention. The second is keys to the back door, which are presents to mistresses or girlfriends that are meant to ensure access, but bypass all the front-door commitments. The third category, which for the jeweler has traditionally been important, is the keys out of the doghouse, or the purchases meant to make amends for bad behavior. Flowers are nice, but of limited power to affect a woman's mind. Nothing says 'Dear, I am *so* sorry!' like a gold necklace or a pair of diamond earrings." I let that sink in before asking, "Albert, are you going for the front door or are you trying to get out of the doghouse?"

"Front, I guess," he says. "It's her birthday soon."

"I see. Why jewelry?"

"For Christmas I got her an extremely high-quality radio that she said she wanted."

"Did she appreciate it?"

"I think so. But I got the impression that I shouldn't get anything that plugs in for her birthday gift. It is in the same family of moves as giving your mother a new catcher's mitt."

Jewelry stores are not keeping up with social change. For instance, in 1993 a study of gold jewelry buying habits found that for the first time ever, women were buying more of it for themselves than men were buying for them. While the key and door thing are still a big part of the business, an important piece of the business has changed forever.

That change requires a new way of thinking about jewelry and selling it, too. All of a sudden, jewelers have to sell two ways from one store. In order to do that, they've got to rethink the premises, which not a lot of stores are doing well, even though this shift is more than a decade old. Jewelry is now closer than ever to fine fashion, at least when women buy it. As with apparel, women are more conscious about how they appear to one another than how they look to men. When a man looks at models in couture, he looks at the woman more than the outfit. Similarly, he's not looking at a necklace or a bracelet the way a woman does—he's not registering the details or the overall effect the same way she does. He's not considering how it will feel to wear it. She most certainly is. Jewelers haven't yet caught up with that distinction.

For instance, most jewelry stores do mirrors badly. There aren't enough of them. And they tend to be awkwardly placed—either on top of counters that aren't near the jewelry cases, or hanging on the walls. Again, the assumption is that the person buying the jewelry isn't the one who will wear it. A shopper is faced with expensive display cases and black velvet swags and high-powered ceiling spotlights that make every diamond sparkle like Liz Taylor's fist. And mediocre mirrors. The assumption is that the mirror scheme doesn't have to perform the same function as it does in, say, Armani. Even cosmetics departments do mirrors better than jewelers do.

This should be easy enough to fix, but the problem doesn't stop there.

The entire jewelry store traditionally plays to a certain fantasy—the one of the guy who's rich and powerful enough to afford something for the woman who's beautiful and desirable enough, with exquisite taste in adornment, to deserve what's here. Once women start buying their own baubles, however, the store needs to accommodate a second fantasy. This one is about dress-up, a game most women have been playing in one form or another since childhood. It's also about self-reward, and making the leap between who she is and who she wants to be.

But it also has to do with the professional woman who is making good money and has been around enough to know what Cartier quality means. She believes she deserves it, and has no problem with buying it for herself, just as she buys Donna Karan or Dolce&Gabbana. She may have a rich husband. She may have *no* husband. She may be married to a man who earns less than she does—in fact, maybe while she's in the store she'll also shop for *him*. The jewelry store now has to create the fantasy that comes with how women adorn themselves, the way Armani or Versace sell their goods to women. Go to those stores and see what the entire trying-on experience is like. It's aimed at the wearer. It assumes she's the decision maker. The dressing room is expensively decorated and immaculate. The mirrors are large and properly placed. The lights are flattering and may even show how she'll look under a variety of kinds of illumination. The sales help is attentive and respectful. A woman tries on an Armani suit or a Versace evening gown and she feels like a movie star. She gets a taste of how the rest of the world is going to see her and respond if she buys that garment. That's what a jeweler now must attempt to do.

There's also another strategy for selling jewelry to that woman, way down at the other end of the spectrum. Because if a woman is shopping for herself, maybe she doesn't need *any* romance or fantasy with her jewelry. We're not yet at the point where diamond earrings in a vending machine will work. But it's interesting to note that Wal-Mart and Sam's Club are now major jewelry retailers, and not just inexpensive goods—even big-ticket diamonds, pearls, and watches. Once upon a time, the person who was likely to buy expensive jewelry would never have shopped at a discount store or buying club for *anything*. But those days are gone. This has been one of the most significant changes in shopping patterns of the past quarter century—that people now go to Neiman Marcus in the morning and Wal-Mart in the afternoon. The walls have all come down, and today there's a lot less shopper snobbery that used to keep all the luxury retailers so contented. Women especially will buy for less if they can. And while Armani is available only at the pricier stores, diamonds and gold and emeralds and pearls can be found anywhere. The woman who decides to buy herself a pair of good diamond stud earrings might as well go to a discounter—after all, she doesn't need to impress or seduce herself.

"So instead of going into Cartier," I say, "let's go visit the discounter next door."

"Is that big 50% OFF SALE! sign in the window a good idea?"

"Probably. You don't see Cartier yelling sale, do you?"

"Hey, how you doing?" That's the manager of the discount jeweler talking. We're in his store now. It's a perfectly nice place to buy jewelry. There are no dark woods or heavy-duty facade to reinforce the feeling that you've entered a magic zone. In fact, there are no exterior walls at all—you just kind of veer in from the mall corridor—and all the display cases are glass with metal or pale wood. The decor is kind of feminine-neutral, with pinkish accents here and there. And the clerk—there's just one—is an affable guy in a plaid sports jacket and red tie.

"We're fine! How 'bout you?"

"Fine!"

"Hey, how often do you have to clean your glass here?" I ask, pointing to the big display case up front.

"Well, let me put it this way—if I had a penny for every time I've done it, I could retire right now. I use a lot of Windex. It gets dirty fast."

Another difference between here and next door is the layout. At Cartier there's a definite barrier between the shopper and the salesperson. The display cases act as a barricade, practically—they're there to hold and show the goods, but they also tell you, the customer, to keep your distance. That design decision is old-school—all stores once operated that way, but today it's fading fast. That layout set the tone for the transaction: it became a face-to-face, head-to-head thing, like the offense and defense lined up against each other on a football field. You, the shopper, had the money, and it was the salesclerk's job to get it from you. Certainly the tone was never overtly adversarial, but the undertone, I think, was just that.

Then, that cosmetics innovation known as the "open sell" became the rage in jewelry retailing, too. In this configuration, all the goods are out in front of the counter where the shopper can touch and try them on, unaided. In so many stores nowadays there are none of the long, low counters that once filled every shop. Even in this jewelry store, the clerk no longer hides behind the counter. He's right next to you, helping you try on the necklace, and looking into the mirror with you.

"You know, I like how the display cases are set up."

"Yep—me, too," he says. "It doesn't help to be standing behind a counter. It used to be that way right here—counter, counter, counter. But when they remodeled it, they took the counters away."

"How much of your business comes in here after being in Cartier first?"

"A lot do, actually. See this necklace here? They sell one like it for many thousands of dollars, solid gold. Ours is costume, but it sells for $139, and, believe me, you can't tell them apart. So most people, if they can save some money and nobody's ever going to notice anyway, they'll do it. Of course, then there are people who have hundreds of thousands to spend on jewelry, and who am I to argue with them?"

"So you stock this store partly in response to what they're selling at Cartier and Tiffany?"

"Yes, indeed. I don't know if my bosses chose this location because it's next to Cartier and down the hall from Tiffany, but it helps. See this choker? You can go to Tiffany and get it for $81,000, that's no lie, or you can get it here for $349. And nobody's going to know whether they're real pearls or not unless they come over and begin gnawing on your necklace!"

"Do you think that ever happens?"

"Not to me it doesn't!"

Albert and I amble a few stores down, to Tiffany. The first thing we see in the window is something the store doesn't even sell—a beautiful black and white photograph of what could be either Paris or maybe Central Park, in the rain. The other most prominent thing here is the Tiffany logo.

"This window isn't selling jewelry, necessarily—it's selling Tiffany," I observe.

"That's a good idea, right?"

"Well, anything's a good idea if it works. I would say it works on some levels really well. The fact is that while Tiffany and Cartier are both world-class names in luxury goods, Tiffany is better known in the U.S."

"There's no Breakfast at Cartier, is there?"

"Not yet. Somehow, Audrey Hepburn and Tiffany became synonymous. She's now their dead celebrity spokesperson."

How this window display works in the mall, though, is an entirely different matter. Here, it seems intended to evoke the Manhattan flagship store and make the connection for the out-of-town mall shopper, especially tourists from abroad. That in itself is remarkable, because, typically, malls don't do much to accommodate foreign shoppers. That's probably because Americans don't think that way. We just don't feel dependent on international trade, even though we really are. Because this mall is near a major metropolitan area, however, the surrounding suburbs are home to many foreigners here either permanently or while working in the states. Lots of Asians—Indians, Koreans, Chinese, Japanese. Lots of Middle Easterners, too, all of whom are familiar with the Tiffany name and reputation. So it makes huge sense to work the brand.

Also, Tiffany is famous for its windows. The Manhattan store puts a great deal of money and effort into them, although they are minuscule by the standards of department store windows. In New York, the windows that get most local buzz around the holidays are Tiffany's and Barney's. The big, glitzy, droll displays at Barney's have become as much a signature as Tiffany's beautiful, elegant, gemlike windows. This window treatment here in the mall is different from what is done in the city. It sells the romance of Central Park in the rain, and being very near to Tiffany, to people who are walking around a mall. That's a good goal.

"Even though the window doesn't have a single piece of jewelry in it?" Albert asks.

"I guess you could buy that silver picture frame in the window. And Tiffany is known for its silver, too. This is Tiffany's being discreet."

"Does all that mean Tiffany will do better in this mall than Cartier?"

"I think that depends on what happens inside. As in most malls, the jewelry stores here are all clustered, so even if you do find something you like in Tiffany, it's very easy to take two minutes to make sure you can't find the same thing a little nicer, or a little cheaper, at Cartier. And this window is very good but not exactly perfect either."

"What's wrong with it?"

"Well, Tiffany is selling New York, that's for sure, and people are fond of New York these days. But Tiffany also is selling a color and a bag. That particular shade of blue, on a shopping bag, announces *Tiffany* even before you see the logo. It's maybe the most successful shopping bag ever. But there's no blue and no bag in the window. Forget the bag—there's not a trace of the blue."

That brings us back to our question of why this merchandise is in the window. The answer seems clear: Because it appeals to women. The windows in the city store play to the fantasy wherein the man gives the bauble to the woman. Here in the mall, perhaps wisely, the window plays to her alone. As we said before, perhaps it's her money, and she wants silver. Or maybe the kids are out of college, and her husband just bought himself that Mercedes two-seater convertible. Now it's her turn for a treat. Either way, more than ever before, it's the woman making the big-ticket luxury purchase. And jewelers have to adapt.

"Hey," Albert says, "there's a smudge on the window."

"You know, the French have an expression for window shopping: They say, *Il faut que je lèche les vitrines.*' Meaning, 'I need to go lick the windows.' And window displays there are often called *lèche-vitrines.*"

"What do you think of this door?"

"Steely," I say. "Sturdy. A real urban doorway. A clear line between out there in the mall and in here at Tiffany's, and there's no accidental crossing between one and the other."

"Not friendly in the mall way, is it?"

"No. Not actually unfriendly, either. Warm, natural shades. The metal is stainless steel, or looks that way, which is kind of stylish these days. But maybe it's a little clumsy."

"How is this different from the store on Fifth Avenue?"

"It's not so different, but here in the mall people have come to expect that they can cross in and out of stores effortlessly. A big, heavy door feels weird. It feels wrong. At the Cartier store there was a doorman, a friendly guy in a handsome suit who would smile at you if you even came close to the door, and he'd open it grandly for you, as though he was certain you meant to spend a lot of dough inside."

"No doorman here."

"Right. Look inside, though, and you'll see the security guard. That's probably the same function Cartier's doorman served, except he also made it easier to get into the place. That was a very smart decision by somebody. Jewelers need a security presence at the doorway, so why not have him also open the damn thing?"

"Have you gentlemen seen anything yet?"

"No, thanks."

"Well, let me know if you do."

"Thanks."

"The other problem for Tiffany and Cartier and every other jeweler," I explain to Albert but also to the saleswoman, who is hovering, "is the changing nature of our relationship to adornment. We have so many ways of adorning ourselves, and of telling the world who we are. Jewelry once was universally accepted as a way of announcing one's wealth and position. It's an ancient means for expressing all that, and continues to hold that place among many of the world's cultures."

Consider the dot-com millionaires—they have (or had) plenty of money, but they didn't spend it on the same things that earlier generations of tycoons did. The younger moguls seemed not as comfortable with the conspicuous adornment of gems and precious metals. They were okay buying houses. Cars. Eminently capable of choosing ostentatious kitchen appliances—Viking stoves and Sub-Zero refrigerators. Home spas. Porsche now sells an SUV, joining Mercedes, Lexus, and Cadillac. That's the status symbol of our era—on the one hand it's a truck, totally lacking in glamour, suitable for hauling kids or lawn-care products. And yet it costs a fortune to own and another fortune to gas it up. It's the status symbol for people who scorn status symbols.

The New Age tycoon may spend $1,000 on a bottle of wine or $8,000 on a laptop computer or $200,000 for an oceanfront rental in Southampton. But he won't drop $50,000 for a piece of jewelry, even one of the highest quality, which could be handed down for generations. He doesn't feel comfortable walking into a jewelry store and plunking down that kind of cash for something that is essentially decorative.

And, once again, we must consider the changing status of women within the lives of men. She used to be comfortable with her role as a mannequin on which he would hang symbols of wealth, power, and taste. You could look at a woman and learn a great deal about her man. Certainly, he wasn't wearing any obvious adornments—that was *her* job.

"Let me ask you something," Albert says. "That dot-com tycoon, is it that he doesn't buy jewelry, or that he doesn't like the idea of buying it in this old-fashioned big-spender kind of store?"

"It's funny you say that," I tell him. "Because the only diamond I've ever bought in my life, I bought at a Sam's Club."

"The place where people go to buy toilet paper in bulk? Now, did you go to the store thinking, 'Gee, today I need to buy a diamond necklace, where should I go?' "

"You know, somebody who's an expert in these matters mentioned to me that if you want to get the most for your money, buy jewelry at Sam's Club. That the jewelry is of the same quality as you find in a jewelry store, but the price is quite a bit lower."

"Did the box say 'Sam's Club' on it?"

"No, actually I didn't care for the box it came in, so I bought another one, something nicer."

"Does your beloved know you got it at Sam's?"

"She will when she reads this. The next year I did get her something at Tiffany. But my point is that this is how people shop today. Not every man needs to feel like the big spender who goes into Tiffany or Cartier or Bvlgari and drops a fortune on gems for his lady. Time has passed that paradigm by, and jewelry stores still haven't figured out what to try next."

"What was the experience like, buying expensive diamond jewelry in a buyer's club with all the crates of cornflakes on palettes?"

"I just told the clerk here's what I want, and she showed me three different versions and I bought the most expensive."

"Were you trying to get in the front door or the back door?"

"It was a Christmas present."

One way the relations between the sexes have changed is that men—especially younger men—often don't have to work as hard as they used to to get in either door. Or maybe today relationships are over quicker. Perhaps if he senses that this woman isn't a lifelong mate, maybe it's better to spend the money on a vacation, something he can enjoy, too, rather than watch her walk out the door wearing the $10,000 Rolex watch he gave her. I mean, how many marriages even make it to the tenth anniversary?

"Or what if she says, 'But honey, what I really wanted was something practical, like a radio?' " Albert says.

"One of the most poignant retail stories I ever heard was from the jewelry business. A jeweler I know described how this middle-aged man came into his shop one day. The guy explained that he was a mechanic, and had a bunch of kids, and so was never able to afford a proper ring for his wife. Now it was their twentieth anniversary coming up, and he had managed to set aside a few bucks to buy something nice. And with that he reached into his jeans pocket and pulled out these crumpled bills, like $250 or so. It was a fairly small sum for this particular store, but the jeweler described to me the pleasure he felt in taking this working man and helping him find a really nice ring, with a tiny diamond in it, for his wife. I mean, that's the kind of moment that happens in a jewelry store. You'll never get that kind of emotional pay-off selling jeans or sneakers or video games. But jewelers haven't figured out how to capitalize on that old-fashioned thing while feeling contemporary, too."

"How might they sell that mechanic's moment?"

"Any number of ways. Maybe a little lifestyle graphic right—"

"What do you mean by 'lifestyle'?"

This was from the Tiffany salesperson.

"Well, like a photo or something . . ." I reply. That's when she notices that I have a small tape recorder along for the ride.

"We're being recorded?" she asks, suddenly suspicious.

"Hey, nice wall," I say, pointing to a large display of Tiffany boxes.

This is an evasive maneuver, but what I'm pointing to is actually a good idea, something I'd noticed before. It takes fullest advantage of the signature blue box: Small, modestly priced gifts, such as silver keychains or money clips, already boxed and ready to go. It provides a huge visual hit of that Tiffany blue, something the store needs. It is designed for gifts a bride gives to her wedding party. The hope is that the customer buys eight, not one. It also offers something affordable to the hesitant shopper who entered thinking there's no way he'd find something in here, while (because it's preboxed) not requiring much salesclerk attention. It is the jewelry store version of the cosmetics "open sell."

"We're being recorded?" she persists, now on full red alert. "Because you can't . . . I didn't realize you had . . ."

"I'm not recording you," I say. "I'm recording me."

"Well, I don't want anything that I said—"

"Neither do I," says a second clerk, who hasn't even been close until now.

"Because we'll be in big trouble," says the first clerk, "because we're not supposed to record or have pictures taken—"

❖   ❖   ❖

We had seen enough of the store, and we're now back in the safety of the mall proper. Albert still hasn't gotten his wife a gift—in truth, he has barely looked at the goods—but each shopper has a unique style, like a DNA fingerprint. Something tells me his style incorporates a great deal of procrastination, followed by a panicky trip (maybe back to this same mall) at the eleventh hour. A lot of men shop that way—it's shopping for people who hate shopping. This is another reason why stores have to operate differently if they want to accommodate male-pattern buying. For Albert, that wall of preselected, preboxed gifts may start looking awfully good in two weeks.

"How about this jewelry store?" he asks when we're a few paces away from Tiffany.

I hadn't even noticed this one before. The windows are large, which doesn't feel particularly jewelerlike. And the first thing you see is color, a kind of pinky-mauvey-rosy shade that predominates. It looks girly, and not in the best way possible. But there in the window, nestled among the swirls and swaths and swoops of fabric, is jewelry.

Inside we find a horseshoe of display cases, all down around mid-thigh level, meaning they're not the easiest things in the world to examine for fully grown men who don't yet feel inclined to bend over or to sit at the little benches before the cases.

Across the cases we face a pair of middle-aged women, extremely pleasant of face and form, wearing pastel-colored fuzzy sweaters and so forth—not at all the stylish keepers of the crown jewels we encountered at the more glamorous shops.

"Hi, ladies!"

"Well, hello," they reply, more or less in unison. Nobody will confuse this store with Tiffany or Cartier. Or the discount place, for that matter, if only because it's hard to imagine any male wandering in here searching for the key to the front or back door. This is an interesting concept, a jewelry store aimed only at women shoppers.

"Wow, pink lights *and* flowers," Albert says under his breath.

"You think this would be forbidding to a man?"

"Gee, this is what a jewelry store would look like if Hallmark decorated it."

On the other hand, the prices here are moderate, perfect for the woman buying for herself or another woman.

"Is there anything we can show you gentlemen?" a clerk asks.

"I'm not sure I can fit my knees under that counter," I say, eyeing a fancy little bench.

"Oh, it's really comfortable," she says.

"Yeah," I reply, "but you're not six-foot-four!"

# 16 A Man and His Mall

CAN A GUY love a mall?

The short answer is no, judging by the behaviors we've seen in our studies. At least they don't love it in the way women do. Some of the reasons for this gender disagreement are obvious. Start by looking at the very composition of the mall—overwhelmingly, the stores are meant for female shoppers. Women's apparel is the number-one category. Men's clothing and shoes are way down near the bottom of the list. Once, malls frequently included stores selling books, stereos, TVs, toys, sporting goods, items that at the very least gave men something to idly browse. It's no coincidence that the only popular mall store bearing the name hardware is Restoration Hardware, which trades in furniture and accessories, and where the closest things to actual hardware are drawer pulls. These are marvelous stores, but go into one and try and buy a ten-penny nail or caulk or an ax, designed for real use rather than for Martha Stewart.

The mall is a tamed jungle, the retail concentrate of the urban environment—a very weird city, one in which there is little to do but shop, with a roof and a smooth floor and air bearing the scent of candle shops and cappuccino.

You go to a mall to shop. There's nothing tentative or halfway about it. You can't just dart in and out, or merely breeze by on your way to somewhere else. You must drive there on purpose, then enter into the parking dance, and leave your car, and then make your way from the lot or garage into the core of the structure.

All this and you haven't even gotten close to a store where you want to be.

No wonder male shoppers are more likely to be found at strip shopping centers. There you can, on a sudden whim, steer in, park within sight of your destination, and then enter the RadioShack or Barnes & Noble or Home Depot or any of the other spots where guys feel most at home. How men shop once inside a store is how they shop *for* stores, too. Men shop like they drive. They refuse to ask directions unless they are absolutely desperate. Inside a store, it is our experience, men will bolt in this direction and then that, trying to find what they came in for. If they don't locate it relatively quickly, they are more likely than women to give up and walk out. Men typically do not penetrate any given store as deeply as female shoppers do. This instinct alone makes malls challenging, for they are the least time-efficient shopping venue. Shoppers spend roughly 25 percent less time in a city store than in a mall location.

Shoppers tend not to go to a mall when all they need are a few very specific things. The mall is for shopping as an activity unto itself, something that most men have yet to embrace. In one store we studied, which sells apparel to both sexes, males shopped only half as many racks as women did. And while men's clothing can be found inside malls, most of it is sold in environments designed mainly for women shoppers. It's at the Gap, where it has become increasingly challenging just to figure out which clothes are for women and which are for men. Or it's at department stores, where menswear is typically off in some remote region.

Men's apparel is still recovering from casual Friday. Historically, men favor uniforms, be it jeans and a Steelers jersey or a Brooks Brothers suit and wingtips. Male apparel shopping once consisted mainly of closet replenishment—replacing garments that had worn out. As casual Friday spread to business casual for every day of the week, the men's fashion industry reeled. In a study for Dockers, we captured video of how some men shop for trousers: They find a pair in their size (whatever they've been wearing) and head straight to the register, without browsing the rest of the merchandise or trying anything on. The time spent in the section was roughly identical to what men devote to shopping for beer in convenience stores.

A similar pattern, one that varies according to region—strong in the West and Midwest, less so in the East and South—is the acceptance of dressing down for men: the high-tech zillionaire who does most of his clothes buying from the Land's End catalog, the entrepreneur who spends on cars and boats but never on custom-tailored suits and handmade shoes. My father owned good shoes, casual shoes, and one pair of sneakers. He bought four suits a year and changed his clothes as soon as he got home at night. I live in khakis, soft cotton shirts, and rubber-soled shoes. The custom of dressing for the arena of work has disappeared for many men.

While some department stores still do a decent business in men's clothing, mostly the business has left the mall. The success of a chain like Men's Wearhouse has occurred in freestanding stores, where men are more likely to go. Smart brands follow men to wherever they're shopping, which is why retailers such as Tractor Supply and Farm & Fleet now sell lots of apparel. "The brands will sell to us stuff they would not sell to Wal-Mart, but they ask us not to advertise," a Farm & Fleet manager told me. "They are scared of their other customers figuring out where else the shopper can find their stuff."

In this very mall, there's a Brooks Brothers store and a few department stores with menswear, but that's about it for anything other than sportswear. There's exactly one men's shoe store, and it is perhaps the sleepiest shop in the mall. But there are nine stores selling sneakers. Guess where men find fashionable footwear these days?

It's interesting to note the single category of apparel that *does* seem to lend itself to male participation, and, in fact, domination—sneakers.

There's an entire generation of American males who have all but abandoned the traditional shoe, by which I mean something made at least in part of leather, usually brown or black, appropriate for wearing with what is quaintly still thought of as "dress clothes." If you're reading this book (as opposed to playing a video game), you probably remember shoes. You may even have worn them yourself once upon a time, and perhaps wear them even today sometimes.

Go to the mall and attempt to shop for these accoutrements of yore, and you may have a challenge on your hands. There are still a few men's shoe stores to be found, of course, but fewer all the time. Invariably, they are among the emptier places in the mall, too. You can just walk in and sense that life has passed them by.

At what point did footwear meant mainly for athletic activity become America's shoe? It's a perfect match, sneakers and the United States of America—the youthfulness, the vitality, the casualness and egalitarianism. Europeans, wearing their old-world, highly constructed, uptight (literally, and straight-laced, too, in some instances), leather numbers sneer at our childlike belief that sneakers are entirely appropriate for all occasions, from the playing field to the office to the mall. In fact, one of the most dramatic differences between malls in North America and Europe or South America is how they sound: There, the ambient noise is the clacking of hard heels on flooring; here, nothing but the odd squeak of rubber soles.

This is one of those trends that was fed from all directions. We experienced a generation of oldsters who maintained their health and disposable income well into their seventies and beyond. They stepped out of the world of work and responsibility and into a kind of second childhood. With what footwear did they take this step? Look around—men and women who would never have been caught dead in sneakers, who came of age at a time when sneakers were thought inappropriate for any nonathletic activity, came to embrace them, for the obvious reason—they feel so good. Combine the rubber bottom, the soft top, and then the miracle fastener, Velcro, and you've got a perfect shoe for the golden years. (It's beyond irony, how our eldest citizens have embraced not only the athletic shoe but also the rest of the active wear costume— sweatpants and sweatshirt, garments blissfully devoid of zippers, metal fasteners, and finite dimensions, and rather held up by elastic, such a forgiving friend to the expanding waistline.)

While that practical embrace of sneakers took place from the aged end of the spectrum, a similar evolution was happening from the opposite extreme. Now it's the old-fashioned shoe that has become the special occasion footwear, while the sneaker is the default item—what most of us wear, given the liberty, even when athletic activity is the furthest thing from our minds. Look around and see—we men have dragged our juvenile getups into maturity, our sneakers and T-shirts and jeans and baseball caps. There was a time when the costume worn by a child and an adult were pretty much distinct. That time is over.

The traditional men's shoe industry was blindsided. It didn't understand how the little sneaker section, which used to exist over in a corner of the shop somewhere, was transformed into a fashion monster that has now overrun everything else in the store. It gave rise to settings where men, women, and children shop for shoes together. The male-only shoe store is one more example of how the traditional masculine preserves are being wiped out, like so many other animal habitats the world over.

The domination of sneaker style is all but complete. Stores organize the merchandise by activity—where once we each owned a single pair of sneakers, now we need different types for running, basketball, cross-training (whatever that is), climbing, and then a pair for wearing when performing no activity at all. The comfort and informality of rubber bottoms has extended fully to all types of shoes, so that even the dressiest styles are connected to the ground via soft, cushiony gum rather than hard, slippery leather. The cowboy boot, America's manliest footwear, once upon a time, in the West and elsewhere, is out of vogue, replaced by the casual boot with a bottom that looks like the tread on a truck tire. Even sandals now are simply sneakers with open toes. You can go from the humblest pair of no-name discount store sneakers for six bucks to the Prada pair for $350, and they're still sneakers.

The retail trade used to have a term to describe the role of men in shopping expeditions: they were called "wallet-bearers." Today, even that supporting role is mostly gestural, since the woman is either paying from her own wallet or sharing the load, making the question of whose wallet pays immaterial. Men in the mall are secondary figures. They come to wait.

But how they wait! This has become one of the most poignant issues in all malldom, the matter of what to do with the men while shopping takes place. We've photographed scores of husbands, boyfriends, fathers, and significant others—loitering, lingering, lurking, hovering, cooling their heels in every conceivable posture. Department stores are particularly inept at accommodating these shopping second bananas. You'll find men perched on the narrow edges of display tables, leaning against walls, sitting on the floor next to their equally glum children. The men and the children are found in identical straits, bored out of their skulls but with nothing better to do than wait for the womenfolk to wrap it up. Video arcades—further juvenilization; nothing for a mature man to do.

Men are pathetically grateful for even a bench here and there, maybe a comfortable chair out of the jet stream of moving shoppers. These furnishings are especially important to have near stores that men abhor to enter. We once studied a mall where a ledge suitable for leaning was immediately adjacent to a lingerie store on a day when push-up bras were on sale. The ledge was fully occupied from one end to the other by males, several of whom passed the time by studying (closely) the women entering and leaving the store, and loudly commenting on their need for the garments in question.

So—woe to the mall that doesn't provide a place where women can park their husbands. At Envirosell we call these "human parking lots." We encourage retailers to think of them in terms of the amount of time likely to be spent there.

It's downright undignified what men are made to go through because mall planners fail to recognize the most obvious fact about shopping—that it is a social activity performed by couples and families, wherein the female takes the lead role but all others must be equally catered to and cared for. In other countries it's even worse. We have a terrific video clip of a woman strolling into a department store, trailed by her husband. She stops, points wordlessly to a chair in the corner, and urges him into it, depositing her bags at his feet. It resembles nothing so much as a woman leading her well-trained dog. In a French cosmetics store, we witnessed a man trying his best to keep up with his wife as she bounced from one counter to another, until he finally gave up—and began strangling her, ever so gently, in an effort to get her to stop. At Diagonal Mar in Barcelona, there's a rest area with couches, giving the men a place where they might actually nap, which is maybe the best solution of all. I feel sure that some enterprising mall management firm is going to develop a concept in which men might pay a little extra but find room to sleep, watch TV, read, even work on computer terminals, while their wives shop. There's already something close in a Toronto mall—a "shoppers' club," called Embarq, where members (who pay an annual fee) can come to park their weary selves. The setup is ideal—there's an area for men (or women, but they don't make nearly as much use of it) and, next to it, a place where kids can work off their excess energies, meaning that Dad can half watch the little ones while watching the game, and Mom can shop in peace.

The gender patterns and attitudes we observe while watching shoppers are stereotypical, true. And the stereotypes don't always apply, because men's mall behavior varies according to age.

Not surprisingly, the younger a male is, the better he likes the mall. Older men are less likely to enjoy *any* form of shopping. Their material needs have declined, especially for anything you can find at Abercrombie & Fitch. The mall doesn't do much to lure the older male shopper; in fact, it does its best to keep him away. The middle-aged male shopper, meaning the baby boomer–age cohort, is headed in that same direction: this guy has never been crazy about shopping at the mall, and age will make him even less inclined.

But the Gen Xer has an entirely different view of the place. The younger male shopper was of the first generation for whom the mall stood for freedom from parental control. He was in the first wave of mall rats. Boomers were taught to scorn the mall for all its suburban prefab lameness. But there's a whole generation who got their first wild taste of independence at the mall. It's where they were dropped off on Friday nights by Mom and permitted to run free (within limits)—to shop, blow their allowance, and socialize themselves into adulthood. For these guys, the connotations of the mall are mostly positive. For them, the mall is real.

# 17 *Who Is Your Dad?*

**W**E'RE approaching an increasingly rare find in malls these days, maybe one that will disappear altogether before long: the record store.

Stop a minute and stand still. Look inside the window. No, look *at* the window, and what do we find? Nothing. Clear, unobstructed glass. Freshly cleaned. No streaks. (Ammonia and newspaper—only way to go.) We know this is a record store because the sign above it tells us so. But the window itself is unadorned by a single thing to alert us as to what form of commerce is being committed here—it serves honestly and earnestly as a transparent means through which to see inside. That's the first mistake.

What do we see inside? CDs, of course. But we don't see the actual silvery discs—we see the clear plastic boxes in which they are contained. The awkward, brittle, generic-looking, cheaply hinged containers that some wizard of retail nomenclature dubbed the "jewel case."

Nothing gemlike about it. It's hard to imagine a less engaging, less inviting package—it's a plastic box with an uninteresting surface and an annoying tendency to crack into shards during normal use (usually after falling under a shod foot). It does the job of holding the CD and keeping it safe, I suppose, but as a way to display the object in a retail setting, it leaves a lot to be desired.

Mall shoppers of a certain age will recall its predecessor, the LP sleeve. It had several advantages over the CD case, primarily its size—a foot square. That alone provided an ample canvas for telling shoppers loud and clear what was inside. It gave the performer and record label the chance to make an artistic statement from twenty paces away. You can hardly *see* a CD cover from that distance. Now tell me about the impact it has on us standing out here in the mall, looking in. From our perch the nearest CD is around twenty-five feet away. It looks slightly more intriguing than an aspirin bottle.

So—big news, a manufacturer has fallen down on the job of retail presentation. Record labels today are dismally bad at many of the things they're supposed to be doing, so this particular failure should come as no surprise. They are in deep trouble lately, most of which they blame on pirated song downloads available via the Internet, thanks to the now-defunct Napster network and its successors. I think the failings of the labels and retailers set the stage for what technology has wrought, and there's plenty of evidence right here in this (or any other) music store.

This window is badly employed even by mall standards, which is say-ing a lot since mall store windows tend to be *so* underutilized. There are many reasons for that fact of life. Due to the structure of retail chains, window displays are designed by specialists and contained in loose-leaf binders stored in a central office somewhere, intended to work equally well in every setting, meaning they don't work particu-larly well in *any* setting. They're not created with an actual site in mind, and so they don't make any allowances for who will be walking by, or from which direction, or under what lighting conditions.

The other reason for lackluster mall windows is a philosophical one, a decision that's been made by nearly every national retailer, so it's practically a pillar of the mall aesthetic: The principle is that from outside a store, you should be able to see in—*far* in. It's why most mall stores don't have solid doorways or defined entrances to mark the threshold between *out there* and *in here*—you can so easily drift from the corridor through the wide-open entrance, almost without meaning to or even noticing. All appealing notions, right?

There's a practical, dollars-and-cents aspect to this, too—efficient design. Because mall rents are high, and because maximum exposure to the corridor is the goal, stores would all like to be wide and shallow; however, many are bowling alleys, narrow and long. In those wide-and-shallow stores it is easy to see clear to the rear wall. This would seem to be an ideal setup—it eliminates the need for the chain to mediate the shopping experience. Why tell shoppers what's inside the store when you can just stand aside and let them see for themselves? Thanks to the absence of brick and mortar or concrete walls inside this mall cocoon, we've been given the possibility of near-total internal visibility. So why put anything in or on the window that might obstruct the shopper's view of the goods?

Well, I can name about a dozen good reasons. The bowling alleys are always trouble. It is tough to get people to the back of the store unless you train them to visit the mark-down fixture at the back, or you put something strong enough visually to tickle their interest. We call that strategy using a mandala—the traditional big altar at the back of Buddhist temples.

But for now let's stick with this CD store. What does it gain by leaving the windows empty? It allows us to see inside. What do we see? Rack after rack of clear plastic boxes. Is this making your mouth water? Does the glint of a plastic box automatically get you excited for the latest from U2 or Christina Aguilera or Tony Bennett?

This is what I was alluding to before—CDs may be a superior medium for storing and playing recorded music (though even that's open to debate), but the LP sleeve was infinitely better as a means by which to display and explain what was inside. It was an ideal and much-beloved package. Labels and artists exploited that admirably—by the 1960s, it wasn't enough to offer buyers a pretty sleeve, it had to contain goodies like photos, lyric sheets, posters, and other bits and pieces of information and whimsy. It became part of the overall package you were buying, and while the record itself was the main event, the rest all became treasured frills.

Maybe the labels didn't realize? Or maybe they did, but didn't care? Either way, the result was the same—they made the fatal decision to package the considerably smaller CD by simply shrinking the LP sleeve. In the case of reissues, that's literally what they did—they took what was designed to be a foot square, collapsed it, and called it a jewel. Did no one notice that what had been a big, bold, and eminently visible poster suddenly was transformed into a postcard? That didn't stop the record industry.

A bad decision by manufacturers usually translates into bad news for retailers, and this was no exception. Here's one result: As you walk by this record store, unless you are already desirous of buying music, there's nothing to goose you into that frame of mind. In every other store in this mall, there's at least a chance that you'll walk by the window, glance up, see a pair of jeans, or a barbeque grill, or a suitcase, and you'll think: *Hey, I just remembered—I need one of those!* Whereas this music store window will probably tickle no such consumerist gene. If there were a poster or sign or other graphic in the window, or if you could gaze into the store and see an actual record cover, you might suddenly exclaim, *Hot diggity, I keep meaning to get that Rolling Stones greatest hits collection, and there it is!* If you started out intending specifically to buy a CD today, you will enter this store, of course. But is that the only customer the store needs to attract? What kind of world would it be if people bought only the things they really needed, only the things they have on their sensible shopping list? A grayer, duller, infinitely poorer world—poorer especially at the bottom line of retailers. A store is supposed to try and make its goods irresistible.

And this is why conversion rate, which is an essential measure of a store's performance, can be misleading. One way to evaluate store health is to see what percentages of shoppers convert into buyers. The higher the number the better, as a rule. Roughly 70 percent of the people who enter this store will buy something, which could be taken as a sign that the retailer is doing a good job. In fact, just the opposite could be true—maybe the store isn't attracting enough shoppers inside its doors, which would result in a too-high conversion rate. It should be working harder to draw more shoppers in; even if the conversion rate falls, sales will have risen.

So: You look inside and see many, many racks containing something shiny. There are a few posters of recording artists up on the walls, but these too are badly deployed—they're mounted flush against the wall, meaning they can be seen properly only if you're standing there facing them head-on. If these were angled slightly outward, to face the front of the store, they might actually be visible from outside, thereby serving a dual purpose. Owing to the shallowness of the space and the glass facade, the entire store effectively *is* the window display. But a very weak window display.

The funny part is that this very record store chain has an outlet not so far away, on a teeming and hyper-busy city street. Rather than being unipurpose, like a mall corridor, that avenue supports many users with many reasons for being there—office workers rush by next to messengers on bicycles next to a few meandering tourists, all amid the usual urban hubbub of taxis and noise and the controlled chaos that is urban existence. In this crowded but untouristy part of the city, most people rush. Some are on their way to the store, but others are rushing past. For the meanderers, they risk being run down like roadkill. How does this outpost of the same chain handle the window thing?

In a completely different way, as you might have guessed. In the city, it's impossible really to see into the store, because each window (and there are several—it's a corner location) is devoted to a different popular recording artist. Now, this isn't purely a matter of chance—these windows get huge exposure, making them valuable real estate, so the record labels pay the store to be featured in these displays. The windows are a profit center in their own right. But they also function well for the store itself. Every window has got something different going on—a huge picture of Eminem's scowl, next to some hip hop diva, next to a constant loop of Weezer's new video. The scale of everything is high impact—they all fill the windows with heads somewhere between three and five times as big as yours. Meaning big eyes, meaning you'll look. Plus, befitting the rocking merchandise, the colors are jarring.

The city store works harder at bringing people in, at jogging the mental shopping list of every passerby, at announcing to the world which piping-hot, right-off-the-presses compact disc the store has just gotten in stock. The mall store announces only that there are CDs inside, should you wish to purchase one. Big difference.

All the actual selling of the consumer is being left to the labels—to their mass-media marketing campaigns, for the most part. The danger, of course, is that all the marketing in the world can't overcome a bad store. Plus, that approach takes a lot of the fun out of shopping. It takes away the motive for the kind of retailer one-upsmanship that used to make shopping such a heightened experience, and still does in other settings.

Let's go in and shop for CDs.

"Hey, how are you?" I greet the clerk, getting the jump on him. I'm the only shopper here.

"Okay!"

"Good!" I cry.

The first piece of actual merchandise that attracts my attention once I'm fully inside the store is . . . a sneaker. Two of them, in fact, two empty sneakers inside a clear lucite cube, which sits atop a plain gray pedestal. There is, also inside the cube, a small white card with type on it, clearly some form of explanation for the shoes. The problem is that the card protrudes from beneath the sole, meaning that it is, let's see, around waist-high on your average adult. And not tilted upward for easy viewing. So picture it: gray pedestal, clear lucite cube, two sneakers, little white card down at your belly button. You actually have to bend over to read the card; I don't care how good your eyes are.

This, believe it or not, despite all the evidence of poor design and planning, is an example of an excellent thing that malls and mall stores could do easily and abundantly, but almost never do at all: cross-promotion. The simple notion that there's a certain amount of overlap among customers of one store and another, or one type of merchandise and another—in this case, between music and sneakers. Who buys music? Who buys sneakers? Young people.

"Hey, can I see those sneakers?" I ask.

"Well, we don't sell those."

"How long have they been there?"

"About two months."

"I don't get it, do you?"

"There's a music magazine that's running a sneaker promotion. It's the urban connection, you know?"

"Who decides where this sneaker goes? Is it corporate?"

"Yes. . . ."

"Even in the Manhattan store, it's at the same place—front right," I point out.

"I didn't know that."

"Except in Manhattan, front right is at a staircase that goes down to the lower level, whereas here it's at the display of top twenty DVDs. Do you think that makes a lot of sense?"

"The sneaker? I guess so. People do look at it."

Good enough for me. This store features a technological selling tool that has made music dramatically more shopper-friendly: Computers that allow you to audition (over headphones) any cut on most of the CDs in the store, just by flashing the jewel box under a scanner and selecting your song. Record stores of old employed listening booths in which you could hear the latest tunes before making your choices. Then this selling tool fell by the wayside. I imagine it got to be costly. Flash forward a few decades and digital technology brings back a worthy vehicle for the enhancement of shopping. You can browse through a book in a bookstore; you should be able to sample recordings here. On this particular setup, according to the sign above the gizmo, you can hear songs from around three hundred thousand titles, all of which have been downloaded into a server.

"And," the clerk says, "soon you'll be able to see trailers for around thirty percent of the DVDs in the store."

"Do you think records are worse than they used to be?" I ask.

"You mean the recording quality?"

"No, the music. For instance, albums used to have around ten songs, and at least four or five were ones you liked, so roughly half was good and half was filler. Whereas today, because a CD can hold so much music, you're getting like three or four good songs and a dozen just so-so."

"There *is* more filler out there," he says. "You get a good mixture, but then again the market is oversaturated with artists."

"Hey, who is that playing now? It sounds like the Kinks from around 1967." I'm pulling this out of the air.

"No, it's Wilco. One of the best records of the year."

"Whatever happened to D'Cuckoo?" I ask. "Do you remember them? They issued one fabulous CD. It was an all-women rock-and-roll band."

"Who?"

"D'Cuckoo."

"I know the name, but I don't know what it was. That's the problem with the market—here one day, gone the next. That's music."

✿   ✿   ✿

It's not just the music store that does windows so poorly, I should point out. In fact, the rest of retailing has fallen almost as low, visually speaking, thanks to the mall. But the worst part is how the mall aesthetic has now infected the urban shopping experience. For if a national chain has the preponderance of its stores in mall settings—which most chains, by necessity, actually do—then the mall window treatments will also be deployed on city streets, where (a) they don't function well, and (b) they degrade the only place left where store windows actually have some life and style left in them.

Take Gap, for instance, not wishing to pick on the chain but finding it impossible to resist. The mall window calls for a few mannequins, spaced at regular intervals, without anything else to stand between the window shopper's gaze and the innards of the store. It's bland, it's uninteresting; and yet it's how most mall windows look, and so it's not jarringly bad. But Gap does its Fifth Avenue flagship store in much the same style. It's how the chain's visual merchandising czar enforces order and organization. As a result, there's a big stretch of suburban blandness blighting Fifth Avenue, totally surrounded by old-school retailers such as Bergdorf Goodman, Tiffany, Gucci, Henri Bendel, Cartier, and so on. The Gap is reasonably well trafficked, in part due to the fact that the area draws so many tourists who may well be comforted by the presence of this mainstay of mall retailing. Maybe to orient themselves in the midst of so much urban hubbub, they gratefully enter this oasis of pale woods, khaki trousers, and mellow Motown piped in through the sound system.

But there's a cost—a little bit more of the cityscape has been claimed by white-bread retail style. Up the street is a huge H&M, a chain (even though its windows are quite a bit hipper than the Gap's, and the store's a lot more crowded, too). Nearby is Club Monaco. All up and down Fifth Avenue and other great urban shopping districts you find outposts of mall-dominated chains. It's taking a toll. The city invented the store window, and now it has returned in some uglier but more efficient form to kill off its father. To call these windows dressed is an overstatement.

✿  ✿  ✿

A few stores away from the music shop we come upon a window sign reading: WHO IS YOUR DAD? To be fair, I should say that this takes place a week before Father's Day, but this makes the sign no less obscure. Is it meant to raise questions of paternity? It's in a store specializing in maps and globes and gear for the intrepid traveler, which does nothing to make the sign's meaning any clearer, at least not to me. It probably seemed very clever and intriguing back in some corporate conference room, where it was unveiled by the visual merchandising agency honchos to the executives whose job it is to sit around in that conference room and make such decisions. Out here in the real world, though, it makes zero sense.

Technology made posters and especially big, lush color photographs a lot easier and cheaper for retailers to come by. With that, dressing the windows made a sudden turn—for the worse. It became quicker and simpler to hire a designer to come up with some fancy graphics and then print a bunch of them in Asia, where printing is cheap, and then decree that they be slapped into store windows and on walls from coast to coast. It used to be somebody's job to step into a store window and dress it—to decorate it and fill it with merchandise in a (one hopes) eye-catching manner. There still are window dressers here and there—in Manhattan you'll find them in the best stores, and everywhere else in America you'll find them in the smallest ones. But in between those extremes, windows are now dressed long distance. They're one-size-fits-all.

# 18 *Malls of the World*

THE modern-day mall may be an American innovation, but it has gone completely global—from Kuala Lumpur to Dubai, from Tokyo to São Paolo. It's peculiar how the idea has morphed: Birthed in the United States by suburban development, cheap automobiles, and land, malls in other places are interpreted through local culture, customs, and needs. Examining the mutation of the concept is one way of looking at the mall's DNA. Iguatemi, a huge mall in São Paolo, Brazil, is a good example of what I mean.

First, some context. São Paolo is South America's largest city. Imagine L.A. sprawl and traffic, with Chicago's industrial base. Pollution and crime are major issues. The city has more private helicopters than anyplace else in the world. Billionaires scoot over traffic, while ordinary citizens may need three hours to get from one side of town to the other. It is not a pretty city. The tall buildings downtown look as if they are melting as the facades have been eaten away by the potent combination of sunshine and dirty air. In spite of everything, it is a great city for business, and it's the center of Brazil's shopping engine. The locals call themselves Paolistas. They work and play hard. I have an office there.

In the early 1990s, we were the subcontractor to an American firm doing branch bank development for Banco Itáu. The American agency lasted about a year and left. Envirosell was asked to stay, and we now have ten years of experience working for Brazilian banks, supermarkets, a huge local brewer, and multinational consumer product companies. Since many grocery stores servicing middle-class markets are in enclosed malls, we have an ongoing relationship with Brazilian mall developers. We learned quickly, no matter which industry we were working with, to discard our North American lens. Brazil has been described as Belgium inside India, in the sense that it has an affluent middle class surrounded by mind-blowing poverty.

It was very helpful in understanding how Brazilians shop to start with banks. In Brazil, big banks are literally big. A typical Itáu branch has more than one hundred tellers and a machine gun tower in the middle of the banking floor. Large segments of the population have no bank accounts and limited access to a postal system. Workers will cash their paychecks and pay rent and utility bills through the bank where their employer does business. A busy branch can feel and sound like a crowded railroad station.

Historically, Brazil manufactures mainly for domestic sale, and many Brazilian conglomerates are vertically integrated. Banco Itáu manufactures its own ATMs, computers, and office furniture. It builds and manages apartments and housing subdivisions for its employees. It is privately held, and the family that owns it must have more than one helicopter. They have never offered me a ride. Brazilians have taken First World innovations and reinvented them to suit their own needs. While the branch bank and shopping mall are recognizable to the foreign eye, they are distinctly Brazilian mutations.

From across the street, Iguatemi mall looks like an Art Deco monolith. The huge, ornate doorway must have been beautiful in the construction drawings. As in many mall designs, the ornamental entrance is unrelated to the entry patterns, or to the demographic profile of who enters where. There's limited walk-up traffic through that grand door.

Design culture loves building triumphant gateways that often can be appreciated only by the policeman directing traffic from across the street. As at many locations serving a high-end market, most of the important users slip in discreetly through a side door. That entrance typically has no charm or aesthetic value.

In Brazil, with its major crime problems, the mall serves as a gated commercial community. At Iguatemi and every other enclosed mall and bank, the first thing you notice are the security guards. These aren't the usual aging rent-a-cops hired to control teenage mall rats. These guys are hard-eyed, aggressive, and ostentatiously armed. They provide what the streets do not—safety.

The presence of police at the doorways and in the concourse turns the mall into a semiprivate club. At Iguatemi, while the stores are attractive, the real action is strolling down the concourse, and it isn't just teenagers you find there. This is a social setting that no American or European mall can duplicate. I am glad I've come to this mall in my dotage; if I'd been here in my twenties, I would have fallen in love every ten minutes. In many cultures, the middle and upper classes dress up to go shopping. While the designer sweat suit is acceptable attire, and you do see belly shirts, Iguatemi puts the general fashion coefficient of any American mall to shame. The social pressure cooker is evident in poses and active eye contact. In a country where many people live at home late into their twenties, the mall is a meeting place for working adults. Many companies run lunch-hour shuttles from their headquarters to the mall.

In North American malls you can be anonymous and lose yourself in the crowd. At Iguatemi, there seems to be the expectation that you will bump into your neighbors, workmates, and possibly your best friend's gorgeous cousin.

The mall as gated community works at being a complete shopping solution, something the American mall might examine. Beyond the supermarket, the corridors leading from the parking lot are lined with small service businesses—watch repair, a locksmith, travel agent, dry cleaning, even a Laundromat that will wash, dry, and fold your clothes while you shop. These shops may not pay major league rents, but they service shoppers and animate underused space.

The retail mix here has only a few names an American audience would recognize. C&A, the European version of JC Penney, is one of the anchors. There is a cross section of global knockoffs trying to ape Gap and American Eagle. In some of the small fashion houses, you find high-end dresses and accessories, bought at season-end closeouts in New York and Miami, transported across the equator to meet the start of the appropriate season launch. There is a distinctly high-end section of the mall signaled by a change in the quality of the concourse seating and a large, aged but sumptuous Oriental carpet in the courtyard.

Brazilian malls are loud. Some of it is because the corridors and concourses tend to be narrow. In a hot climate, stone and tile flooring helps keep the mall cool, but they also amplify the cacophony. The biggest difference is the sound of footwear. In the United States, the rubber-soled shoe reigns everywhere, especially on shopping trips. While some American women may wear high heels to the mall, they are a minority. American women have learned to feel stylish in sneakers. At Iguatemi, the echoing clatter of feminine footwear is pervasive. High-heeled sandals, spike heels, and mules go with the miniskirts and short shorts. The voices, too, are louder, to compete with the clatter and also to announce one's presence. You can't hear the jukebox playing in many people's heads, but you pick up the cadence and swing in the walk.

The contrast between Brazil and Japan could hardly be greater. Safety is not a concern in Japan. Street crime is almost unknown. Japan has an efficient and widely used public transportation system. Public safety is not just about facts, but also about perception. Unlike anyplace in North America, it is common in Japan to see young children commuting alone across Tokyo to school. The early morning and afternoon subway trains are crowded with schoolchildren aged seven and up, all in uniforms. The youngest travel in small packs, and as they age the packs only grow. In that safe world, the role of a mall as safe haven is unnecessary. Japanese kids can comfortably range far afield, and they crowd the hip urban shopping districts.

There are elegant malls in Japan, including a new one across the street from Tokyo Station called Maru-Biru. It is part of a large office complex, where numerous buildings share the same name, or nearly so. Like all Tokyo street names and numbers, the mall defies logic, and I had a hard time even identifying it from the outside. The mall anchors a shopping strip between Tokyo Station and Ginza, the major shopping district. It's a little sterile and lacks animation. That mall focuses on young, single, employed women, and at lunchtime it rocks, but still the scene is very corporate and restrained.

Japanese consumers vacillate between two opposing impulses. They can be extremely frugal and practical. But they also exhibit a fevered obsession with high-end products and brands. The Japanese are forever looking for a bargain. Relative to the United States, everything from housing and transportation to beer and vegetables is expensive. The meeting of Japanese prudence and luxury shopping tastes creates retailing and business anomalies. In stores, two examples stand out.

Don Quixote is a popular chain in Japan. The origins of the name are a mystery. The name is not used in the Western form, but rather translated phonetically into Japanese and presented in Kanji. It is the Japanese equivalent of the American Dollar Store, or the German chain called Aldi (now found in some U.S. communities), only bigger and with a wider range of products. Often stuffed into aging multistory buildings, the stores are warrens selling everything from canned goods and household products to apparel, home appliances, and electronics. It is easy to get lost. The price promotion signs look hand-done and are everywhere you look. The store presents itself unapologetically as a maze, which is its charm. The Japanese love it for the discounts. The perception is that nowhere is anything cheaper than at Don Quixote.

Another stop on the search for a low-cost shopping fix is a new store in Tokyo called Three Minute Happiness. The copy on the sign outside reads—Just Three Minutes/Enjoy Shopping/A Happy Feeling. It's a retail vacation featuring broad aisles and a simple arrangement of wildly disparate merchandise—"stuff for living," as it is described, arranged not by category but by price. You can find cosmetics, notebooks, housewares, toys, all just paces away from a coffee and ice-cream bar, where you buy a coupon from a vending machine and present it to a human server. It's a store conceived and designed to deliver a cool, pleasurable, highly organized, 180-second experience in the midst of urban madness. Nothing is expensive, everything is fun, and it's all in your face. With small cosmetic samples at ¥100 or ¥200 ($1 to $2), it's a shopper magnet. Both stores play to the consumer's love of value in completely different ways. They are radically different flowers springing from the same root system.

At the other end of the Japanese consumer spectrum is the love affair with luxury brands. Many such brand names do huge business in Japan. Oscar de la Renta, Calvin Klein, and many others license their names to Japanese stores and product manufacturers.

Historically, there is a unique signature to Japanese design, from the brushwork on paintings to the simplicity and grace of ancient buildings and the richness of Japanese textile design. That tradition has influenced Western design for more than 150 years. While you still see that history in twenty-first-century Japan, the best examples of high-end retail are in distinctly foreign settings, such as the Hermès, Prada, and Louis Vuitton stores in Tokyo.

Around the corner from the Imperial Hotel, where I stay, is the new Hermès store in Ginza. Mornings on my way to Starbucks, I pass the crowds waiting for the shop's ten o'clock opening. White-gloved security guards keep the docile hordes in line. It is a lovely store where product, display, and architecture are unified.

How do you explain the particular fervor many Japanese have for high-end brands? It surpasses what we see even in the United States and Europe. It is especially curious in Japan, which has struggled with economic stagnation of almost two decades. Japanese families endure punishing commutes, long workweeks, and expensive but modest housing. But they spend serious money on luxury products and have an almost mystical belief in their value. Just as previous generations may have hoarded gold coins, some Japanese today seem to believe that a Prada bag tucked in a closet is an investment.

To senior executives at luxury goods firms, the Japanese devotion to designer labels is a mixed blessing. The companies love the money—the Hermès and Louis Vuitton shops in Tokyo generate some of the largest sales-per-square-foot revenues of any retail location on Earth. A good Hallmark Gold Crown card store in an American mall may do $500-plus per square foot. A great Gap might do $700 a foot. A French or Italian luxury goods store in Tokyo brings in more than $7,000 a square foot.

What worries the European luxury goods manufacturers is the degree to which their native customers react negatively to crowds of Japanese tourists filling the shops in Paris and Milan. To a European snob, there is something distinctly déclassé about seeing your favorite bags getting on and off the tourist buses. Japanese customers are right to suspect that some products are being deliberately withheld from stores that serve the Japanese market. Some high-end shops in Paris and Milan limit the number of bags they will sell the individual Japanese tourist, but will look the other way when a well-dressed European wants to make the same multiple purchase. Outside the Louis Vuitton store off the Champs Elysée in Paris, Westerners are often approached by Japanese tourists asking if they will make their purchases for them.

As you leave the central urban core and make your way to the residential suburbs, the retail excitement and innovation drop off. The shopping centers serving much of the middle-class Japanese market are unassuming on the outside and aging on the inside.

Nara is a bedroom community of Osaka, Japan's second-largest city. It's home for teachers, middle-aged salary men, and Japan's increasingly visible retiree community. Nara is also one of the centers of Japanese Buddhism. Sprawling temple grounds, carefully groomed and maintained, attract thousands of tourists and pilgrims every year. To serve that trade, Nara has Palace Hotels, conference facilities, and expensive restaurants. Beyond the temples and facilities for tourists, the commuter line bifurcates the community like a noisy brook. Like much of Japan, Nara consists of densely packed pockets of housing surrounded by small farms. From the windows of the mall you see rice-field landscapes right out of the sixteenth-century—surrounded by pint-size strip shopping centers, modern bridges, and train lines. It is a weird vista.

The traffic on the narrow, two-lane roads approaching Nara Family Shopping is backed up for almost half a mile on the sunny Saturday afternoon we visit. Even from afar the mall looks to be more than fifteen years old; on the outside it is nondescript and the paint is peeling.

There's a line of over thirty cars waiting to park in the tiny lot. We end up appointing a designated driver, who spends the next two hours circling while we shop. While most Japanese shopping centers have parking, a lot of the traffic arrives on foot, since many malls are adjacent to commuter rail stations. Bicycle traffic can also be significant. I expected the Japanese to have developed an innovative bike parking system. They have not. In many locations, bike parking is subcontracted out and a uniformed employee is constantly moving locked bikes around to maximize space.

The commuter Japanese bike is solidly utilitarian and functional. This isn't glam bike country, and so theft is not an issue. The bikes are locked, but any urban American would laugh at the modest security measures, easily foiled by a Swiss Army knife. The basic bike comes with baskets and simple child carriers.

On the weekend the mall is populated by the elderly and young families. For both groups, convenience and proximity are trade-offs for the aging building and narrow selection. Employees' smiles are perfunctory and presentations routine and uninspired. Only the kimono shops have any dignity. The vinyl flooring is worn through in places on the first floor. Even the coin-operated kiddie rides in the concourse look ancient. As in many shopping centers, the escalators have been slowed down to accommodate an aging customer base. In homogeneous Japan, a tall, bald, bearded foreigner is not a common sight. My head brushes the bottom of signs hung from the ceiling. While Don Quixote has a sense of discovery, this place has a faint smell of stagnation. You sense the vast gulf between twenty years ago, when Japan seemed destined to take over the world, and now, where it sits at the edge of demographic and economic catastrophe.

Land is precious in Japan, and malls tend to sprawl upward rather than out. While all shopping involves a series of physiological constants—from how our eyes age to our tendency to be right-handed—the implications differ depending on where you go. The design of the signs and graphics is pure chaos to me—not at all in keeping with the serene Japanese aesthetic we Westerners have always admired. But thanks to a pictorial alphabet, the Japanese see and absorb graphic information differently than we do. The Roman alphabet may be easy to learn, and basic reading skills can be taught at an early age, but our system is not efficient. While a bright American kid can read the newspaper by age eight or nine, a Japanese student gains full literacy two or three years later. Much of their early education is about training visual memory. That ability to compress complex information into a series of symbols drives both the haiku and the richness of Japanese animation. It is also why text messaging is so popular in Japan, where words can be entered phonetically, making it easier and faster to compose. For the rest of the world stuck with spelling out words on a twelve button numeric keypad, we struggle to find a clumsy shorthand. On retail signage, the impact is harsh. The use of graphic symbols is coming, and our evolving mall directional signs and maps are good examples. We want recognizable iconography that is more efficient, and easier and faster to read.

Japanese malls are modeled after the country's department stores. Below ground level is where you find the takeaway food operation. As at many non–North American malls, food shopping is a major draw. For most Japanese it's a daily event, and the mall shops package their wares in single servings. The ground floor tends to be where groceries are sold. The middle floors are for general merchandise, like Target or Wal-Mart, with a mix of smaller merchants. The top floors are for restaurants.

The crowding in Japanese shopping is polite and mannerly—however hurried a person is, there is an acceptance of the pace, a resignation to the waiting. I am always surprised at the order in this country, from people all taking their lunch breaks at the same time to the controlled body movements and postures. As you walk the streets, you can pick out the Brazilian-born ethnic Japanese who have returned to the motherland. Their hips swing, the stride is longer, and the shoulders move differently.

It is not surprising that outside Japan, the Japanese tourist is a shopping machine. Much of the problem Japanese retail faces is the perception of ordinary citizens that they are not being offered what they deserve. Japan continues to innovate in developing consumer products and electronics. Yet we have seen few homegrown retail concepts translate elsewhere. American and European retailers have come to Japan with mixed results. Sephora and Boots, the English drug chain, have come and gone. McDonald's, Gap, Eddie Bauer, even Carrefour, the French hypermarket giant, are all struggling in Japan. The Japanese mall needs to reinvent itself and become more relevant in the twenty-first century. Given that Japan is aging faster than any other First World nation, we are looking for leadership on serving seniors. The shopping mall is one place it has to happen.

✼    ✼    ✼

Spain and Portugal have gone through remarkable transformations since the deaths of dictators Franco and Salazar. The countries have skipped fifty years ahead into the twenty-first century, having had the chance to examine what the rest of the developed world did right and wrong.

The most successful fashion chains in the world today are Zara and Mango. While Zara has a few locations in North America, Mango is an unknown in this part of the world. Amancio Ortega, the founder of Zara, comes from northern Spain and has built a retail organization that functions in seventy-plus countries around the world, selling inexpensive yet fashionable apparel. Both stores, but particularly Zara, are staples in non-American upscale malls across the world. They have set the bar for fashion with rich merchandising and lightning-quick responses to the marketplace. It spots trends quickly and exploits them to the max. Jennifer Lopez gets seen in some designer outfit, Zara copies it and has it in stores less than two weeks later. Both chains have dealt the traditional department store industry a serious blow.

The key to the store's success is the degree to which it gets its customers to buy at full price, a concept that has almost disappeared in the American market. Its high-fashion, modest-cost positioning trains you to buy it, if you find it, because two weeks from now it not only will not be on sale, it will be gone forever. The chain manages to get the right product to the right place in the right sizes. The stores are well designed. Zara has not flexed its muscle in the United States, preferring growth in easier markets. However, it's only a matter of time before domestic players like American Eagle, Old Navy, and Ann Taylor get a formidable rival.

European mall developers have been making pilgrimages to the Vasco da Gama and Colombo malls in Lisbon, Portugal, for more than five years now. Both malls were designed and built by the Portuguese developer Sonae, which is also a major shopping center developer in the Brazilian market. Vasco da Gama Center, named for the Portuguese navigator, is designed to look like a modern-art rendering of a sailing ship. It is one of the few modern malls built to look good on the outside, based on the premise that a distinctive external appearance will drive traffic and attract interesting tenants. Like the Guggenheim Museum in Bilbao, or the Tate Modern in London, the exterior architecture is part of the marketing effort. The Vasco da Gama Center is what results from a cooperative visionary relationship among developer, government, and architect.

European retail also differs from the American variety due to the history and role of the merchant. In the United States, retailing has always been a middle-class profession. The price of admission is a little money and the willingness to work hard, rather than education or social background. Few MBAs from America's top schools start their careers in retail. American merchant history is about immigrants and outsiders gravitating to retail as one of the few career tracks open to them. That nouveau-riche history is what makes American retail both brash and innovative, while at the same time leaving it vulnerable to staleness as the entrepreneurs give way to the managers and bureaucrats.

On the other side of the Atlantic, the merchant has always had social respectability. Four centuries of purveying products to wealthy aristocrats has developed the European sense of how to sell luxury goods. The Spaniards, French, and Italians are particularly good at it. Prada, LVMH, and Gucci are all merchant brands with long histories. The Brits and the Dutch have long traditions of merchant banking, the middlemen in buying and selling, tying retail into a comfortable, wealthy establishment.

My European colleagues tell me that Barcelona is the second-most popular weekend destination in Europe, after Paris. It is one of the continent's most beautiful cities. For those people who took exotic stimulants in the 1960s, the Catalonian architect and Barcelona native Antoni Gaudí possessed godlike qualities. His cathedral looks like melted candle wax, his apartment buildings undulate like belly dancers. What substances were they ingesting here in the late nineteenth century?

While Paris impresses, Barcelona seduces. One of my favorite stores in the world is Vinçon, which sells tools, furniture, and household products. It's visual merchandising plays in a different league than the rest of retailing. Even its paper shopping bags, which change with the season, are distinctive and collectible. It is retail theater that may not be transportable or conducive to chain ownership. Its owner is committed to art and design, and, while the store makes money, it feels like a labor of love. In the same tradition as our own Restoration Hardware and Williams-Sonoma, the store manages to help you fall in love with merchandise regardless of the price.

That is what makes stores like Vinçon stand out. It has managed to sustain its edge. In a city that's home to Vinçon and other shopping landmarks, it's not surprising to find interesting malls. Diagonal Mar in Barcelona is part of a huge redevelopment project started around the time of the 1992 Olympics. It's designed to be the commercial center of a district of high-rise apartment buildings and office towers. It gives residents the opportunity to shop, congregate, be entertained, and dine in an elegant pedestrian setting.

While the project is still incomplete, it wins both praise and catcalls. When you drive into the garage, there is a system for directing you to a parking place. It doesn't always work perfectly, but at least it's a system. Like Iguatemi, it has a formal entrance, which seems to have no relation to where most people actually enter the mall. On the day I visited, the car/taxi drop-off point was piled high with trash. Likewise, the bus stop across the street was forlorn. The mall's windows are largely empty, and the paint of the crosswalks is faint.

And yet, the third floor of the mall opens onto a magnificent plaza facing the surrounding apartment buildings and office blocks. It leads shoppers to restaurants and movie theaters on the top floor. The mall offers a broad selection of dining and is open late into the evening. At night it is a very busy place.

Like an American mall, Diagonal Mar is built with two anchors. At one end is FNAC, the French music, book, and electronic superstore that also sells concert tickets. That combination works well; I've seen FNAC mall stores where crowds have gathered early in the morning, waiting for the ticket window to open. At the other end is Sfera, a chain owned by Corte Inglés, the Spanish department group. Neither anchor store is a stellar contributor to this mall. FNAC is an urban format misplaced in a suburban setting. At the mall lease line are the ticket windows and registers, which make perfect sense for FNAC but are not particularly inviting to the passersby in the mall. Corte Inglés has the same problems that many North American department stores are facing—it is a tired concept that has trouble going up against its more nimble fashion specialty store competition.

On the inside, Diagonal Mar looks like an American mall. There are the predictable skylights on the central corridors and common areas. It is the details that make it distinctive. The tile work is unusual. Shopping carts from the mall grocery store are left on the concourse, as customers visit other stores on their way home from the supermarket. There are some long, gently sloping shopping cart escalators. There's a small lounge with sofas and chairs. This is Spain, and so, in spite of the signs, people are smoking everywhere. In one of the common areas, a Volkswagen Golf is being painted according to designs submitted by local schoolchildren. My Catalonian colleagues tell me Diagonal Mar has shifted the axis of the city and taken a blighted area and turned it around.

While malls are an American innovation, a lot of the most interesting development work is happening outside North America. Some of it is fueled by a better combination of government and private funding, but it is also about changing the rules and making the mall a more complete solution to consumers' needs. One thing the American mall must examine is how comfortably to integrate food shopping into the format. Particularly with high-concept, upscale grocery chains like Wegman's and Whole Foods, the idea is not inconsistent with the upscale mall's image. Iguatemi and Diagonal Mar offer customers shopping, entertainment, good eating, and a comfortable environment in which to watch people and socialize. They manage to duplicate the total urban experience, more or less. As the First World ages, the thought of riding an elevator from your apartment to the supermarket begins to sound sensible. In that spirit, I'd take Barcelona and Diagonal Mar over Miami Beach and Collins Avenue, its main drag, any day.

# 19 *Where the Girls Are*

IS THIS where you go inside?"

"Yes," says Brianna. "Because this is the entrance that's closest to Pac Sun."

"Does everyone call it Pac Sun?" I ask Britney.

"Yeah."

If you need to ask what Pac Sun is, you've obviously never spent time at the mall with anyone named Brianna *or* Britney *or* Ariel, as we're doing now. It's a chain of stores called, properly, Pacific Sun, specializing in clothing and accessories with a California surfer/skate flavor, lots of T-shirts and hoodies, and the like. If you wonder why it is that a bunch of adolescent girls living in New Jersey are so devoted to the surfer aesthetic, I do, too, but it seems beside the point to ask. The mall, like the city, is capacious, and serves any number of subcultures and even sub-subcultures simultaneously, and without making a big fuss about it. It's the endless and nonchalant ability of commerce to

157

give us what we want without calling it to our attention. Probably we're all better off this way.

"Would you ever shop *here*?" I ask, referring to the big department store through which we've entered.

"With my mom. Not really," Britney says, making a face. The other girls giggle.

"I go here sometimes," says Brianna.

"Yeah, me, too," says Ariel. "I buy perfume here."

"Okay, let's stop a second," I say. We're in a department store, at the perfume counter. This does not strike me as a place particularly well aimed at teenage girls—it feels like the domain of their mothers, per-haps, of middle-aged women who seek (and pay for) cosmetics and moisturizers and paints and fragrances to emphasize and amplify what-ever natural beauty they bring to the party—but here we are all the same.

"I wear Calvin Klein," says Ariel.

"I wear Tommy," says Brianna.

"Polo," says Britney.

"Excuse me," I say to the saleswoman who has come over to where we're standing. "About how many of the shoppers in this department are around the age of these girls?"

"A lot," she says.

That's surprising because this counter does absolutely nothing to at-tract young girls. There's a big lush photograph of a semifamous actress who's on the brink of incipient middle age and is in the news for having borne a child to her much-older actor husband.

"And you girls shop here because . . ."

"It's on the way," says Brianna.

"Do you ever look over there?" *Over there* is the shoe department.

"I gaze, but I don't *look*," says Ariel.

"Yeah, my mom is always the one who goes, 'Aren't they cute?' and I'm, like, 'No.' "

"So where do you usually go from here?"

"I go to Musicland."

"First?"

"It depends."

"Do you like music more than clothes?"

"Mmm, not really."

"If you had to decide between buying jeans and CDs, which would you choose?"

"Jeans."

"Jeans."

"Jeans. Because it's always better to have more clothes. And you can always go online to get music."

Pac Sun is drawing us in its direction, but on the way we pass Old Navy.

"Would you go in here?"

"No."

"Why?"

"It looks like what forty-year-olds wear."

"Yeah. Older people."

"Like my mom."

"Teachers."

A death sentence.

"Teachers would wear this to school?"

"No. Some of it is too . . ."

". . . revealing. For teachers."

We pass American Eagle, which appeals solely to teenagers.

"Here?"

"I don't wear preppy clothes."

"Me neither."

"We have friends who shop here, but not us."

"Amanda."

"Or Holly."

"We grew out of preppy."

More death.

"Okay, everything so far has just been leading us to here, right?"

We're there. Pac Sun.

"How often do you come to this store?"

"I was here two days ago."

"How many times a month?"

"Four, at least."

"Same."

"Five or six."

"Eight."

Eight visits a month. Imagine if these girls had money!

"You all come Fridays after dinner?"

"Pretty much."

"Then we come Saturday, too."

"What's there to do in here?"

The answer's obvious, but I like hearing it.

"Oh, look at clothes."

"Look at what other people are wearing."

They're still new enough at this to be aware of what they're doing. Twenty years from now they'll all be here, or someplace just like it, but it will be so reflexive that they won't even have to think about why.

"I like the guys' T-shirts. But I would never wear them."

"They have funny slogans."

"Do you always find new stuff? In other words, if you come in again next week will the store look pretty much the same as it does now?"

"No, they'll have new stuff."

This is the challenge for any store catering to mall rats—the kids come back so often that you're forced constantly to change the displays. Otherwise, they get bored and stop coming at all. It's one reason stores need to know how often the regulars return—to see whether the windows and front tables should be changed every week or every seventeen days.

"Now, correct me if I'm wrong," I say, "but this is what you'd call a surfer store."

"Yeah."

"Yeah."

"Yeah, like California skateboarding . . ."

"And what does that mean to you?"

"Well, it's the kind of music we like."

"What kind?" I'm thinking: *Surf music?*

"Rock."

"Punk."

Oh, right, *that's* surfer music today. Not the Beach Boys.

"Like tell me who, specifically."

"Get Down Boys. Blink-182. Adema. Linkin Park."

"Jimmy Eat World."

"When you watch a rock video, are you noticing what clothes people are wearing?"

"Yeah."

"So you watch a video and see clothes like these, and it's obviously supposed to be some kind of California scene, and you're in New Jersey, but still somehow it registers with you?"

"Pretty much."

"I also shop here because it's different from everyone else. Like today a lot of kids around here are more into rap and less into this kind of thing."

"What do those girls wear?"

"Baggy pants and a tight T-shirt that says 'Baby Phat.' "

They smirk in unison.

"What kind of person is that girl?"

There's a pregnant pause.

"I guess we'd call them *thugs.*"

They seem a little uncomfortable with this, but no one can come up with anything better.

"Thugs rather than punks?"

"Yeah. They all have attitude. Bad attitude."

"Where do they shop?"

"There's a store called Against All Odds."

The store names do a good job of differentiating the tribes—you've got Pac Sun versus Abercrombie & Fitch versus Against All Odds. It sounds so young, until you think about Nordstrom versus Versace versus Ann Taylor, and you realize that retail tribalism doesn't end when we become adults. It's just that the signifiers become a little more subtle (to us adults, I mean).

"So you have thugs and preps—"

"Hold on a second. What is preppy today? How's it look?"

"Clean cut."

"Not too tight."

"Everything ironed, and they're like cheerleaders or they like what-ever's popular in music."

"Whatever's in, they like."

"Okay. What other kinds of kids are there?"

"Skaters. Skas. Punks."

"I think that skaters and punks are the same. And then you have thugs."

"Between all those, you have half our school."

"And then you have the rest, the people who just dress normal. Like they all have the same style."

"But you also have people who used to be skaters and then just changed overnight to thugs. Like overnight changed their whole wardrobe."

"Everybody has to have their own place to shop, then, is that right?"

"Kind of," says Britney. "Although my mom shops here."

"At Pac Sun?"

"Uh-huh."

"Interesting."

"See, she does try to do fashion, and she dresses young so she can feel younger, but . . ."

That *but* hurts.

"So your mothers *could* shop here?"

"Yeah," says Brianna, "but mine shops at Old Navy."

"My mother doesn't care anything about fashion," says Ariel.

"So where does she shop? She has to buy something."

"I don't know *where* she shops."

"Britney, what would your mother buy here?"

"She'll choose like the dorkiest thing here."

"Show me what she'd pick."

"*That,*" says Brianna.

"Yeah, that dress right there."

"Hey," says Ariel, "I *like* that dress."

"No, not the blue one. Actually the *pink* dress."

"You wouldn't wear the pink one?"

"No."

"No."

"No."

I'm sure this conversation would come as a surprise to the executive suite at Old Navy, since they imagine their chain is aimed directly at girls such as these. In that company's master plan, today's Old Navy shopper migrates tomorrow to the Gap, and then, once she's a little older, all the way up to Banana Republic. But reality has a way of intruding on even the best-laid merchandising plan.

"I'm a little surprised to learn that, in your view, Old Navy is such an adult store," I say. "Would any of you shop there for anything?"

"I do."

"Don't."

"I don't usually find anything in there."

"They changed from when they first started."

"And made it worse?" I ask.

"Yeah."

"Their clothes fit weird."

"Baggier. The jeans got baggier."

"And they've got a funny shape."

"Do you think the jeans are bigger and baggier because there are more older shoppers there nowadays?"

"It's not *that* kind of baggier."

"What kind?"

"More like for rappers."

"Oh! Like thugs, you mean?"

"Kind of."

Another reason to stay away—thugs *and* moms.

"How much time will you spend here in Pac Sun?"

"An hour."

"That feels like a long time. What will you do during that hour?"

"I'll try on a dress."

"And I'll try it on like fifty times."

"Wow. Will you try on stuff from every section of the store?"

"Pretty much."

"Will you buy anything?"

"At least one thing."

"So if you come here once a week, you'll buy one thing a week."

"At least."

"Maybe a T-shirt?"

"Maybe. Or shorts. A necklace."

"How much will you spend? How much is that sweatshirt?"

"Like $40."

"Like $50."

"So you could end up spending fifty dollars every week here?"

"Sure."

"That comes to, what, around $2,500 a year. That's a lot of money."

"It is."

"Yeah, here I sometimes feel things are overpriced. Like $18 or $20 for a T-shirt."

"A plain T-shirt."

"I always go to the clearance rack to see if I can find anything there."

"It's always the first place *I* go."

But lest you go forward under the impression that Pac Sun is the zenith of the teenage girl mall experience, think again. We were discussing the glories of the mall itself when Britney says, "There's only one store missing here."

"What's that?" I ask.

"Hot Topic."

"Hot Topic," Brianna agrees.

"If that was in this mall, that's the first store we'd go to," says Ariel.

"But it's at a different mall, one that's farther away," says Britney.

"What's the best store in the world?" I ask.

"Hot Topic."

"Hot Topic."

"Hot Topic."

Can you imagine finding this kind of unanimity among adult shoppers? This level of rock-solid certainty? Life loses focus as we grow older, and I'm not talking about eyesight here. Teenagers are the ones whose love for the mall is pure and constant and unshadowed by doubt or ambivalence. Do these girls worry about whether their love of buying and owning masks some unmet spiritual need, some emotional dead zone deep inside? No way. Teenage girls may be ironic about a number of things, but stores and shopping and acquisitions and malls are not usually among them.

"They have interesting things that would make you stand out, like express yourself more," says Ariel.

"Clothes, jewelry?"

"Yeah. Shoes . . ."

"Perfume . . ."

"Shoelaces . . ."

"Boots . . ."

"Patches . . ."

"Patches. And that's like the ultimate fourteen-year-old girls' store?"

"Teenager store."

Okay, we're back out of the store and strolling the mall. We come upon Victoria's Secret.

"How about this store?"

"I don't go here," says Britney.

"Too expensive," says Brianna.

"I don't even think my mom shops here," says Ariel.

"This place is more like . . ."

"More like what?"

"Like . . . *lingerie.*"

"Fancier."

"Not like everyday. Not like teenager."

"When did you get that lip piercing?" I ask Britney. Something about walking by Victoria's Secret brings my attention back to how the bodies of these adolescent girls have been adorned, permanently in some cases, by contemporary fads.

"Last month."

"Did your parents have any objection?"

"Not much. My mother said fine, you know, as long as you're going to take care of it, then go ahead."

"I'm not allowed to get any piercings, but I want to get so many," says Brianna. "When I turn eighteen, I'm getting every one that I want."

"My parents aren't that strict about it," says Ariel. "I got my belly pierced for my birthday."

"Your fourteenth?"

"Yeah. But like they don't want anything piercing my face. When I'm sixteen, they said I can get my tongue pierced if I want."

"And you're going to do it?"

"Yeah. My tongue and my eyebrow."

"I want my tongue," says Brianna.

"Why?"

"Because it's fun!"

"How could getting your tongue pierced be fun?"

"It's just interesting. It looks cool when you talk."

"Okay, but do you all imagine someday being, I don't know, adults and mothers, or holding a job? Do you figure someday you'll be a lawyer and talking to the judge with your tongue and lip pierced? And your eyebrow ring? Or do you figure you'll take it out?"

"Yeah, like if I got my belly button pierced and then I was having a baby, I'd definitely take it out, because that would be disgusting."

"How about tattoos?"

"The only thing about tattoos is, everybody has a tattoo nowadays."

"Yeah. Not everybody has a piercing yet."

"But why do you want one?"

"I don't know. It expresses you, I guess."

We've somehow wandered right to the food court.

"Now, usually, we eat."

"Where?"

"Always the food court."

"Not one of the freestanding restaurants?"

"Never."

"Where in the food court?"

"We don't know. That's why it always takes so long."

"This is really most like a hangout, isn't it?"

"Yeah."

"Where, besides the mall, do you girls actually go?"

"Not counting school?"

"Yes."

"Or home?"

"Yes."

"Well, sometimes we go and like walk around our neighborhood."

"And hang out with friends."

"Hang out with friends where?"

"At people's houses."

"But tell me, is there any nonmall, nonhouse place where you can go?"

"Well, there's always the movies. But people don't want to spend that kind of money all the time. It's like $8 every time you go."

"But that's not really hanging out. We go sometimes to the park."

"Sometimes."

"Or to get Chinese food."

"Yeah. We just walk around town and see what we can find stupid to do."

That sounds a lot like most adolescents.

"But other than that or the park, everything you do involves spending money."

"Yeah, that's the way life is. You spend money when you go out, or you stay home and talk on the phone and pay for minutes."

"Do you girls ever meet boys here?"

"Sometimes."

"At the arcade."

"Yeah, that's where you see them."

"And they whistle and stuff. You just keep walking, but . . ."

"Do they whistle because they're too shy to talk?"

"Yeah."

"I guess."

"Is it obnoxious?"

"It's just the way they are."

"I think they're trying to have fun."

"Do you ever go shopping in the mall with boys?"

"I don't know."

"It's weird, because they shop for different things than we do."

"They shop at some of the same places, but they just pick something out and like get it. They don't take the time we do. They don't try stuff on."

"I don't think they have to."

"Yeah, they can look at the label and see it's size thirty-two and the certain length they wear and then just buy it. But for us it can be the right size but everything fits different."

"Do boys go to Pac Sun?"

"Uh-huh."

"Do they spend an hour?"

"No way. They spend five minutes in the store and then the rest of the time just walking around the mall, seeing who they can bother."

"Whereas you girls can spend hours just shopping."

"Yeah, well, we do but we alternate. We shop, hang out, then shop some more."

"We'll get all our shopping done in the first two hours, and then we'll spend the next two hours just walking around and stuff."

"Looking at people."

"Do you go anywhere other than to the stores and the food court?"

"The video arcade."

"To meet boys or to play?"

"To play."

"See, now I always imagined that the video arcade is more of a guy thing."

"I play all the time."

"I do, too."

"I don't waste a lot of money buying games, though, because I need other things. And I don't have time to play video games constantly, like some boys do."

"I play much more than my brother does."

"Who else is at the arcade?"

"Mall junkies."

"Those are the kids who are always, *always* here. Either inside or sitting around on the steps outside the mall, in nice weather. Like the people who no matter when you come to the mall, you see them here. It's like they never leave."

"A lot of them are the kids who live so close that they walk to the mall."

"When did you girls really start coming to the mall?"

"From birth."

"No, I mean coming by yourselves. Not getting here alone, but spending time here without parents."

"I used to come when I was in the sixth grade. That's when I was allowed to spend time here without my mother. She would like drop me off here with some of my friends, and then she'd come back at a certain time to pick us up. Or I'd call her at home when we were ready to leave."

"Do you remember what it felt like the first time?"

"It felt cool to be out somewhere without your parents along."

"Yeah, and you could do whatever you want and buy whatever you want, 'cause you had your own money."

"I think I came the first time with my friend Rochelle, and we went to Pac Sun. I think I bought a shirt, and then we just walked around. For hours."

"Are you girls allowed to go in other kids' cars yet?"

"No. I can go in my brother's car. He drove us here last week."

"What did your mothers do when they were your age?"

"Like, where did she hang out?"

"Yes."

"I don't know. I don't think she was allowed out much."

"Yeah. Like, when they were our age they were pretty much at home."

"Things must have changed, because my mom says 'I'm letting you do things that my mother would never let me do. Like, she would never let me go shopping, or do things to my hair like color it or get it cut or anything like that.' "

"Yeah, when they were our age, I think they were playing with dolls."

"How old is your mother?"

"Right now? She's forty-three?"

"Do you like her?"

There's a lot of nervous giggling at this.

"Sometimes."

"Sometimes I don't really like her, but . . . I guess I'm closer to my dad. I don't know why."

"Yeah. My mom always tries to be my friend, and I get so mad."

As you may have noticed, teenage girls love malls, but as shopping machines they are not without their flaws. For all the time they spend in stores, they have the lowest conversion rate of any demographic, meaning the percentage of female teenage shoppers who buy something is at the bottom of the pack. They are inefficient, in other words, which is not to say that efficiency in these matters is all, or even paramount. Their inefficiency stems for the most part from the fact that they are not in total control over what and how much they purchase. We saw how much preshopping they do—they comb through mountains of clothing, trying on a great deal of it in an approximation of the fashion-show games they may have played in childhood. Then, with Mom in tow, they return to the stores to plead for the items that truly seemed most awesome.

And for all their inefficiency, they (along with their male cohorts) still manage to constitute a $200 billion annual marketplace. If you do the math, every American teenager is the source of roughly $200 a week in total retail purchases. It is true that many American teenagers work—from baby-sitting to taking after-school shifts at the local fast-food restaurants. But most are living off the largess of their families. Their money is spent almost entirely on discretionary purchases. They are, to the economy, pure gravy—they manage, even with limited productivity, to represent a lot of buying power, making them tycoonlike in their contribution to the cosmic bottom line.

They are trendy, impressionable, and emotional in their spending habits, too, easy to reach through the dependable medium of TV. They also possess something their predecessors couldn't imagine: consumer credit. The typical college freshman carries somewhere around $2,000 in ongoing credit card balances, the result of having been importuned on countless occasions since high school. They have time, boundless desires, and money. Is it any wonder that retailers crave their attention?

# 20 *The Mall Touch*

WHERE do the exhausted, the played out, the spent, the irredeemably mall-sore go for relief?

They climb into a big blue polyurethane-lined coffin, one that's throbbing with slamming, pulsating jets of warm water, whereupon they experience mall ecstasy.

They go to Aqua Massage.

There's a line, so we'll have to wait a few minutes for our turn. It's a good chance to contemplate this phenomenon, which strikes me as a venture that could succeed only in the mall. Maybe that's due to the psychic kinship shared by an enclosed shopping center and an enclosed massage machine. They're both so spectacularly fake that they outdo reality.

If this is your first time, let me describe. It's a large box, maybe the size of a refrigerator. It opens like a coffin, into which you climb, with only your head sticking out. (It's not for claustrophobes.) Then the blue vinyl lining fills with water, and you are pleasurably pummeled in a fashion not previously seen outside the car wash. At no time are you ever touched by a human being, and you keep on all your clothing except your shoes. These are seen as the advantages of this contraption. You pay by the minute, usually somewhere between $1 and $1.50.

It's not a hoax or a con, either—these machines were originally meant to be sold to physicians and hospitals for physical therapy. But they didn't catch on, until some smart businessman got the idea to put one in a mall. Today there are around two thousand in use in the United States. It's a franchise business, meaning that all over this great entrepreneurial country of ours, there are men and women dreaming Aqua Massage dreams of wealth and glory and malls.

You want to go first?

# 21 *Short Hills or Seoul?*

I PROBABLY spend more time looking at the ceilings and the floors than most people walking around the mall," Ron says.

Ron may be one of the few people I know who has spent even more of his life in malls than I have. He's a store designer—a position somewhere between architect and interior decorator. I like him because he's both the most honest and most cynical mall store designer I know.

He grew up blue-collar in Brooklyn, worked his way through college selling records at Korvette's, graduated with a degree in architecture, but couldn't find a firm that would give him a job. He compromised and took a gig with a store-planning agency. He's now devoted more than twenty-five years of his life to the trade, has his own firm, makes buckets of money, and has not just the inclination but also the right to say what he thinks.

"What do you see up there on the ceiling?" I ask as we stroll.

"Details. Lighting. Lights are extremely important in a mall, because inside the stores it's a totally enclosed, controlled setting, and you've got to make things visible to shoppers, first of all, and then you've got to highlight the things you really want them to notice. No shopper thinks about lighting when they walk through a store, which is how it should be. If you notice it, it's probably because it's either too dim or too bright. Some stores manage this better than others. Smaller ones have an easier job because they have less to illuminate. Most mall stores are built wide and shallow, meaning most of the storefront is right there along the corridor. As a result, there's already decent light coming in."

"How about the big stores? How about the department stores?"

"They've got a tougher challenge. Walk around just about any department store, and you'll begin to pick out the dark spots. You've got a lot of territory to illuminate—say, 150,000 square feet of selling space, and ceiling lights will run you around $25, $30 a square foot. It's a lot of bucks. It's tempting for the store to say, 'You know what, maybe we can just do an acoustical tile ceiling with surface-mounted fixtures' instead of something more powerful that will also be more costly."

"To me, Macy's all seem dark."

"They are. That's because they don't spend enough on lighting. That's what I meant—if you notice the lights one way or the other, there's usually a problem. It's even worse for department stores because their best shoppers tend to be older ladies."

Ron's hit on something there. As we age, the lens in the human eye turns yellowish. Thus, a fifty-year-old sees colors differently than a young person. In addition, those older eyes let in roughly 20 percent less light. Now, most designers of stores and restaurants tend to be young, meaning what they think looks bright enough is too dark for customers middle-aged and older. This is why I have a flashlight key chain—to read the menus in trendy restaurants. Not only are they too dark, but also the young menu designer in all likelihood made the type-face too small for my decrepit eyes.

"Whereas," I say, "when I go into Neiman Marcus, I usually find a big skylight somewhere, and it floods the store with natural light."

"Right," says Ron. "Natural light sends a message—it says we spent some money. It's ironic, that sunlight is more expensive-looking than electric lighting, but it's true. I have no idea why. It doesn't make a bit of sense."

Nowadays everybody's getting skylights. They show up in most newly constructed suburban homes, even the midrange models. The new Wal-Mart prototype uses skylights!

"What else are you looking at, besides lights?"

"I'm looking for impact. I want the store to tell me what it is."

"Do you mean first impression?"

"I want the store to begin talking to me even before I know exactly what particular things I'm going to find inside."

"Show me an example."

"Let's go see the J. Jill store."

J. Jill is part of a significant trend in American retail, wherein some catalog houses are going into the bricks and mortar store business. L.L. Bean, Coldwater Creek, and even REI, the outdoor store, are all examples. L.L. Bean's outlet in Maine is on the top-ten list of tourist attractions in the state. The firm's move into shopping mall country is a very big step. What makes the transition interesting is how a brand so well developed and focused in two dimensions translates into three, and how the successful catalog customer service model changes once the interactions are face-to-face.

A J. Jill catalog is a romance novel's interpretation of how a beautiful, mature female artist might live: walks on the beach, a studio flooded with natural light, the soft textures of a weaver's loom. All the models are over thirty, there is some sexy gray hair, and all the waistlines are gently concealed. The photo layouts are brilliant, and the clothes are soft and romantic, definitely not urban.

"Okay, here we are. What do you see?"

"First, this very soft curtain. No other store in this mall uses fabric at the doorway. In this case it sets a nice tone, and it is a very distinct entrance. There's some topiary up here and a little stone thing on the entrance floor. You're getting some variety in terms of surfaces and textures—the same way the catalog uses texture to evoke the lifestyle. So you are being made to recognize that you've crossed the line from out there in the mall to in here, inside the store."

"That's kind of an exception to the mall rule, isn't it?"

"Kind of."

"Is there a downside to doing it the other way—the usual way?"

"Several that I can think of. For one thing, you might not want every visitor to the mall inside your store. If you're selling high-end goods, for instance, that could be a negative. Which is why, as a rule, the fancier the store, the more definite the line between inside and outside."

"This isn't a fancy store, though, is it?"

"Not at all. But they still have taken some trouble with the entrance. I think their typical customer is a woman who is fairly style-conscious. So it should make what I was talking about before—some kind of specific impact on that woman. Look, once we step inside there's a little fountain here, so we get a sonic hit, the trickling water, plus some soft music. The whole effect slows you down, and that's good, too. There's something very feng shui about what they've done. You get a good, positive, relaxed feeling from the environment itself. It's not casual and noisy, like a store appealing to young trendy buyers. It doesn't have loud music and rock videos on TV monitors and bright lights and all that stuff. But it isn't haughty high-end luxury either—it doesn't say stay away unless you've got a lot of money to spend."

"What does it say, then?"

"I don't know exactly, except that it's saying something—you can tell that much from when you walk in. The point isn't to say everything all at once. In fact, you want to tell a story over the course of the entire store, not just in the first six feet. There's something to be said for starting out a little mysteriously. With luring people inside and letting them discover what you're about."

"I try and tell retailers that all the time, but it's maybe the hardest idea to impart. Part of shopping is discovering. It may even be a very important part of its appeal. It feels as though it's tapping into some primordial instinct we have for hunting or gathering—we like the actual process of finding things. When we enter a store for the first time, our senses are fully alert and our eyes are moving all over the place. We're sniffing the air, and our ears are scanning for clues about what kind of place this is. That's part of what makes shopping a fun thing to do. It's what distinguishes one store from another."

"The merchandise doesn't really do that, does it?"

"Less and less so. Stores used to have strong personalities, and they expressed it through merchandise. Bloomingdale's sold one kind of thing, while Bonwit's sold another, and Lord & Taylor another, and Macy's something different from all those. Today you find the same brands, the same designer labels, in all those stores. It leads to a certain predictability."

"This store seems to have some personality, though, doesn't it?"

"It does, in a weird way. For instance, most designers would do all the walls in white, for a simple reason: It shows off the merchandise better. It makes it pop."

"What colors are these, a kind of taupey shade, right?"

"Yeah. We store designers would all look at that and say it's dangerous because it doesn't highlight the clothes as well as it could. And all the graphics are what I would call organic—there are pictures and other things hanging on the walls, but they're not photographs or posters of the merchandise, which is the way most stores would go. They're not selling goods, they're creating a mood."

"Why is that not what most store designers would do?"

"Because in the end, the store and everything in it are intended to do one thing—sell goods. It can be beautiful, but if it doesn't help the store to carry out its main function, is it good? I don't think so."

"What else do you see?"

"The fixtures look like they were chosen by a decorator rather than by someone who designs retail interiors. I'm talking about these bamboo tables, for instance. Or those baskets. Look at that nice, antiquey-looking lamp. A woman might have that in her dressing room at home. Nothing here looks like it came from the usual sources for store furnishings. Everything's been tweaked a little."

"What would it all look like if it were done according to the rulebook?"

"White walls. Light-colored wood fixtures, maybe, or just plain chrome racks and so on. Ceiling-mounted lights. It could be dressed up from there, but there would probably be less stuff to distract your eye from the clothes. On the walls, there might be photos of models wearing the actual goods being displayed nearby, with copy making the connection. A bit more institutional-looking, less like some individual person went out and picked the furniture and wall coverings for this particular store. And maybe there would be less mood overall, but the merchandise would be more prominent in the mix. Here, the room itself got all the attention, while the clothes are displayed in a very simple way—almost like whoever designed this didn't know much about presenting merchandise."

"What do you think the effect of this store will be on the shopper?"

"I imagine she'd want to stay in here a little longer. It's a nice room. It's a break from the rest of the mall. It actually feels like the kind of boutique you'd find in the city, on a street downtown maybe. That's why I like this, because it will give the shopper an experience that's different from most of what's out there, and it's someplace that begins speaking to her in a distinct voice the second she walks in."

"Is there any reason *not* to do a mall store this way?"

"Maybe some shoppers will look at the store and be turned off by the boutiquey feeling, and they won't wander inside. If this were a big, bright typical mall store with the usual, durable fixtures, it might be more welcoming to your average shopper."

"But then we'd like it less."

"Exactly."

"The world of visual design in stores seems to have declined. Retailers aren't spending the money they once spent, and they're not taking any stands in what they do. All the decisions are being made in a central office, and made so they can work in every store equally well, meaning they've got to be somewhat generic. They no longer see the store itself as a kind of stage on which the merchandise is presented."

"It depends on which store you're talking about, but for the most part you're right. Back in the old days, in the 1960s and 1970s, you had big retail executives with big egos, and they sought out creative designers and hired them to come up with distinctive looks. The designers were like hired guns, and they went back and forth depending on who had hired them for what. Then, the trend shifted and the retail chains began hiring in-house design staff. It was a smart move for them because it took the best designers off the market and away from their competitors. Designers ended up exposed to less, and they were influenced by less, too. As a result of all that, the design world became static and even a little stale—you had one client, and you came up with something, and then you just worked on refining that. It took some of the edge away. That's why the whole world of retail starts looking the same."

"Less one-upsmanship among you designers."

"Yes. We were just hired by the fashion division of a huge Korean corporation. They own a chain of stores throughout the country. They're positioned somewhere between Ralph Lauren and Burberry—they're like the Polo of Korea. And I spent some time there recently, and it amazes me how throughout Asia the brands are all totally formed by American images. The stores, the clothes, all the collateral stuff—the ads, the graphics and visual material, its all blond-haired, blue-eyed imagery. Indonesia, same way. Japan. On the highway, as you approach the big retail-entertainment complexes, the billboards all show people living the dream suburban American lifestyle, with hammocks and golf clubs and blue-eyed, blond-haired families. The Koreans hired us because they wanted to buy what they called 'New York style.' They came to New York from Seoul and interviewed a bunch of firms looking for a representation of simply that. They didn't really know what they wanted, except that it look like New York—like something you'd find in SoHo. They wanted that quirkiness, that style you find there, and they wanted to box it up and ship it to Korea. Which is what they hired us to do."

"And you did a good job of it, too, I imagine."

"The best. Soon you won't be able to tell Seoul from Short Hills."

Okay, so now we're in a fancy department store, in fact, *the* fanciest department store in this particular mall, and we're not in just any old part of the store but in one of the fanciest sections (though not *the* fanciest—that's just around the corner from where we're standing).

Yes, we're standing in ladies' clothing, so to speak. And when we look into the department, we see: sleeves.

Not disembodied sleeves, of course—but the view from this particular spot is of women's suit jackets and blazers hanging in racks, and the racks are positioned in a way that saves space, a result of which is that the sides of the jackets—meaning the sleeves—are what face the shopper. You can tell quite a bit about a jacket by looking at the sleeve, it's true—the color and fabric at the very least—but a jacket must be seen from the front to experience it. This will come as no surprise to the executives of this famous department store chain, and yet somehow, standing here, what we see are sleeves.

"What can be done?"

"Well, there's actually a very simple solution. You could chevron the racks. Angle them, so instead of the shopper looking head-on into the sleeve, they'd see a three-quarter view of the front of the first jacket in each rack."

America's store shelves and display racks would almost universally be improved by making this change. That's because the way shelves and racks are stocked is fundamentally at odds with how people move. We walk facing forward. In order to look directly at a box of cereal or a bottle of shampoo on a supermarket shelf, we'd have to turn and face squarely sideways. But of course it's impossible (or at least dangerous) to walk facing sideways. And so we tend to examine shelves and racks and so on from an angle. If the merchandise was angled to face us, we'd see it head-on.

I could easily devote all the working hours of a week to strolling the retail aisles of America making just this simple change. And believe me, the shopping experience would be instantly improved for all parties, resulting in higher sales and lower shopper frustration.

"And there's another advantage to chevroning. When you angle the racks, you actually eat up more floor space than the other way. So you have room for fewer goods on display."

"And what's good about that?"

"Well, we've tested this with shoppers, and they think it looks like there's more merchandise out there, not less. So you can fill up the selling floor using fewer goods, which means lower inventory costs."

"What happens to sales when they chevron the racks?"

"We measured that. They go up some. Not a huge amount. But there's always a bump."

"So if chevroning the racks would show the jackets off better, why don't they all do it?"

"Well, because of a problem that's widespread in retail but especially so in malls: no storage space. Once upon a time, department stores had vast warrens of stockrooms and storage areas. When these mammoth retail emporiums dominated downtowns, they had all the space in the world for storage and offices and all manner of backroom operations."

"The mall killed that?"

"Real estate prices did. High rents did. Today the pressure is on to make every square foot count. Nobody can afford stockrooms. Everything goes straight to the selling floor."

"And that's why they can't chevron—it's too crowded."

"Correct."

"Is that also why sometimes it seems as though too many clothes have been put onto the racks, especially ones with hangers? They're jammed so tight you can't pull anything out."

"There's been a fundamental change in how the space in retail businesses has been apportioned. Imagine your house with no closets. That's retailing today."

"Even in a fancy store like this."

Every so often I'll get a call from some group asking if I'll testify in court against a big retailer for not being as wheelchair-accessible as the law requires. I reply, "Look, I am very sympathetic to what you're trying to do, but, in terms of the state of retailing, there aren't a whole lot of choices." You build a store today and plan for maximum selling space. You also try and make as much of it accessible to wheelchairs, baby strollers, and shopping carts as you can. The dilemma is how much of your design and construction budget is going to get chewed up by accessibility issues. Yes, there are real travesties out there, spaces that totally ignore the spirit of what the Americans with Disabilities Act is supposed to accomplish. Prada opened a store in SoHo in 2001, and it won lots of praise for its fabulous design. I have yet to be in it when the elevator works.

Retailers are frustrated because they are aware of the accessibility problem. From the designer's point of view, getting the basics right, from ramps and railings to bathrooms and doorways, is hard enough. The store has to do the best it can, and it's our responsibility to point out where it fails. However, making a legal issue of it ignores the most powerful marketplace rule, which is, if you are offended, take your business elsewhere. Store planners, particularly when working with older buildings, have a difficult time complying with the ADA. If you leave enough space for a wheelchair to go from the central corridor to the farthest recesses of the store, you have to leave a lot of empty space between fixtures and racks.

I have been asked to testify as an expert witness on behalf of handicapped shoppers. I have also been approached by big department stores also asking me to be a witness in their defense in ADA cases. I understand both sides of the issue, and so far I have chosen not to get tangled up in *any* court cases, although I am very willing to talk off the record to both sides. When merchants seek my advice on how to deal with ADA lawsuits, I suggest that they confess not only to the 267 violations they were charged with, but to admit that they were probably in violation of the law in about 3,000 other instances, too. And if the law were broadened to make America's stores baby stroller–accessible, the number of violations would be double that. Then, I say, they should explain to the court that they could probably afford to fix fifty of those accessibility problems a year. If the ADA is really going to help, it will be used not to sue businesses but to help them prioritize their violations and fix the worst ones.

"I'm looking at that far wall there," Ron says, "and I can't even see *all* the way through—even though they have merchandise allegedly on display there."

We approach what, on some store designer's computer screen, must have looked like a wall display rack of women's silk blouses. Given the average adult human's eyesight, the display would be completely visible and thereby effective at, say, twenty-five feet. Unfortunately, there's no unimpeded view of the wall from that distance. In fact, you can't see the blouses until you're around five feet from them. There's a lot of merchandise on the selling floor. But at a certain point each display gets in the way of all those surrounding it. The clothes begin to cancel one another out. You find it difficult just to maneuver around everything. And your eye can't keep it all sorted out—it creates a visual jumble. It's not simply unappealing—you are actually incapable of taking it all in, and so you don't.

"What the heck is that red thing?"

Up above the wall rack of blouses, maybe ten feet off the floor, there's a shelf. On the shelf is a big red shiny ceramic something. Behind that is a wall hanging—fabric. Also bright. Yellow.

"It's what they call a design element."

"No, look, it's a vase!"

"Yes, but it's a vase with no practical purpose. You'll notice it isn't actually holding anything. Clearly, it was intended to catch your eye from far away. It's a decorative piece, but it has a job, too. It's supposed to tell you that there's something over here to see."

"The silk blouses that are obscured by all those floor racks."

"These blouses are $200 each. And this rack alone holds about twenty of them. So, that's $4,000 worth of goods hidden from customers. Put yourself in the place of the shopper looking for an expensive silk blouse. Does a crowded rack of merchandise obstructed by a floor display signal 'fancy silk blouses'?

"I mean, are the visual clues we all rely upon adding up? There's not a great big sign that proclaims 'really expensive high-quality silk shirts over here!' Stores speak to us in subtle ways. The way these blouses are presented to the eye has to give shoppers a fair amount of information about them. One formerly reliable clue was this: The less clutter, the more costly. That's the rule in the store itself, or in any given area of it, or on any rack or shelf. At the Dollar Store, you expect to see merchandise jammed into every nook and cranny. Just like you expect to find linoleum floors and metal racks and plastic signs and fluorescent lighting. Whereas in this place you want carpeting and marble and polished wood and a nice, upholstered chair. Beautiful and clean dressing rooms. And a certain amount of spaciousness on the selling floor—it says that the goods are so costly that they cover a *lot* of rent."

We stroll closer to the escalator, where there are . . . more racks. The very fact that these racks are off the selling floor and in the passageway, where foot traffic is highest, indicates that the merchandise on them is cheaper. All the cues are working properly—discounted clothing, so you have to stand in traffic to shop it. But still good stuff, because it's a good store.

"Isn't there something wrong with having discounted good stuff sold within view of nondiscounted good stuff?"

"I think there is. These sale racks attract bottom-feeders—shoppers who maybe browse this store on a regular basis but never or hardly ever buy because the prices are high. Those women see these racks out here, and it's like a jackpot: the goods they covet at a price they can afford. But what effect does that have on the full-price shopper? Maybe she sees the action out here near the escalator and never even makes it farther in, to the pricey stuff. Maybe she buys two sweaters out here instead of one in there, which means the store's not getting the markup it might have gotten. Or maybe she sees the sale merchandise and the cheap racks blocking the way and decides that she'll begin shopping elsewhere—maybe in one of those ultra-high-end Italian designer boutiques elsewhere in this mall. Maybe for her, shopping away from the riffraff is an important factor."

"It sounds like a risk for the store."

"I think you're right. But there's the potential for reward, too, which is why the store does this. On the one hand, you want to take full advantage of the space and of your brand identification. Look at what nearly every luxury brand has done in the past decade or so—they've all searched for ways to sell things to less-affluent customers. There are moderately priced Mercedes-Benzes now. Armani has high-end stores, midprice stores, and stores for young shoppers interested in jeans and T-shirts. Every big-name designer has what they call a bridge line to pull in the younger shopper with less to spend. These stores are no different, and when you consider how department stores are dying out like dinosaurs, it becomes doubly important not to miss a bet. But they have to be careful not to turn their good customers off. The store can be a dynamic space, where more than one thing happens, where today's discount shopper can become tomorrow's luxury customer. But it has to be done in an orderly and controlled way."

"Does this look orderly and controlled to you?"

"Could be. But having so much merchandise on the full-priced floor, and having it within sight of the discount racks, is probably not anybody's big plan. It just happened this way, I bet. Now look up ahead for the opposite situation—where the store proper gives way to the designer boutiques. What they call the vendor shops."

Here's where the identification issues really become complex, be-

cause this out-of-the-way corner is where the world-class labels—
Chanel, Gucci—sell out of little boutiques within the larger store. But
the conditions that prevail elsewhere aren't totally absent here, as is
evident as soon as we get close to the beautiful and expensive-looking
table behind which business is transacted.

"Now, what do you see there?"

"The table?"

"On it."

"Office junk."

"Well put. We're looking into a part of the store where probably the
average garment costs upward of $10,000, and on the table where that
sale is recorded is a slightly scuffed blue plastic three-ring binder.
There's also a $1.19 pen, some blank sales slips, assorted other cards
and pieces of paper, a telephone that wouldn't look out of place in a discount electronics store, and various other items required by the person
who runs this department. Under the table is a small trash can with a
plastic bag liner. Am I missing anything?"

"I think you got it all."

"It doesn't say 'Chanel,' does it?"

"Not to me."

"I guarantee you that when the Chanel executives come through
here to visit, all that stuff gets stowed somewhere out of the way. You
need paperwork and staplers and pens to do business. But why does it
all have to be out here? And why doesn't Chanel provide the proper
tools—like a beautiful leather-bound book, or a silver pen, and an ap-
propriately glamorous trash basket? This stuff belongs behind the
counter in a discount drugstore. You can't really expect the clerk to
leave the selling floor every time she has to make a phone call or order
something or write a letter. And there's probably no meaningful back-
office space for those tasks. But Chanel has to recognize the design
equity in everything—the clothing but also the trappings, the furnishings, and so on. If the salesperson came to work in jeans and sneakers,
Chanel would fire her on the spot. But they don't object to her using
Wal-Mart–level desk accessories."

The details of visual merchandising are critical pieces of merchant
magic. How stores present themselves has become a form of commer-

cial art. Andy Warhol started his career as a window dresser and advertising illustrator (his specialty was women's shoes). I've been in the
most exquisite shops on the most exclusive blocks all over the world,
and I've witnessed just about everything a person can do to exhibit
goods for sale. I've seen artful displays that hush a room as profoundly
as anything in the Louvre or the Uffizi. But my all-time favorite retail
vignette is still the towering stack of canned foods found in supermarket aisles. Executed properly, on a massive scale, it stops me in my
tracks every time. A mountain of peas! An ocean of V8! I look and wonder, How long did it take that clerk to pile up a thousand cans of pork
and beans? Were there any shaky moments when the whole thing was
about to come crashing down? And how did he feel once he was
through, when he stood back to check on its symmetry, and to make
sure all the labels were facing the same way? Did it fill him with pride?
I sure hope so—I admire the diamond room at Harry Winston and the
private couture salons at Barney's. But for sheer retail balls, you can't
beat a twelve-foot-tall pyramid of canned cocktail nuts.

There's something about typical mall design, with its straight row of
flat storefronts, that discourages shoppers from stopping. Granted,
they must stop all the time, otherwise no store would ever be entered
and nothing would be purchased. Still, the monotony of the storefront
line allows you to walk in a kind of ambulatory trance—you're passing
one sheer, absolutely flat wall of glass after another. There's nothing to
slow you down, nothing that catches your eye by jutting out into pedestrian space. When you look a few paces ahead of where you are, as
walkers normally do, you can just barely make out what's in the upcoming display windows. If there's glare you may not even see that
much.

This is what we're faced with in the mall—sheer walls of glass, absolutely even and regular, with nothing to break the plane. The leases
demand that each store stop at the same exact spot, and there are se-
vere limitations on what (if anything) can be placed out beyond the
wall of the store. We shoppers circulate without even seeing how un-
natural this is. Walk down a city street, and there you'll find endless
variations on the vertical facade, a multitude of planned or sometimes
completely ad hoc deviations from the flat front wall. You need to pay

attention, if only so you don't trip over merchandise that's been dragged out there.

Just the other day I was walking by a store specializing in leather bags, briefcases, coats, and so on; a clerk noticed three tourists staring in the window, so he casually sauntered out there to join them in conversation. As I passed they were all standing shoulder to shoulder, pointing at a suitcase. Good retailers do their best to make the storefront as porous as possible, something that rarely happens in a mall. The poignancy of this occurs to me whenever I happen to visit a mall on what they usually call "Sidewalk Sale Day." On these occasions, stores are permitted to bring a rack or two of merchandise out into the main thoroughfare; some malls even allow stores to drag goods out into the parking lot. It's a real novelty, and speaks volumes about our vestigial connection to the street—seeing how the mall attempts to evoke the sidewalk is enough to make you laugh.

Some mall stores do at least acknowledge that important things can happen right at the outset of the store, in the entrance. At both the CD store and the sneaker stores, we see video monitors mounted high, facing the doorway. They try to send their energy and pop culture signifiers out into the mall thoroughfare to snag shoppers. Even better, they're noisy and feature lots of motion and light and color, which would grab your attention anywhere, but especially in the bland confines of the mall. Here, when Jay-Z raps in your face, you notice, whether you like it or not.

Music stores especially have to deploy these attractions judiciously. For instance, we know that a mall's demographics shift depending on the time of day and day of the week. On a Tuesday morning at eleven, you've got stay-at-home mothers and their small children. You may lure them in with the latest Bon Jovi video, but they're not buying 50 Cent. Even earlier in the morning, when the mall walkers are out, the store might do best to blast some Sinatra. Most music stores now sell DVDs, too, so movies can also be screened on these monitors, especially when there are likely to be few music fans in the mall. Maybe by day they could run the new Richard Gere movie on the monitor. On a Friday night, however, teenage tastes rule the mall, and kids are the music store's prime audience.

A sneaker store doesn't have those particular considerations to make. But it does need to maintain its image within the mall, and the music and videos it plays are an important part of that. As America's taste in pop culture has gone urban/African American, kids who have never set foot outside of these middle-class white-bread confines are rocking styles that are straight (more or less) outta the Bronx and Compton. Nowhere in all suburbia does this exist more vividly than in the sneaker store. It's where the latest look to win the imprimatur of Allen Iverson can be had by any tow-headed fifteen-year-old with $100 to spare. Here and the music store are where urban culture manifests itself most tangibly in the lives of suburban kids and adults. Go ahead and laugh— once again, the retail arena is where we all finally learn to get along.

✿    ✿    ✿

We've just come upon the mall toy store. Toys are another category largely gone from the mall. Money is the reason, of course—you need a lot of space to compete in the toy market today. For Toys "R" Us, it makes a lot more sense to build a freestanding store. The mall has gotten too expensive. There are some toy stores left, but they tend to be small and specialized, like the ones focusing on toys for all the little geniuses, of which there are no doubt many. Who has average kids anymore? Today, even kids understand that average won't cut it. This toy store isn't anything spectacular, but they do one thing that no other store in this mall can do: place little windup swimming frogs and remote-control cars out ever so slightly in the corridor, the better to attract the attention of passersby.

"Ron, what do you think of how some stores come out into the mall itself?"

"It's a great idea, assuming mall management lets you get away with it."

"They usually frown on that, don't they?"

"It's in the lease—you either can or can't put freestanding signs out there, for instance, or if you can, they can only be so far away from the wall, and only signs of a certain type, and so on and so forth. Otherwise, you'd have every store in the mall dragging stuff out here."

"I imagine the toy dancing bear gets a little more leeway than, say, a rack of T-shirts."

"I think you're right. It's a form of entertainment."

"Yes, it is. Speaks volumes for the rest of the mall, doesn't it?"

"Well, there's not much in a mall that entertains kids, is there?"

"No, and that's a problem. Malls really try a kid's patience."

"So this becomes the reward, right? A trip to the toy store."

"While Mom is shopping somewhere nearby, I bet Dad and the kids stand out here and stare at the remote-control cars. You could easily kill four minutes just doing that."

We stop and stare at the remote-control car and the swimming frog.

"You have to drive that thing carefully so it doesn't go too far out into the mall, don't you?" Ron asks the grinning teenage salesclerk who's steering the car.

"Yep, otherwise they'll give me a ticket," she says.

# 22 *Other Venues*

I WANT TO get out of this mall.

When malls came along, it seemed as though they had commandeered all the considerable shopping energy in America. In fact, they did contribute to the downfall and even death of a great many downtown shopping districts, in cities but also in small towns, villages, even in suburbs, which in many cases were as old and venerable and self-contained as any urban district.

But big enclosed malls never really did render urban streets or even suburban strip shopping centers obsolete as places where retailing thrives. In fact, while malls are really good at certain forms of shopping, they're vastly inferior in others.

Take bookstores. They are moving out of malls everywhere, largely driven by high rents. But they also discovered that they have higher conversion rates away from the mall—that more shoppers actually buy something in freestanding stores. That's because in a mall, the book-

191

store is a handy place to browse around and kill a little time without really meaning to buy anything. Also, today's mega-bookstore usually includes a café, which often is the most profitable real estate in the store. But in a mall, shoppers are likely to get their refreshments elsewhere. So the café doesn't serve its primary function—that of keeping people in the store longer.

I want to spend a few minutes here thinking about how malls compare to other shopping venues. And since I'm a guy, and since I'm now weary of the relentlessly female-driven atmosphere of the mall, I want to start by thinking about a store selling consumer electronics and technology toys. Pretty much a full-service place, where you might go for anything from batteries and solder guns to telephones and remote-control toys to flat-screen TVs and digital cameras. I say it's a guy kind of place because in one sense it is—stores like this have replaced the auto store and hardware store as spaces where a man can roam idly and probably find a few things he wants or even needs. (Whoever has enough speaker wire?) But women buy a hefty amount of the technology on display, so the stores need to attract and work for both genders.

What happens in this store when it's located on a city street, or in a suburban strip shopping center, or in an enclosed mall? Well, in a city, roughly one in ten passersby will stop inside. Slightly more will enter in a mall. But in a strip shopping center, more than four out of every ten people who pass will go into the store.

A dramatic difference, and one that's fairly simple to explain.

In a city, lots of people will pass the store, most of them with absolutely no intention of shopping there. Maybe they're on their way to shop elsewhere. Maybe they're racing back to work from lunch. Even this one in ten figure would be high in, say, midtown Manhattan. Strip centers are, by their nature, destination sites—typically they'll have fewer than a dozen stores, so a high number of people are headed for a particular store.

The gender mix in this electronics store will also be affected by its location. In the mall, nearly four in ten shoppers are female, but only half that many in the city or the strip. Among mall shoppers will be women for whom visiting a techno store is not a high priority—she'll see the window and be reminded that she needs a monitor for her desktop or blank videotapes.

For a store such as this, the prime demographic is males under forty. In the city and strip, roughly four out of ten shoppers are men between twenty-six and forty. In the mall, only 10 percent or so fit that description. This should be seen as alarming news for the mall store, or at least for merchants who need male shoppers. The mall is attracting too high a proportion of males younger than twenty-six—mostly teenagers and under, I'd wager—or older than forty, probably *much* older. The prime group of male consumers is shopping at the strip, which is more its style, or in the city during a lunch break or after work.

City and strip shoppers spend more time in the store. Undoubtedly, this store gets better, more committed shoppers at the strip or in town. In fact, city shoppers usually are in and out of stores much faster than those in a mall, which makes the disparity even wider than the numbers show. It also reflects that in a mall, especially for men, it's tempting to leave a store the second it begins to bore you, since there are at least a hundred more from which to choose.

The difference in conversion rate is significant. More than half of all strip shoppers will buy something, best of the venues. If the store doesn't have exactly what he wants, he may compromise, since there's no guarantee he'll find it elsewhere. And if he doesn't find what he wants, he'll probably find something else he needs. In the city, a similar, but not identical, dynamic prevails—if one store doesn't have what he's looking for, maybe his travels will bring him by another store that will. But maybe not. He'll either buy nothing here and gamble on finding it elsewhere, or, like the strip shopper, he will settle on the next best thing. In the mall, you've got a lot of guys idly browsing, with no intention to buy. Also, it's easy to go from one store to another until you find exactly what you want. As a result, conversion rate in the mall is lower.

❀ ❀ ❀

The comparative numbers are different for clothing stores, such as a well-known emporium specializing in reasonably priced sportswear for both sexes. In this category, strip shopping center locales are more or less irrelevant—you tend not to find big apparel stores there.

The percentage of shoppers who use fitting rooms is almost identical in city and mall—one customer in five tries at least one garment on. But it's interesting to look at the difference in how often shoppers must wait for dressing rooms. In the city, one shopper in four waits; in the mall, it's four in ten. This isn't necessarily due to crowding—it's because people move faster in city stores than they do at the mall. City shoppers are on the move; mall people are there with no other tasks to juggle. We tend to absorb the velocity and rhythms of our environments. It's not just that mall shoppers are slower. In many instances city shoppers and mall shoppers are the same people. We all go with the flow.

The same velocity applies in transaction time—in the city, average time at the register is one-quarter less than at the mall.

When it comes to apparel, mall shoppers spend longer inside the store than city shoppers do. They also shop more items, and they are more involved in the *act* of shopping. In the mall, they're more likely to look at the price tag and read the label. What's the significance? In part, it means mall shoppers will be more deliberate. There's also the sense that the mall shopper isn't quite as committed to buying anything at all, whereas in the city the same person finds what she wants, examines it, tries it on, and hurries to the register.

Our final grounds for comparison is the outdoors outfitter—the place to go for clothes and equipment for the rugged life (or for people who just want to dress that way). These shoppers spend twice as long in the strip center store as in the mall; they shop twice as many departments and almost a third more items. Nearly half the strip shoppers convert to buyers, compared to around one-third of those at the mall. Strip shoppers are twice as likely to use the fitting room. The strip store gets more couples, the mall more singles. The mall gets more unplanned visits.

# 23 Scenes from a Mall

I AM A SUCKER for Jackie Chan, it doesn't matter how stupid the movie is. I got hooked years ago by a fight sequence in an appliance store that integrated refrigerators and ovens into the action. While I fall in and out of love with Hollywood actresses, my fascination with Jackie is constant.

I'm giving in to the filmic urge, but only after I feel I've done enough mall talking and walking for one day. That's the wonderful thing about having a cinema this close to shopping—you can build your day around it. It's a fitting reward after an outing of ambulatory acquisitioning—a nice dark place to sit for two hours.

Movie houses are expensive to build, even the bare-bones, thin-walled, cheap-seated cinderblock specimens you tend to find at the mall. But it's usually worthwhile from the developers' point of view. The marriage between the mall and the movie was born of a practical impulse—you were already drawing people to the premises, and there was plenty of parking available, especially at night. In the early days, the mall was the bait that attracted moviegoers. Now it's turned around to some degree—there are plenty of people who come for the movie but fit in an hour or so of shopping.

Mall shoppers and movie fans tend to be the same folks. Shopping and movies are both popular leisure activities. But in the mall the fit has not been properly worked out. Most times, it's hard even to find the theater. There will be a tall sign outside, the mall version of a movie marquee, announcing the films playing. But beyond that, you can walk the entire mall and never see an ad or a sign announcing the presence of a theater. If you don't pass the theater entrance (and it's usually in an out-of-the-way corner), you might forget it's there.

You'd think the cinema operator might want to make it as easy as possible for shoppers to take in a show. If that were the case, there might be a box office within the mall itself, a kiosk or counter where you could learn about what's playing, find the show times, and buy your tickets in advance (or pick up tickets ordered over the Internet). Somewhere in this mall, Hollywood's latest masterpieces are running. But you'd never know it. Nowhere are there measures being taken to turn shoppers into moviegoers—the theater operator isn't distributing discount coupons for early-bird admissions or supersize sodas and popcorn. There are some posters advertising current films—but nowhere does it say if those movies are playing at the mall. There should be a digital sign somewhere announcing ATTENTION, SHOPPERS: THERE ARE STILL TICKETS AVAILABLE FOR THE 2:30 SHOWING OF THE NEW JACKIE CHAN MOVIE.

There *is* plenty of movie-related merchandise for sale in here, but it's all over the mall—DVDs and soundtracks at the music store, movie screenplays and bios at the bookstore, licensed items like action figures and cartoon character lunch boxes at the toy store. Nobody has brought it all together and tied it in with the presence of a cinema here in the building. There should be a major movie presence at the food court. There, as we've seen, everybody's sitting and eating with nothing to look at, not even a window. It's a perfect place for a big video screen showing trailers for what's playing now or coming soon. Food court diners skew young compared with the rest of the mall, so it's a terrific way to reach the prime movie audience.

When you arrive at the theater—once you find it—you come upon a similar lack of retail sensibility at work. This is evident the instant we walk in the door of this fourteen-screen multiplex. Back when theaters showed just one movie at a time, your approach to the building filled you with anticipation. Everybody walking alongside you and every person milling outside in line was going to see the same film. It provided you with a shared entertainment experience that's in short supply today in the land of the twenty-screen cinema and the one hundred–plus channel digital cable TV system. I think this is one reason live sports and rock concerts have maintained their appeal—there's electricity in the air when people convene to watch a single event. Americans today long for that kind of pop-culture communion from time to time. It's a big reason we're all in the mall.

Today, when we arrive, we're split fourteen ways. This is more like an airport than a movie house—everybody is arriving at staggered times with different destinations. At the airport, business-class flyers rush in next to families headed to Disney World beside snowboarders off to Sun Valley; here, some of us are headed to the new animated feature, others are bound for the slasher bloodbath, others for the hot-date movie. We're barely in the same building psychologically. Visitors to the Cineplex and the airport share the same food, time, and bathroom anxieties. We all race from box office to popcorn line, then wander around looking for the right theater. Once we've figured that out, we mill about, waiting for the line to form.

How could this chaos be harnessed? Nobody has ever accused Broadway of being a hotbed of retailing energy, but even there, a few sensible tricks are deployed. True, everybody is there to see the same show, a unanimity of purpose that makes packaging it a lot easier. That is a unique situation, granted, but some of those tricks would translate to the movies. What happens after you've gained entrance into the movie lobby? Almost nothing. You can stand around and look at those dumb cutouts promoting upcoming films. If you're hungry, you join the concession line. Some theaters provide video games, which do occupy a certain number of customers and throw a little profit to the bottom line as well. But the games are aimed at adolescent tastes, so there's a good portion of the crowd that's either annoyed by the noise or will just ignore the machines altogether. It would be a great place for classic video games. Donkey Kong and Ms. Pac Man. As well as a place to showcase video games tied to specific movie properties.

Our research shows that, on average, moviegoers arrive eighteen minutes before their show starts. That's an eternity by retail standards, and they're all in a well-defined space with nothing to do.

Broadway shows usually take advantage of the lull by offering show-related merchandise. This could happen here, too—as I noted earlier, there's no place in the mall where our movie fixation receives any retail expression. But this would be a perfect spot for DVDs, soundtracks, T-shirts, posters, books, action figures, you name it. I'd build a store on wheeled racks, so it could be pulled back against the wall when the lobby's mobbed. Otherwise, this would be a great place to shop, if only because the lobby-waiting experience is so dull.

But let's back up to the entrance. There, a highly practical need is going unmet. We've got fourteen screens, maybe ten movies in all, quite a few of which opened yesterday. Naturally, I arrived knowing what I wanted to see—but what if it was sold out? I didn't have a plan B, and this theater is doing absolutely nothing to help me come up with one in a hurry. I stand in line at the box office with nothing more compelling to do than eavesdrop on the bickering couple behind me.

The cash register experience here is no more linked to entertainment and movie stars than the one at Wal-Mart. All I've been given to look at is a sign up ahead, at the box office, which lists relatively tiny movie titles, even smaller show times, and the price. Standing here is boring and tells me nothing about what's playing on the other thirteen screens. If one is sold out, I'm in trouble: I'll be under big pressure to choose an alternate fast and get out of the way.

Or, let's say I showed up at the theater not completely sure of what I want to see. It happens more than exhibitors seem to realize. Maybe I just wanted to see *something*—that's more likely in a mall than any-where else. Right now, this theater is doing practically nothing to entice me into a seat.

What would serve me is, once again, the movie trailer. This is one of the truly genius inventions of the cinema business—it's a staple of our lives, and often it's the source of more entertainment than the movie it means to advertise. Right at the theater entrance, a bank of video screens would be entertaining for those in line, informative for those who are still trying to decide, and a good way to attract us back to the theater soon. Best of all, it's dirt-cheap. Somebody could also clip the best reviews from newspapers and magazines and put them up on an easel. We're not necessarily looking for film criticism here—all we want is the plot summary, the movie stars' names, and maybe a quick thumbs-up or -down. Something we could absorb fast. In principle, it should happen in two places—outside the box office and inside the lobby. Art movie houses tend to do this well. I have yet to see it at the mall.

I also don't understand why all fourteen theaters in the complex are the same. They may differ in size, but not in design. On any given weekend, a typical Cineplex has a very predictable assortment of movies—family, teen, guy movies, and date or chick flicks. In your fourteen-theater complex, some number of theaters would, in my plan, be set aside for family and teen movies only. The seating and flooring would reflect the abuse the theater is going to get. They could even be hosed down if that's what it takes to get the Pepsi off the floor. The location of those theaters relative to concessions and bathrooms would also be taken into account. The action-movie theaters would have more legroom; the date theaters would have armrests that fold away and a section of love seats that sell at a premium price.

There's also nothing done to recognize that we're in a mall. Here, for example, you tend to get people who are shopping in small groups—families, or bunches of friends. They attend movies that way, too, different from the usual cinema configuration of an adult couple, or two friends, or single adults. Here, then, a simple thing like selling food to match group size would make a difference. You should be able to get the family meal—two large sodas, two small ones, a couple popcorns, maybe some Raisinets, for a special price. Or even something geared to couples. On Broadway, again, and also at sports arenas, they sell alcoholic beverages. A theater looks the same on Saturday afternoon when everybody's here for the SpongeBob SquarePants movie as it does on Saturday night. Does that make sense? The lighting in the lobby, the amateurish slideshow movie-trivia quiz that runs between features—

nobody is tailoring it to the people in the room. In a world desperate for guerrilla marketing opportunities, the three-dimensional engine that a Cineplex represents is poorly understood.

The movie business is built on the blockbuster, the film that will open huge and then tail off. The theater is getting maybe ten cents out of every admission dollar, which makes all the other sources of revenue that much more important. It's no surprise that the concession stand is a theater's only chance for profitability. But we were taken aback to learn that roughly 11 percent of all customers who get in line at the concession counter step out of line without buying anything. They worry that all the good seats will be taken, or that the show will start, so they bolt into the theater empty-handed. Maybe the line is moving so slowly that they talk themselves out of that big infusion of sugar water, starch, and chocolate they had planned. In every retail setting, some people abandon the line. But nowhere does it happen at anywhere near this level. The movie theater business has a lot of work to do in managing its environment.

A movie's success is indicated by how many people come to see it on the first weekend it hits the theaters. A studio may spend five dollars marketing every seat it sells on that first weekend. The cheapest and most effective marketing medium and audience development point is the Cineplex itself.

Every night of the week, in every movie house in the world, are the loyal customers, the people who are most likely to return repeatedly. Almost nothing is being done to ensure that they return soon. Nobody bothers to collect their names or e-mail addresses, even though they are the industry's lifeblood. There are no coupons for future ticket discounts, or even fliers.

Once the movie ends, you are ushered through the ugliest exit corridor you've ever seen and ejected into reality. You may see a stray poster, or a cardboard cutout to tell you what's coming next July. Whatever dreamlike state Paramount or Miramax has put you into is rudely interrupted by crowds at the bathroom and the rancid smell of spilled faux popcorn butter on cheap carpet.

# 24 *The Postmall World*

I'M TIRED. I don't think I can go on much longer.

Part of my mall-sickness may be due to the fact that I just polished off my second Cinnabon. (I didn't see the need to mention the first one.) But maybe I'm all malled out. Maybe you are, too.

We've all entered the postmall era. I don't mean that the ones we have are going out of business. We'll still visit them and spend our money there. But as a defining concept, as a relevant institution, as a contemporary form of commercial organization, the mall's heyday is history. These shopping centers will never look as shiny and inviting and wonderful to us as they once did. We're never going to love them the same way again.

Do I mean that the mall is a flop? Maybe. I suspect there was a fundamental flaw in malls from the very start, something that virtually guaranteed that their growth cycle would last just a few decades. Less than forty years ago they were still novelties. We had yet fully to comprehend what they would someday mean to us, how they would transform American retail culture for better and worse. In the boom years, the 1970s and 1980s, a new mall would open somewhere every three or four days. Aging cities and towns quaked with terror every time a new one broke ground, and with good reason, for all it took was a couple of suburban shopping centers to devastate a traditional retail district. Malls were the Godzillas of shopping.

Today, you don't see many malls being built in North America. We're all malled up—new ones succeed only by cannibalizing older centers. We barely replace those that close.

I put a large amount of the blame on the mall's fatal flaw—its lack of mercantile DNA. This is an industry driven by real estate, not retailing. If a mall is in the right spot, it will almost surely thrive. It lives by the axiom that guides all real estate: location, location, location. Beyond opening the doors and turning on the lights, what kind of retailing savvy has the mall exhibited? How has it kept up with and responded to the social and economic changes of the past two or three decades? Ask yourself this: What have been the coolest recent innovations at the mall? The food court? Ferris wheels? In the past, attractions you could find only at the mall kept shoppers interested. In 1990 a new Disney Store could cause a noticeable bump in attendance. There hasn't been a hot novelty for some time. We've had malls in abundance for more than three decades now, and we shoppers have explored all the corners and crevices, every store and pushcart, every Build-A-Bear workshop and rock-climbing wall. Developers didn't plan a future for the mall, and so far none has arrived.

There are examples of developers trying different approaches. In Tokyo there is a "nostalgia mall," aimed at older shoppers. It specializes in the consumer goods they marveled at in their prime. In an otherwise flat economy, the Ichome Shotengai is booming. The mall used to appeal exclusively to young shoppers, who are rabid shopaholics in Japan, but they began running out of money just as the population of elderly rose. It's like a museum of consumer goods. I wish somebody here would try specialty malls with a little imagination. I fear I'm in for a wait.

Two-thirds of America's biggest malls are more than twenty years old. That's not ancient, as buildings go. But the featureless, flavorless architecture of many of these monstrosities will give future generations no good reason to rehabilitate them, whereas we found plenty worth salvaging in aging department stores, railway stations, hotels, and other public edifices.

Strong malls will continue to prosper. Failures may go through two or three incarnations as malls, but then, inevitably, some other use comes along to "repurpose" what would otherwise be a very large white elephant. "Most centers, if they don't make it as a shopping mall, are ideally positioned to be easily converted," a spokesperson for the International Council of Shopping Centers was quoted in a newspaper article, perhaps too candidly. "It's the whole nature of a mall. At their basic heart, they're just a collection of boxes."

The makeovers that succeed are news, and the rest are aging roadside ruins. One particularly American transformation is the mall that undergoes a change of ethnicity. We've always had specialty shopping centers devoted to one or another immigrant culture. Koreatown Mall, in Los Angeles, is maybe the most famous in America. In Atlanta, a failed outlet center first became an Asian mall and, more recently, Hispanic. All kinds of shoppers, not just the obvious ones, are drawn to exotic novelties. As I'm writing this I read that in Charlotte, North Carolina, a failed mall has been taken over by a trio of Vietnamese sisters who have dubbed it Asian Corner, the planned home of retail, restaurants, and groceries to serve the ten thousand Vietnamese residents of Mecklenburg County. I have no doubt that it will also be an attraction to the region's non-Asian residents looking for a slightly unusual mall dinner or shopping trip.

Near Atlanta, the Buford Highway Farmers Market brings live eels, ginger cakes, and other delicacies from all over the world, especially the Third World, to the area's newly arrived influx from Southeast Asia, Latin America, the Caribbean, and Eastern Europe. An estimated 700 immigrant-owned businesses now inhabit what had become a run-down commercial strip shopping center. This did not take place according to any developer's plan but thanks to happenstance and necessity and pluck, the way outbreaks of retail vitality have always occurred. American commerce relies on this recycling mechanism; as one group moves up and out, there's always somebody coming in right behind them—newer, poorer, and boiling over with energy and optimism and resilience. We all know how successive waves of immigrants revitalize residential areas. Less noted is how they bring new blood to aging retail environments. It reminds us how merchandise, bought and sold, has served historically as our primary means of cultural exchange.

The country is dotted with mall repurposing. The Bell Tower Mall, in South Carolina, was taken over by Greenville County and is now County Square, a complex of governmental buildings. The cinema has been turned into a courthouse. Inspired, the nearby Carolina Center Mall is planning to turn itself into a recreation development with athletic fields and an arena, perfect for hosting volleyball and soccer tournaments, and maybe a movie theater, too. The hope was that all this activity would draw kids and parents, enough to support as well a little retail and a few restaurants—the two businesses that once filled the entire mall. The Downtown Mall in Tupelo, Mississippi, was wiped out when another mall opened just outside town. Now it's the city's convention center. In Dallas, twenty-year-old Prestonwood Mall failed and was then converted to a center for telecommunications and Internet companies. Malls are being turned into light manufacturing centers, warehouses—churches have bought a number of failed shopping centers. Westchester Mall, in High Point, North Carolina, was put out of business when a bigger, better shopping center opened nearby. The mall was acquired by First Wesleyan Church and is now a religious complex including sanctuary, bookstore, and nursing home. They call it Providence Place.

Even one of our most culturally significant malls—the Sherman Oaks Galleria, in the San Fernando Valley, backdrop for the movies *Fast Times at Ridgemont High* as well as *Valley Girl*—has been remade. The roof has been removed, and now a townlike complex with lots of open-air street-level activity fills the site. Movie animation studios have moved into a spot formerly occupied by a department store. Overall, the space devoted to retail has shrunk by more than a third.

o     o     o

Technology has also taken a bite out the shopping mall. Take your average thirty-year-old today and compare her monthly obligations to those of her mother. The contemporary middle-class American has a lot of expenses that didn't exist a generation ago. Say $100 a month for a cell phone. Throw in another $50 for cable TV. Add $20 or so for your Internet service provider. Maybe you own a desktop computer and a laptop, and every two years you're replacing one or the other, or both; spread that cost over a year and it's another $100 a month. DVD rentals. Download on demand. TiVo. There, you've got at least $300 a month that will never be spent inside a mall—$3,600 a year for each of us. A fair chunk of that money used to go to shopping and restaurants and, by extension, the malls.

Another piece of the puzzle is our relationship to our cars. While we love our vehicles, we increasingly hate driving them in heavy traffic, and congestion is no longer strictly a rush hour experience. Few North America malls are tied into any public transportation system. At what point will the aging First World population walk away from their cars? My mother, at age eighty, plots with her condo-complex neighbors about getting to and from the store when she no longer feels comfortable driving. In Sydney, Australia, the hot apartment complex combines great views of the harbor with an elevator that drops you to a mall that includes a grocery store and delivery services. The mall has to imagine itself into our demographic future and see where it stands.

We baby boomers are in a postshopping mode, psychically speaking. We're not as thrilled as we used to be at the mere prospect of buying, of being in the presence of multitudes of objects, talismans, fetishes, beautifiers, intensifiers, glorifiers, junk. If we needed it, we bought it, more than once. Now we're feeling bought out. We're bored. People in their twenties and thirties always looked slightly askance at our consumption binge. They're not quite as sold on the idea of salvation through shopping. An awful lot of today's middle-class disposable income goes for adventure and vacation, intangibles that nourish something more than Calvin Klein's bottom line. The fact that malls didn't find a way to keep up with the zeitgeist's every twist and turn also explains their overall failure of imagination. Teenagers and children are still excited by the mall, but it's all still new to them, isn't it? Give them time—when you consider all the blandishments and temptations they'll be exposed to, they should become jaded a lot faster than the

rest of us. And face it: What's the alternative to shopping for those adolescents? Almost anything that smacks of the outside world and independence looks good when you're twelve.

The fact is, the mall is trapped by its success as a place to bring the
family. It has never found a more sophisticated way to envision itself.
The food court is a shrine to lowest-common-denominator food—it's
pizza and burgers and ice cream and cookies, a menu guaranteed to
please any four-year-old. To my knowledge, nobody is experimenting
with the mall food court. I could easily see splitting a really big one into
two halves—one for juvenile diners of all ages, the other a bazaar of
high-quality, higher-priced dining for mature palates. Ideally, the layout would permit you to seat your kids in their food court and keep an
eye on them from yours. Keep waiting.

Because some of us are too busy to spend as much time at the mall
as we once did, retailing has gone chasing after us elsewhere. The mall
has been successfully re-created at airports, for instance. It's a sound
notion—especially today, when we're instructed to check in at least an
hour before flight time. That means you've got thirty minutes with
nothing to do and a limited area in which to do it, since you've already
gone through the security screeners. The airport in Pittsburgh has an
extensive retail section, and not just junk for tourists—you can buy
clothes and shoes. Denver has one, too, as does Reagan National Airport in Washington. Especially for time-pressured business travelers,
these airport shops save a few trips to the mall. I could tell that airports
were taking this seriously when a national airport manager association
invited me to speak at its annual conference. Retailing there has to
adapt a little to the location—for instance, shoppers tend to be toting
clumsy carry-on bags, so aisles need to be wide.

The Internet bubble has popped, but still this shopping venue represents a dramatic change in the retail landscape. Online shopping
plays to the heart of the mall audience—middle-class, middle aged
and younger, pressed for time, already in front of the computer every
day. The promise of mall as community is being realized at eBay, the
flea market of the twenty-first century. There, and at good shopping
sites such as Amazon, there's an experience superior in some ways to
the real world. Amazon seems to recognize also that the future of any

shopping medium isn't based on its popularity with Silicon Valley male geeks, but on how it plays with overworked and overcommitted women in mainstream America. Look at Amazon's most dazzling innovation—one-click buying, whereby, with a single click of the mouse, the sale is rung up and ownership of the goods has transferred from them to you. The world of retail has yet to figure out a painless, graceful way to handle the transaction itself—the cash register experience. Whether you're at McDonald's or Nordstrom, the exchange of money for goods takes place in essentially the same way, and poses the same potential for anxiety, frustration, and unhappiness.

The cash register and the credit card machine look like prehistoric tools—the stone axes of retailing. The basic design of the transaction point hasn't changed in fifty years. Yes, we've added bar code scanners and better credit card machines, but the physical act and even the transaction time is about the same. If anything, the experience has gotten worse because the process has been depersonalized. Even as supermarkets have experimented with self-scanning stations, a significant percentage of customers refuse to use them. They want the final opportunity to see what they are buying before it disappears into a shopping bag. Technology has tried to solve the transaction issue with something called source tagging, an advanced version of the bar code we find on most packages. A source tag reader can tally everything in a shopping cart without the merchandise even being unloaded. The practical problem of ensuring that every product coming into the store has the correct source tag has proven difficult to manage.

Internet retail is still hampered by the fact that you still can't really *shop* online, if by that we mean look at and touch vast amounts of merchandise. But the Web is a great place to buy certain things, such as books, music, videos, software, appliances, electronics, toys, drugstore stuff, anything for which you have a fairly sure notion of what you want. You can info-load at the store, select the exact thing you desire, then go buy it online and save the taxes and, sometimes, shipping, too, or do it in reverse, info-fuel online and make your decision in-store. But if you enjoy, for instance, the experience of exploring a bookstore in hopes that something will catch your eye, you'll have to go to a real store. I buy some books online, but two-thirds of my purchases still take place in stores. Most clothing will continue to be bought in stores, but you can replace the staples as needed online. If you live in thirty-four-waist, thirty-four-length, pleated-front, cuffless, relaxed-fit khakis from the Gap, you can easily buy them online. A lot of us have found our personal uniforms—jeans, button-down cotton shirt, whatever—and those items you can buy just as well online as in stores.

Malls have for the most part remained clear of much Internet influence. Some have tried creating a virtual mall online, but it's expensive to wire every store to permit online shopping with real-world pickup. Some malls have websites listing stores and phone numbers, but that's a fairly low-tech use. At Fashion Show Mall, in Las Vegas, they use the Internet to attract a steady stream of tourist-shoppers by setting up a bank of stand-up terminals and offering free minutes of online access. Last time I was there, the place was packed with tourists checking their e-mail.

The cell phone also may play a role in the future of the mall. In Europe and Japan, cell phones seem to work everywhere, while in the United States phone users are often driven outside or to odd corners of the mall for good reception. The cell phone as a shopping aid allows contact with your buying adviser; a photo-equipped phone can bring that person right into a store aisle or dressing room. But if the phone doesn't work inside the store, the point is moot. At Envirosell, we have started to track the phone conversations that happen in stores and their apparent effect on buying decisions. It's remarkable how predictably the conversations begin:

"Honey, I'm here at the mall, what did you say you wanted?"

All technology and tactile experience aside, the principal condition that is strangling the mall is time. The bulk of the mall's core customer base, particularly the women between thirteen and fifty, has never been busier. A time-poor customer has brought about the success of two postmall shopping center trends.

The first is actually the postmall version of a premall suburban fixture, the strip shopping center. These have always tended to be somewhat random collections of stores, mostly locals. It was where you'd find the dry cleaners next to the Italian deli next to the car wash next to the beer distributor. Today's version is sometimes called an "affinity center." These developments are bigger than their predecessors, and more sophisticated in design and layout, although the storefronts are still visible from the roadway, and parking is still right out in front. The innovation is in the selection of stores. There will be no more than five or six, all national chains, usually big, so-called "category killers." They'll all appeal strongly to the same well-defined demographic group. It's like a mall for people who are sick of the mall. It's for people who are saying: "Look, the mall is okay as a place to spend an afternoon with the family once every few months, but I don't want to go there every time I have to shop. There are 107 stores in our mall, four of which I actually frequent. So I'm much happier to find a shopping center that's got Barnes & Noble, Bed Bath & Beyond, Best Buy, and Starbucks. Or, one with Home Depot, Staples, Old Navy, and Blockbuster Video. I can buy 90 percent of what I need there, and my trip takes no time. Parking is a breeze. And I don't have to deal with all the noise and nonsense. I've seen a hundred Disney Stores already, and I don't ever need to see number one hundred and one. And besides, I *always* thought the mall was bogus."

The second and more exciting innovation is what have been called  Main Street developments, or "neo-villages"—twenty-first-century attempts at re-creating urbanesque (or is it small-town?) American shopping. Mashpee Commons in Massachusetts is a good example. These take up less room than the typical mall, although they're expansive in their own way. There are lots of stores, many of the same ones we find in malls everywhere, and focusing on the same basic categories.

But these centers do their best to look like communities. It's genuinely fake—some include phony facades that extend upward two or three stories, although the store itself is all on one level. They're made to look like that staple of old-school retailing, a storefront with the owner's quarters upstairs. But these are so charmingly artificial that they seem theatrical, almost like movie sets. Unlike at the mall, some genuine thought has gone into the architecture here, an attempt to make it pleasing to the eye and human in scale.

Developers have created entire little villages this way, complete with pavements and streetlights and vest-pocket parks. On each little grid of streets you find big national retailers right next door to locally owned restaurants and even some service businesses, like the shoe repair or a post office. You never lose sight of the fact that you're in a manufactured simulation of a real town or city shopping district. It's all a nod to Disney, but again, you can't help but admire the effort. Some of these even include some housing nearby.

There's nothing particularly new about this. All over Europe, you see mixed-use developments that include shopping malls. There, the complex is also likely to include a good supermarket, one with an extensive selection of prepared foods to go. That's the kind of thing that encourages daily after-work visits to the mall. On the outskirts of the development may be small, locally owned service businesses, a drop-off pick-up laundry, the dry cleaner and key maker and hardware store. There could be some office space. There will surely be a residential component—maybe apartment towers or housing clusters or both. A hotel is also a possibility. And very close by will be mass transit—a commuter train stop perhaps, or a bus line. It's remarkably villagelike, appropriate on a continent that perfected the small-town form of social organization long before our country even existed. Recently, I saw an odd version off the highway between Milan and Genoa, where somebody built an outlet mall as a fake town complete with false facades and plastic moldings. It sits in a fog belt for much of the year, which makes its appearance even stranger.

Main Street complexes have their charms, but they are also much more efficient than the mall as a place to shop. You can hit and run—dash into a single store and be out of there in fifteen minutes. You can arrive with the desire to visit three stores, find yourself attracted to one or two more, visit those, and still get out feeling as though you've accomplished everything in a compact time frame. Or, you can go thinking that you'll kill a few hours, visit some stores, wander the streets, get in your dose of people watching, and experience it that way. I think these urbanesque layouts speak to some ancient part of our souls, the love of browsing and exploring and window shopping. Discovery is one of our most satisfying emotions. "There has to be emotional content to the shopping experience," said Limited Brands CEO Leslie Wexner, speaking on the subject of a neo-village mall near the company's Columbus, Ohio, headquarters. I think he's right.

Nearly all of these involve one thing—pedestrians walking on concrete pavements and asphalt streets, with real curbs, and out in the open, exposed to wind and rain and cold and heat and all the rest. In one sense, it's just a mall without a roof. But that may be a critical difference: Ripping the roof off this sucker may be all that's required to liberate shopping and keep it real. After so much time inside the air-conditioned bosom of the enclosed mall, breaking out sounds a little like heaven.

There's something poetic about all this, isn't there? The mall was a little *too* hermetically sealed for our tastes. This trend renews my faith in humanity.

Okay—what did we miss? Not a thing that I can tell. And we can always come back, right? The mall isn't going anywhere, but I am. I've had it for today. You can stay if you want. I'm going home.

# *Endcap*

NOW WHERE the hell did I park?

# Acknowledgments

TO MAKE this book possible, Lucia and Willie Tonelli had to give up their father, Bill, for many weekends in a row. I would like to thank them for their sacrifice.

Alice Mayhew, David Rosenthal, Emily Takoudes, and Scott Gray at Simon & Schuster have gently guided this book from inception to completion. Glen Hartley, my agent, continues to provide sage advice and direction. My assistant, Jenny Bonilla, has done much of the crafting and polishing. She has more patience and style than I do. She's also given me the opportunity to sit in the dressing room at Nordstrom and eavesdrop on shopping soap operas.

A few people agreed to walk the mall with me. To protect the innocent, they will remain nameless. Our conversations formed the basis for the dialogue constructed in this book. I thank them for their time and willingness to share.

It has been a long three years since *Why We Buy: The Science of Shopping* was published. It exists in nineteen foreign editions and has a life of its own. Here in the United States and elsewhere it continues to sell and make its way into classrooms and training programs. I have been surprised by the passionate response of readers across the globe. It has made my life both miserable and wonderful. Thank you.

It has been difficult at times, balancing the role of author with my

primary job as chief executive of Envirosell. I am grateful to my colleagues who tolerate the role changes I go through. Our core group at
Envirosell has worked together for more than ten years. Barbara Weis-
feld, Tom Moseman, Craig Childress, and Anne Marie Luthro continue to be steadfast contributors and companions. Neither this book
nor *Why We Buy* would have been possible without their support.

Every three months I go through a mantra at one of our weekly staff
meetings. Envirosell is answerable to three things. First, we are answerable to our clients. They pay the bills, and their belief in us is important. Second, we are answerable to what we think is the truth.
Finally, we are answerable to one another. We have no distant share-
holders or management, which in the world of research and consulting
makes us unique. As a small agency, we cast a remarkable shadow. We
have a series of clients whose support has been critical to helping Envirosell prosper. Bob Cecil and Dave Edmondson at RadioShack, Ann
Marie Stephens at Circuit City, Deborah Grassi at Wal-Mart,
Francesca Schuler at the Gap, Robin Pearl at Estée Lauder, Marc
Scorca at Opera America, Connie Olsen at Godiva Chocolatier, Scott
Lamensdorf at Philips Lighting, and Kevin Armstrong, now at Cosi,
are just a few.

Our offshore network has been particularly important. Giusi Scan-
droglio and Mario Scatigna in Milano, Mitsuyo Uchida in Tokyo, Kita
Mastopietro and J. Augusto Domingues in São Paolo, Manolo Barber-
ena in Mexico City, and Greg Thain in Moscow.

I have a special relationship with Japan. While it is impossible to cite
all my Japanese friends, the few who follow are special. Hiroshi
Hayakawa bought the Japanese rights to *Why We Buy* in spite of the
fact that his imprint specializes in mystery books. I am grateful for his
courage and vision. I have worked closely with Kenji Onodera at
Hakuhodo, the Japanese advertising agency. I could not ask for a more
responsive and dedicated colleague. Through Onodera-san's guidance
and direction, Envirosell Japan has had a successful launch. Shiota-san
and Asano-san at Sony Music Communication have been advisers,
friends, and fine dining companions. Kazuo Nozaka is the most elegant
and serene man I know. Nozaka-san is the founder of Humanold, an
AARP-like service organization for Japanese seniors. His guidance,

counsel, and example have been valuable to me both as a businessperson and as a man. Finally, Kaz Toyota has been my agent and friend for many years.

I have been led to and through malls across the world by Suat Soysal in Istanbul, Momo Toyota in Tokyo, Aki Toyota in Nara, George Homer and José Luis Nueno in Barcelona, John Hitcham in the United Kingdom, Peter Childs in Paris, Haakon Dahl and Christian Sinding in Oslo, Jean Pierre and Celine Baade in Strasbourg, Alberto Pasquini in Milano, and Tatiana Voronina in Moscow.

No thanks to the airline industry, I have a close network of friends working the retail and consumer-product circuit. There is rarely a place where I land that I can't find someone I'd be delighted to share a meal and opinions with: Judy Bell at Target in Minneapolis, Jim Lucas at Draft in Chicago, Lauren Askew at Monk Design in Baltimore, Carmen Spofford at the Bon in Seattle, Terry Shook and Kevin Kelley at Shook Kelley Design in Charlotte, Erika Szychowski at E°Trade in San Francisco, Karen Hyatt at Hewlett Packard in Corvallis, Bob Gorrie at Gorrie Marketing Services in Toronto, Don Whetstone at Walgreen's in Deerfield, Allen Klose at Blockbuster in Dallas, Alberto Ulloa at Coca-Cola Central American in San Jose, Costa Rica, Paul Kelly at Brown Thomas in Dublin, Patrick Lehman at Express in Columbus, David Blackwell at Ford in Detroit, Jim Ratner at Forest City in Cleveland, Ron Askew at the Integer Group in Denver, Tim Heard at the Brown Shoe Company in St. Louis, Joe Nevins at Bergmeyer in Boston, Tom Kass at Blain's Farm & Fleet in Janesville, Robert Hanson at Levi's in San Francisco, Mark Kolligian at CVS in Woonsocket, Kevin Kwiakowski at Pfizer in New Jersey, Philip Davis at Asprey in London, Mike Ernest at Sara Lee Direct in Winston-Salem, Ed Harsant at Staples in Framingham, Ken McGovern and John Menzer at Wal-Mart in Bentonville, Arnold Schmied at Silhouette in Albany, Dave Williams at Best Buy in Eden Prairie, Bobbi Brooks at RLG in Atlanta, and Jeff Williamson at the Phoenix Zoo are just a few.

It is not that in the New York metro area I have any shortage of merchant and marketer friends. Richard Marcus now lives here; our gain is Dallas's loss. Barbara Stoebel is a veteran cosmetics executive. She is always funny, insightful, and grounded. Rob Ceretti is the past president of the New York Chapter of the Institute of Store Planners and the principal at R. Ceretti & Associates. Lisa Monteleone works for Bvlgari in New York City, but serves stores across the hemisphere. Michael Gould and Jack Hruska at Bloomingdale's have facilitated our work for years. Watts Wacker, or W2 as he calls himself, lives outside the city in a place we call Connect the Dots, but I give him the benefit of the doubt. Watts is glib and inspiring. Kate Newlin reinvents her life every year or two. Anyone with the courage to adopt children after age forty deserves kudos. Wendy Liebmann is the founder of WSL Strategic Retail. She may be the most perfectly groomed person I have ever known. Richard Kurtz is one of my market research mentors. He reminds me that the spirit of life is about staying curious.

I am asked often why we, at Envirosell, continue to get good press. Envirosell had a PR agent for about ten minutes many years ago. I have no regrets about dealing directly with the media. I am happy to talk on and off the record. *New York Times, Washington Post, Los Angeles Times, Philadelphia Inquirer*: The list is endless. I am particularly grateful to the business press—*Business Week, Business 2.0, Fast Company, Fortune,* and *Fortune Small Business,* all of which have been very generous to us. I talk to *Women's Wear Daily* sometimes once a week, not bad for a fashion nerd.

Small parts of this book have appeared in DDI, the retail design trade magazine where I have a short bimonthly column. Group publisher Karen Schaffner and editor RoxAnna Sway have been generous with their time and support.

My Canadian grandmother would have been tickled pink with the attention given Envirosell and my last book by the *National Post, Toronto Globe and Mail,* the CBC, and media outlets across Canada. I think it is because the Canadians are concerned with manners, and *Why We Buy* is focused on retail manners.

A few people look out after me. They tolerate my bouts of ill temper, understand the zombie nature of jet lag, and take my late-night calls. Some of them I see often; others almost never. None of them know how important they are to me. Rip Hayman, Jeff Hewitt, Rob Hewitt, Teresa Sarno, Wilton Conner, Christine Lehner, Carol White, Hutch and Kate Raymer, Liz and Hazem Gamal, Pierre and Colleen Cournot,

Holland Williams, Michael Monroe, Lisa Underhill, Reed Valleau, Joseph Gugletti, Mitch and Mary Ann Wolf, Stan Beck, Peter and Asiye Kay, David Searles, Joe and Sandy Weishar, Joe and Jean McGuire, Sara and Jeff Bowen, John and Medora Barkley, and Mark Gillen.

My companion, who gets the best and worst of me, is Sheryl Henze. I call her Dreamboat, and she is.

A small group of us run an old 1924 forty-eight-foot yawl called the *Klang II,* which sails out of Nyack harbor. Mark, Lisa, Christine, Bill, Rip, Martin, Willie, Fred, Mike, and I meet, sail, drink, tell bad jokes, and discard stress. Their companionship has made aging a pleasure.

If this volume has urban attitude, I am merely the conduit of the training I received on and off the street. Fred Kent and Bob Cook were my early bosses at Project for Public Spaces. Harvey Flad at Vassar College and Barry Boots at Columbia University gave me my first education in Urbanism. Roberto Brambilla and Gianni Longo are two New York–based Italian architects and authors. At their Institute for Environmental Action, they exposed me to both the joy of writing about design and taught me to play and think in city scale. While Roberto has retired to develop luxury property in exotic locations, Gianni remains a remarkably effective pixie at generating sense and consensus in troubled communities across the United States. Peter Katz, the author of *The New Urbanism* is an urban policy wonk and fellow misfit, always willing to have a serious conversation at the drop of a hat. Finally is my old friend Sari Dienes, who died in 1993 at age ninety-four. She described herself as a painter, printmaker, and troublemaker. Sari was the most observant and resourceful urban person I have yet to know. Her Hungarian-accented English still sings in my ears, from our late-night citywide ramblings: "Oh, Paco, Paco, look at that!"

# Index

'Evaristo uses her sec[...]
Empire with a gleeful dis[...]
haven't suffered such irreverence since *Carry on Cleo* . . . it has
great charm and vitality' *Daily Telegraph*, Books of the Year

'This is a belter of a book. Told at breakneck speed by an incredible
talent. This novel deserves to win every award going. Bound to be
a bestseller and a classic' *New London Independent*

'Wildly imaginative' *Red Magazine*, Pick of the Month

'*The Emperor's Babe* is an undoubted triumph . . . it
is a beautifully crafted work' *Wasafiri Literary Magazine*

'Evaristo rewrites history in her extraordinary tale of Roman
London . . . *The Emperor's Babe* breaks all the rules. A world
where ancient and contemporary zeitgeists converge, it offers a
whole new take on the concept of the London novel . . . an
hilarious, streetwise tragicomedy' *The Voice*

'Evaristo is youthful and daring, with hidden depths of wisdom
and hilarity, and she has delivered an entirely new concept for the
historical novel, as well as the London novel' *Independent*

'There are few books more quirky and original than Bernardine
Evaristo's new offering *The Emperor's Babe*. Evaristo has
managed to capture, with contemporary clarity, humour and a
host of quirky characters, what London might have been
like 2,000 years ago' *New Nation*

'Irreverent, fun, and amusingly anachronistic . . . The
gladiatorial scene is not to be missed . . . Consistently
amusing, clever and inventive' *Library Journal USA*

'Smart, imaginative and readable . . . a rich farrago of historical
fact and outrageous fancy' *The New York Times*

'A vividly imagined albeit distinctly modern look at a woman's
role in Roman times by a talented writer with a fertile
mind and playful spirit' *Publishers Weekly*

## ABOUT THE AUTHOR

Bernardine Evaristo is the Anglo-Nigerian award-winning author of several books of fiction and verse fiction that explore aspects of the African diaspora: past, present, real, imagined. Her novel *Girl, Woman, Other* won the Booker Prize in 2019. Her writing also spans short fiction, reviews, essays, drama and writing for BBC radio. She is Professor of Creative Writing at Brunel University, London, and Vice Chair of the Royal Society of Literature. She was made an MBE in 2009. As a literary activist for inclusion Bernardine has founded a number of successful initiatives, including Spread the Word writer development agency (1995–ongoing), the Complete Works mentoring scheme for poets of colour (2007–2017) and the Brunel International African Poetry Prize (2012–ongoing).

www.bevaristo.com

## ABOUT THE COVER ARTIST

Jon Gray / gray318 grew up in Suffolk and Essex and studied graphic design at the London College of Printing. While studying he took a summer internship at a publishing house and has remained in publishing ever since. He has worked as a freelance cover designer for twenty years and his work has won awards on both sides of the Atlantic. His website is www.gray318.com

# THE EMPEROR'S BABE

*A Novel*

Bernardine Evaristo

PENGUIN BOOKS

PENGUIN ESSENTIALS

UK | USA | Canada | Ireland | Australia
India | New Zealand | South Africa

Penguin Books is part of the Penguin Random House group of companies
whose addresses can be found at global.penguinrandomhouse.com.

Penguin
Random House
UK

First published by Hamish Hamilton 2001
Published in Penguin Books 2002
Reissued 2017
This Penguin Essentials edition published 2020
002

Copyright © Bernardine Evaristo, 2001

The moral right of the author has been asserted

Printed and bound in Great Britain by Clays Ltd, Elcograf S.p.A.

A CIP catalogue record for this book is available from the British Library

ISBN: 978-0-241-98984-5

www.greenpenguin.co.uk

MIX
Paper from
responsible sources
FSC® C018179

Penguin Random House is committed to a
sustainable future for our business, our readers
and our planet. This book is made from Forest
Stewardship Council® certified paper.

PENGUIN ESSENTIALS

*The Emperor's Babe*

'A daring experiment in verse fiction which came off
triumphantly . . . its lurid scenarios pulsated with a hybrid vigour'
*Independent*

'Readable, sexy, delicious . . . I loved this book' Helen Dunmore

'Exhilarating . . . wildly entertaining then deeply affecting' Ali Smith

'One of Britain's most innovative authors . . . Bernardine Evaristo
always dares to be different' *New Nation*

'Evaristo remains an undeniably bold and energetic writer, whose
world view is anything but one-dimensional' *Sunday Times*

'Audacious genre-bending, in-yer-face wit and masterly
retellings of underwritten corners of history are the hallmarks of
Evaristo's work' *New Statesman*

'Evaristo is a gifted portraitist, and you marvel at both
the people she conjures and the unexpected way she reveals
them to you' *New Republic*

'Bernardine Evaristo is one of those writers who should be read by
everyone, everywhere. Her tales marry down-to-earth characters with
engrossing storylines about identity and the UK of today' Elif Shafak

'Bernardine Evaristo can take any story from any time and turn
it into something vibrating with life' Ali Smith

'Sexy, clever and ingenious: a verse romp set in Roman Londinium.
Why must fiction always be in prose?' *Independent*

'Exot' . . . . . . . . . . . . . . . . . . . . . . . this is amazingly

SWANSEA LIBRARIES

6000370743

'Evaristo's strikingly original *The Emperor's Babe* makes you feel that you are reading something that has never before been attempted, a sensation to savour. Written in fresh, zingy, witty language that combines tags of Latin, historically authentic references and twenty-first-century teen slang, it is a fast, exciting read whose occasional bittersweet notes build until it turns like a ballad from comedy to tragedy . . . *The Emperor's Babe* is a modern work of art that uses the literary tradition with such light assurance that everything seems new. Brushing off the dust of 1,800 years like a cobweb, Evaristo's golden lads and girls dance in the sun before us, glistening, frail and real. Vivat Zuleika' *Sunday Times*

'*The Emperor's Babe* is unexpectedly sassy, funny, engaging and very sexy. Honest to God, you'll love it' *Sunday Independent* (Ireland), Books of the Year

'If there is any justice in the world, *The Emperor's Babe* will be a huge hit. Fictions like Evaristo's, overflowing with energy and originality, are as rare as the sautéed peacock brains she has her heroine consume . . . Evaristo's triumph is to transmute politics and history into a glittering fiction whose words leap off the page into life . . . brilliant' *The Times*

'Evaristo's skill lies in taking standard metaphorical models and twisting them in the most unusual, original, inventive ways. *The Emperor's Babe* is exactly what the title suggests: the adventures of a sassy, sexy girl about town . . . It's also funny, engaging and a daring evocation of the possible genesis of black British history. By puncturing the imperial pomp of Latin vocabulary with the cut and thrust of modern street talk, Evaristo demystifies much of the gilded decorum Rome evokes . . . The punchy poetry is perfect for the rhythm of the emperor's babe, the epitome of all that is fast, fresh, funky' *Independent on Sunday*, Books of the Year

'Evaristo's delicious *The Emperor's Babe* is, as they say, something completely different: a fresh and original historical novel, narrated in verse' *Bookseller*

'It is a highly enjoyable romp' *Guardian*

a verse novel you can't put down' *Observer*

For Nicholas

| CITY AND COUNTY OF SWANSEA LIBRARIES | |
|---|---|
| 6000370743 | |
| Askews & Holts | 06-Oct-2020 |
| | £8.99 |
| SWGW | |

The one duty we owe to history is to rewrite it.

— OSCAR WILDE

# CONTENTS

Epilogue

PROLOGUE

## AMO AMAS AMAT

Who do you love? Who *do* you love,
when the man you married goes off

for months on end, quelling rebellions
at the frontiers, or playing hot-shot senator in Rome;

his flashy villa on the Palatine Hill, home
to another woman, I hear,

one who has borne him offspring.
My days are spent roaming this house,

its vast mosaic walls full of the scenes on Olympus,
for my husband loves melodrama.

They say his mistress is an actress,
a flaxen-Fräulein type, from Germania Superior.

Oh, everyone envied me, *Illa Bella Negreeta!*
born in the back of a shop on Gracechurch Street,

who got hitched to a Roman nobleman,
whose parents sailed out of Khartoum on a barge,

no burnished throne, no poop of beaten gold,
but packed with vomiting brats

and cows releasing warm turds
on to their bare feet. Thus perfumed,

they made it to Londinium on a donkey,
with only a thin purse and a fat dream.

Here in the drizzle of this wild west town
Dad wandered the streets looking for work,

but there was no room at the inn,
so he set up shop on the kerb

and sold sweet cakes which Mum made.
(He's told me this story a mille times.)

Now he owns several shops, selling everything
from vino to shoes, veggies to tools,

and he employs all sorts to work in them,
a Syrian, Tunisian, Jew, Persian,

hopefuls just off the olive barge from Gaul,
in fact anyone who'll work for pebbles.

When Felix came after me, Dad was in ecstasy,
father-in-law to Lucius Aurelius Felix, no less.

I was spotted at the baths of Cheapside,
just budding, and my fate was sealed

by a man thrice my age and thrice my girth,
all at sweet eleven – even then Dad

thought I was getting past it.
Then I was sent off to a snooty Roman bitch

called Clarissa for decorum classes,
learnt how to talk, eat and fart,

how to get my amo amas amat right, and ditch
my second-generation plebby creole.

*Zuleika accepta est.*
*Zuleika delicata est.*
*Zuleika bloody goody-two shoes est.*

But I dreamt of creating mosaics,
of remaking my town with bright stones and glass.

But no! Numquam! It's not allowed.
Sure, Felix brings me presents, when he deigns

to come west. I've had Chinese silk, a marble
figurine from Turkey, gold earrings

shaped like dolphins, and I have the deepest
fondness for my husband, of course,

sort of, though he spills over me like dough
and I'm tempted to call Cook mid coitus

to come trim his sides so that he fits me.
Then it's puff and *Ciao, baby!*

Solitudoh, solitudee, solitudargh!

# LONDINIUM TOUR GUIDE (UNOFFICIAL)

One minute it's hopscotch in bare feet,
next you're four foot up in a sedan in case

your pink stockings get dirty. No one
prepared me for marriage. Me and Alba

were the wild girls of Londinium,
sought to discover the secrets

of its hidden hearts, still too young
to withhold more than we revealed,

to join this merry cast of actors.
She was like a rag doll who'd lost its stuffing:

spiky brown hair kept short 'cos of nits;
everyone said she was either anorexic

or had worms, but Alba was so busy
chasing the dulcis vita that she just burnt

everything she ate before it turned to fat.
She'd drag me out on dangerous escapades,

we were partners in crime, banditos, renegades
she said there was more to life

than playing with friggin' dolls, like causing
trouble and discovering what grown-ups

did in private without getting caught.
We were gonna steal from the rich,

give to the poor, keep seventy-five per cent
for ourselves and live in one of them mansions

with a thousand slaves feeding us cakes,
all day every day, but until such time . . . Her dad

owned the butcher's next door but one.
Mine couldn't care less what I did.

His precious Catullus got the abacus and wax,
I got the sewing kit and tweezers.

He was *even* bought a ponytail for his curly
little head, so's he fitted in at school

with all those trendy Roman kids.
Bless his sockless feet. *Imagine.*

Some days we'd tour the tenements
of Aldersgate. He'd trail behind

like a giant sloth, his big muddy eyes
under sleepy hoods (just like his father's),

and plead with us to slow down;
I'd tell him to *futuo-off, you little runt,*

leaving him behind as we raced towards
the slums, swarming with immigrants,

freed slaves and factory workers (usual suspects).
We'd play Knock-Down-Ginger, throw stones,

break windows, then leg-it down an alley
outa-sight, arrive home breathless

and itching with flea bites and jigger-foot.
What with the alfresco sewerage running

between paving stones, now
in my neighbourhood, summer evenings

were spiced, trout fried on stalls, fresh
out of the Thames, you could eat air

or run home for supper in the back-a-yard
Dad called an atrium. That's

if the rush-hour traffic allowed, carts
clogged up the main drag to the Forum, unloading

produce from up-country or abroad.
Sometimes, I'd hear a solitary flute through an open

window, and stop . . . . . . . . . . breathing.
Later we'd sneak out for the vicarious thrill

of the carnal experience. Like two toms,
we'd prowl the darkened alleys, our noses

sniffing out the devastating odour of sex.
Peeping through candle-lit shutters,

we were amazed at the adult need to strip off
and stick things in each other.

Men and women, women and women,
men and men, multiples of all sorts

groaning in pain. Absolutely fascinatio!
And then we encountered death,

Lucan Africanus, the baker of Fenchurch.
I was the daughter he never had, he said

(though his eyes spelt *wife*),
gave us fresh bread dipped in honey.

Our thanks? To raid his store one night,
find his great, black, rigor mortis self

in a cloud of flour, two burnt buns for cheeks,
too much yeast in his bowels, emptied

on the floor. That stopped our missions,
for a while. Some nights we'd go to the river,

sit on the beach, look out towards
the marshy islands of Southwark,

and beyond to the jungle that was Britannia,
teeming with spirits and untamed humans.

We'd try to imagine the world beyond the city,
that country a lifetime away that Mum

called home and Dad called prison;
the city of Roma which everyone

went on about as if it were so bloody mirabilis.
We'd talk about the off-duty soldiers

who loitered in our town, everywhere,
they were everywhere, watching for lumps

on our chests, to see if our hips grew away
from our waists, always picking me out,

plucking at me in the market,
*Is our little aubergine ready?*

'No, I'm not, you stinking pervs,' I'd growl,
skedaddling hotfoot out of their reach.

Sometimes we'd hear grunting
on the beach and imagine some illicit

extramarital action was in progress,
we'd call out in our deepest, gruffest voices,

*Hey, polizia!* and rock with laughter
'cos we'd interrupted their flipping coitus,

we'd hear them tripping over themselves
as they scuffled off and then everything

changed, I got engaged. I wasn't allowed
out no more, I had to act ladylike

and Alba said it wouldn't be the same
once I'd been elevated.

# THE BETRAYAL

> Time to leave your mother, dear.
> You're ready for a man.
> – HORACE

First I heard of it was overheard
when I came home unexpectedly early

from the baths 'cos it was overcrowded
and as usual they told *me* to come back later.

As I dawdled up our street, busy
with shoppers – tired of having to say *Salve!*

and *Bene*, *gratias* at every step to neighbours
who didn't give a toss about how I felt,

wondering if Alba could come out to play,
glad that spring was here after a long winter

when I'd had to wrap my feet in rags
or else they'd fall off –

I saw a fancy sedan parked up outside
our shop and four bronzed sedan-bearers

wearing white linen skirts with gold stripes,
leaning against the wall, waiting.

I ran the rest of the way, found the shop closed.
I heard voices, put my ear to the door.

'Sì, Mr Felix. Zuleika very obediens girl, sir.
No problemata, she make very optima wife, sir.'

'Glad to hear it, for when I saw her at the baths,
she stole my heart. Indeed,

she is so . . . exquisita, so . . . pulcherrima,
such a delicious surprise in this, shall we say,

less than dazzling little colonia.
She reminds me of the girls back in Ægyptus,

where I spent most of my teenage years,
my father was governor there, you know,

I liked the mysterious, dark ones
from the south, who would oil my limbs,

waft soundlessly around me leaving
the lingering scent of musky sandalwood

from Zanzibar in their wake.
I have been looking for a wife for some time,

and naturaliter, I wanted someone young,
someone specialis, a rare flower.'

'Sì, Mr Felix. Zuleika very specialis girl.
Yes, always at home, quietly sewing,

very placid, no back-chat.'
'Good. I have enjoyed bachelorhood

to its utmost, Anlamani, but the fiend loneliness
has become a most unwelcome friend.

I intend to make this my far-western base
and I need to warm my home with a wife.

I am a man of multiple interests: a senator,
military man, businessman, I undertake

trading missions for the government,
and I'm a landowner,

I've just bought Hertfordshire, you know.
Yet I have never been interested

in the plethora of simpering debutantes
who are paraded in the cattle-market balls

every season, mothers thrusting their powdered
wrinkled cleavages at me, supposedly

on behalf of their darling twittering daughters.
My own dear mater died young, you know,

she was so *very* benevola, I missed
her terribly when I was a boy. I still do.

Perhaps that is why it has taken me so long
to tie the knot, so to speak.

To form an attachment is to risk its loss,
is it not? I have been looking for a nice,

simplex, quiet, fidelis girl, a girl
who will not betray me with affairs,

who will not wear me out with horrid fights,
unlike my pater's subsequent three wives,

who made my life hell, *and* his,
who were of the hedonistic breed

of aristocratic matronae, determined to compete
with the husband in all spheres,

ever boastful of their sexual shenanigans,
humiliating the dear gentle man in public

and prepared to argue until dawn on matters
of politics, world affairs and the arts.

Have you heard that women now dress up
in male attire and compete in chariot races?

It has got quite out of hand in the fatherland.
Nor do I want one with cumbersome baggage.

Is my load not heavy enough?
I will of course see to an educatio for her,

and lessons in elegantia, she is of the age
where she will learn quickly.

Do not worry about her dowry, it is of no
consequentia to me, of course

you will benefit greatly from this negotium.
I think we can safely say that your business

is due to expand considerably.'
'You are very benignus gentleman, sir.

Road has been uphill, almost vertical, for years.
A boost to oeconomia most welcome, sir.'

'Say no more. You have my patronage.'
I looked through a large crack in the door

(there *were* many) and saw an old man,
much taller than my small father,

who was so thin, that day his stoop resembling
a frozen bow. The man was much fatter

than Pops too, he was in a word: obesus.
His smooth olive-skinned face wore

the haughty expression of a true patrician,
his thinning brown hair was cut

in the fashionable pudding-bowl haircut,
his orange-and-white-striped toga

was of sumptuous linen that fell in elegant folds,
he wore several gold rings with bright stones

and when my eyes moved slowly down
I saw his legs: thin, hairy *and* bandy.

At which point my own took me rapidly
down the street, not even stopping at Alba's,

no words could form yet.
I ran until I reached the sloping banks

of the River Fleet, far away from the docks,
and then I screamed at the water

until my throat was sore and my spittle
had dried up, not caring

that all the fishermen thereabouts
stopped mending their nets and stared.

I stayed for hours and when it was dark,
the beach deserted, I stripped off, threw

my tatty green dress on to pebbles,
walked into the cold water and swam far out,

shivering. It was what I needed,
to calm me down. I had done it before.

When I turned round, the city was lit up
with lamps, and torches flickered in windows

and doorways of houses on the hills.
l knew I had to accept my fate. I *could* throw

countless tantrums, I *was* an expert,
but it would go ahead, regardless.

The man's voice carried such utter imperium,
and he expressed such an awful desire for me.

I swam towards the lights, forcing myself
to conquer the cold water,

before my body seized up with cramp.
And what about Mater dearest?

Dad would have sent her on an errand.
I thought of how she spat out words

like the gristle of fetid beef, hating
her adopted language, even now:

*Zuks! Fetch Khu-kh-umba! Cabb-age!*
*Hasp-ara-gush!*

She'd wave an arm at Dad,
her underarm loose like soggy papyrus.

*More! More!* – finger and thumb rubbing
together in a greedy money-making gesture.

*Nubia good!* He'd turn away, serve
another customer, joke with them,

while she scowled, pulled her voluminous
black robes over her head, slumped

into a corner, still as a sack of potatoes.
As a kid, I'd crawl into her covers,

make my breath hers.
A sweet tooth had taken the rest away,

her cheeks were dried out and grooved,
she had given birth when most wombs

nourished ghosts, walked with stillborns
riding her back. She dragged me down streets,

I flew like her robes in fierce wind.
Darling Catullus came three years later,

a miracle on account of his sperm bag.
I hadn't been left to die outside the city walls

exactly, but, aged three, I knew who
would inherit the key to the Kingdom of Pops.

*I have suffer so too you will have suffer.*
Her eyes were nigrosine, whites browned,

liquefying only when she rocked Catullus
to sleep with softly sung Nubian ditties –

cross-legged on the mat which served
as couch and mattress behind the counter

of our first vegetable shop in Milk Street.
Ulcers sprouted in my mouth, sleepless,

Dad lanced them, I bit my tongue
so's not to awaken the Baby Jesus,

was desperate to run into the night for ever,
to find the river and disappear in it,

I was swimming in the dead of it,
my frozen limbs struggled up the beach,

my dress instantly soaked. I ran back
through the deserted streets,

feeling my blood warm up, my joints
becoming fluid again, the only sound

was of my sandalled feet on hardened earth,
my harsh panting breaths. I called for Alba,

she heard from the back where they slept,
but she came quickly to the door,

took one look at me, ran back inside, returned
to wrap me up in her grey blanket

that scratched my wet skin like thistles.
She made me sit down, just the two of us,

few dared walk around after dark.
She rubbed my back. 'Zeeks. Wassup?'

## THE BETROTHAL

His pupils
are soaked in desire,

float in a crisp January sky,
show no mercy,

even as mine plead
innocence.

A small gold link
to my heart

lies in the damp crevice
of his supplicant palm,

spiders crawl
up his forearm,

I am level
with his beige linen

abdomen, black leather girdle,
slung low.

'The Ægyptians,' he proclaims,
'discovered a most delicate nerve

on the finger anularius,
the only one, indeed,

with a direct line
to our greatest gift:

The Human Heart.
And so with this ring, I thee betroth,

Zuleika,
cherished daughter

of our man from Nubia, Anlamani.'
He takes my limp hand,

fills
the trembling gold

and withdraws
ever so,

ever so,
ever so

slowly, to applause, but
I flick my hand down,

so that Cupid's cute
little handiwork

tinkles on the ground,
amidst gasps.

My eyes lock his in
then,

and smile.
He has just made

of my greatest gift
an exile.

## OSMOSIS

### I

A straw mat, an earth floor,
snow that blew in as we lay, three

in a row, my vigilant Dad shaking
pools of water off the cowhide blanket,

for our poor wooden shop offered
little protection from the storms of winter.

### II

He and Mum, way back when,
the family heirloom, he whispered,

was a human chain belonging to the King of Meroe,
with no breakages for generations,

their own mother, his concubine.

> *Is my mother also my aunt?*
> *Am I your daughter and niece?*
> *Am I my own cousin?*

III

Dad looked hurt. They shared
the same profile, I thought tribal.

'There are some things,
you can only share with your own.

When you're a slave you dream
of either owning slaves or freeing them.'


IV

A famine, plague or flood
(the story always changed), the king

died, the palace was in chaos,
they fled 200ks to Khartoum in a caravan,

exporting sacks of sorghum,
lentils and melons.


V

They travelled for a year
before they reached, slept in forests

or inns, sold amethysts and chrisoliths
stolen from the palace, she resisted

every step onwards, yearned
for the city of Meroe, and safety.

## VI

They bypassed Rome
and its many Ethiops, too congested

they were told, but they heard
of Londinium, way out in the wild west,

a sea to cross, a man
could make millions of denarii.


## VII

I shivered behind his itchy shawl,
he mumbled in his sleep, bristling

with plans, flames burnt
under his clothes, I slid my fingers

into hot armpits, he squeezed, I felt
him draw the ice from my veins.


## VIII

Breasts bursting with milk
for the coming Son of Christ

pushed against my back, stealing
my heat, knuckles poked into my spine,

until I melted into sleep and awoke,
not knowing where I began.

# TILL DEATH DO US

### I

The white stucco villas of Cheapside
are usually out of bounds to scallywags

like me and Alba. Guards shoo us away.
(She has not been invited.) Today

they bow as if I were the emperor's wife,
when my horse-drawn carriage, *if* you please,

arrives at a villa with its very own latrina.
and enough rooms to fill the Forum.

Janus-faced gits! I am the same girl
I was last week. Or am I?

### II

A *lady* uses powdered horn to enamel
her teeth, dontcha know, and powdered

mouse brains keep her breath sweet.
I am pampered by maids, an ornatrix is weaving

Indian hair into my own, six pads – Vestal-stylee.
They are painting me white with chalk,

my lips and cheeks with the lees of red wine,
*Don't talk!* Black ash is dabbed on to my eyes,

*Keep still!* I'm the It Girl of Londinium, yeah!
Alba would crack up.


### III

A girl sits in a silk-embroidered loincloth,
all tarted up with a wedding to go to.

A lemon tunic, a heavy saffron cloak,
a bright yellow veil are all draped over her,

then a wreath of myrtle and orange blossom,
and around her neck, a metal collar. *Here, Fido!*

A lady *never* leaves her cubiculum,
without putting on the slap. Jove forbid,

I should ever again be seen au naturel.
*Someone watches me in the mirror.*


### IV

The haruspex ripped out the guts of a pig,
blood ran down his arm on to the pretty floor.

*Ubi tu Felix, ego Zuleika*: then Felix *kissed* me.
and the room whirled with dancing girls

exposing their breasts and guests
poured red wine into each other's mouths,

clowns juggled knives and dwarf acrobats
did cartwheels and I entered the statue

of Minerva in the corner, alabaster and wise.
*I would soon be alone with him.*

V

Felix had to wrest me from Mum's
loving embrace (*what* a performance).

Our cortège turned the midnight streets
into bacchanalia, torches and flutes led the way,

everyone sang bawdy songs and people
danced out of houses, past the baths

and up Cannon Street towards his manor
at the Walbrook Stream. He carried me

over the threshold. I glanced back to see if Alba
was in the crowd, watching.


VI

Flames flickered by the marital bed.
He laid me out, peeled off my layers

like humid rose petals, he sucked my *toes*,
called me *mea delicia*, opened my legs

and held a candle to my vulva until flames
tried to exit my mouth as a scream

but his hand was clamped over it. I passed out.
Pluto came for me that night,

and each time I woke up, it was my first night
in the Kingdom of the Dead.

# METAMORPHOSIS

*Martius*: doctor recommends months
of recuperation each time his sewing

is undone, this becomes my world, to adjust
to married life, I am not let out, he says

he is too selfish to share his new bride
just yet, imagine this is our honeymoon,

you are in a cocoon, will emerge
with the manners of a true lady, one day

he will take me to his holiday villa
in the Bay of Neapolis, you have never seen

the like, my dear, stop the tears, my love,
accept your grand new status, I wander

around the villa, grander than any me and Alba
imagined, leading off the atrium

are cubicula, triclinia, bathing rooms
built just for me, the tablinum full of books

where he receives his clients, peristylium
at the back full of bushes and flowers, a kitchen

leads off it, the slaves' quarters hidden
behind trees, by the front door the household

shrine, all this is mine but I am a stranger
here, listen out for him, where is he?

Will he call for me? *Aprilis*: when he leaves,
I fear his return, when he returns, I fear

he will never leave, Mum and Dad visit,
stand like country bumpkins, stare at a twenty-

foot ceiling, speechless, a professor
comes daily, I am reading Juvenal

and his witty works, push my back
into his at night, when he is out I fear

he will never come home, when he is here,
I fear I will be left alone, again,

I am becoming a spectre, I think, *Maius:*
he wakes me up at dawn, three leather trunks

are stacked in the atrium, a chariot
outside will take him across Gaul towards Rome,

he has important duties to perform,
he must report back to HQ, attend

to his business interests. 'The silk route
from China for one, Persian bandits

are plundering my caravans of silk, pirates
are seizing my shipments of grain

from Alexandria, the Med is a war zone,
I must see to all that so we can have all this.

Go out into the town, enjoy, I'll assign
a bodyguard but, for goodness sake,

don't show me up and walk,
take a train of slaves and a sedan.'

# TWO HOT CHICKS

'Is it a girl? Is it a ghost? Is it a glamour puss?
Is it a grand dame? No, it's me mate, Zuky-dot!

How've you been, darlin'?' Venus's droll
contralto floated over the empty wooden tables

in her twilight bar Mount Venus, at the junction
of Ludgate Hill and St Paul's Churchyard.

It was late, not quite the done thing for a lady
to be ordering a pint just up from the docks,

in fact to be out alone at all. But Venus and me
went way back to when I was a mite

of seven, scavenging for leftovers at the market
of a Saturday evening in the years

before Dad became a 'man successfully made'.
Venus showed me how to tell the difference

between an overripe apple and a maggoty one,
helped me carry my assortment of cabbages,

turnips, radishes and wotnots home
much to the snooty disdain of Dad,

waiting in the road for supper to arrive,
for Venus was a sight to behold, and some.

'It's a long story,' I called back, all gung-ho,
braving a room acrid with stale beer and vino,

trying to step daintily in my posh new sandals
on a sawdust floor covered with broken glass,

testament to the previous night's round
of ribaldry, rivalry and lewd rhetoric.

We embraced, tears came into my eyes,
partly because she'd just come from the baths

and had overdone it with a mixed potion
of lavender, rose and honeysuckle perfumes

and partly because it had been so long
since I'd been held without it being a precursor

to a demand for sex – non-negotiable.
She fingered my gold dolphin earrings,

her dark blue eyes sparkling with amusement.
'Upmarket tomfoolery, eh. The real thing, luv?'

I had left home that afternoon with wings
on my heels, ordered the sedan-bearers,

bodyguard and train of status symbols
to trot ten paces behind, made a dash for it,

up Bucklersbury and out of sight, headed
for Gracechurch Street, popped in to see Alba,

who was chasing headless chickens in the yard,
before plucking them for display outside.

She couldn't believe it was me.
She moaned she had no time to herself now.

I moaned that was *all* I had. She asked
why I hadn't come out to play,

but I couldn't explain.
I knew she wouldn't understand.

I could tell she was angry. She was catching
chickens, then letting them go.

'Stop and talk to me,' I begged. 'Please.'
'I said it would change, Zee. Look at you,

all poshed up, I went to your house twice
but the guards told me to scarper.'

'It wasn't me,' I replied. 'It's him, it's my . . .
I've missed you so much. It's been awful.'

She stopped running, came over,
awkwardly, not knowing what to do

with her hands, whether to hug me.
'Me too. Look at all that make-up, Zee,

and that dress, you look so grown up.
So when do I get to go to your manor?'

'When I can fix it. Tranio's the head honcho
when he's away, so it won't be easy.'

'I feel sorry for you, Zee.'
'Thanks!'

'No, I'm not being bitchy. I'm just glad
I'm still free. Come and see me soon.'

She disappeared inside the house.
Two doors up, Mater and Pater

were serving a queue of bemused customers.
Dad was chatting his usual bollocks,

about really being the exiled King of Meroe,
the last of the great pharaohs.

'My palace bigger than governor's. Yes. No lie.
I made good, see. Look Zuleika here,

married to Roman nobilitas. Veritas princess?
Clothes so fine? My blood, see.'

Blah, blah, bloody-blah. Mum glared at him,
as usual, whispered loudly he'd taken

to gambling, wanted a villa like Mr Felix.
'Nothing good enough now.

Him want quick-come money.'
She'd found a backgammon board

with rolling dice in the yard, confronted him,
but did he listen to her? She moaned

he spent most evenings in a seedy den
by the river front with a bunch of low-lifes.

I tried to furrow my brow with concern
but felt I was watching a B-rate play

with C-rate actors, sitting in a D-rate seat
at the amphitheatre.

I asked after Little Bro Catullus
(aka *He Who Can Do No Wrong*), was told

he was at Maestro Caesar's over the way.
Took this as my cue to leave, though I just

studied him from a distance while Caesar,
bald as a pumpkin, cut his locks in the middle

of the thoroughfare, waved his knives
at passers-by who got too vocal

with their complaints, had slashed a face
or two in his time, you see.

There the Little Usurper sat, fat brown
cheeks gleaming, full petulant lips,

wearing the smug demeanor of one
so dearly loved he'd been bought a dog,

a parrot *and* a blooming nightingale.
Then Caesar's knife plunged suddenly

into his neck, blood spurted out, Catullus
released a spine-chilling scream, his eyes

rolled back, he fell off his stool
on to the ground, writhing. Yeah, right. I think *not*.

I took to my old stomping ground,
the narrow backstreets, hawkers poked sulphur

matches in my face, or lamps for sale
or bread or second-hand shoes.

'Oh, come on, miss, be a benefactor
to a poor beggar, why don't you?'

'Abi!' I said, telling them I never walked
with cash and that the jewels were fake,

then pushed them roughly aside,
as they had done me, oh not

so many moons ago. A flower-seller
sold vibrant bouquets, an ivory-vendor

sold tusks from Kenya, mirrors hung
from shop doorways, the scent of oils

from Arabia and Ethiopia floated
out of perfumeries, others sold spices

and cotton, there were pearl-sellers,
goldsmiths, robe-makers, cloak-makers,

cabinet-makers, embroiderers, dyers,
tanners, workers sitting on stools outside,

or doors wide open to shops;
money-changers lurked in doorways

like dirty old men, luring me
to make my fortune; I heard horn-tuners,

horses' hoofs, barrels on gravel, chisels
on stone, saws on logs, knives

scraping leather, coppersmiths' tapping,
children's laughter, grunting pigs, sausages

frying in saucepans, chanting schoolboys
sitting under trees, I heard shouts,

bells, gongs, chimes,
how I loved and missed it all.

Outside the Forum, Dinesh the bow-legged
mystic was still doing his old

cobra-in-a-basket act with a reed whistle,
though the viper was geriatric,

could no longer writhe its alluring,
double-jointed body in a dance

that would feed Dinesh's family daily.
He stood alongside the local loonies

on wooden crates who predicted
the destruction of empire or that Christianity

would soon come west, cracking jokes
about virgins giving birth or how

to walk on water without getting your feet wet
or the ten best ways to rise from the dead

or declaring Jupiter is really a woman
or that raw eggs give you a longer hard-on

or parading in a papyrus placard announcing
that the world will end in the year 300 –

to a crowd of onlookers who kept up a steady
supply of rotten fish and pigs' entrails.

Inside the orators were out in full force, juicing
every syllable for its music, competing

to speak the most passionalissima Latin
to a lively audience. I slid in at the back,

desperate to know about the world I lived in.
They spoke of the great Septimius Severus,

who had gone from African boy
to Roman emperor, had spent many years

travelling the empire from Germania
to Syria, back to his hometown in Libya,

who would surely one day visit Britannia,
this far-flung northern outpost of empire,

defeat the fucking Scots, Pict and Saxon
bastards who made a steady onslaught

on our cities and towns, spear every last man
of them, burn their villages, castrate

their infant sons, occupy their women,
colonize their terra firma, make them speak

our lingo, impose taxes, yay! and thus
bring Pax Romana to this our blessed island.

Vivat Emperor Sevva!
Vivat Emperor Sevva!

* * *

'The first time is always the worst, Zuky-doo.'
Venus had listened to each scene in my drama

*Girl Weds Rich Old Man Who Locks Her Up.*
'I know, believe you me, I couldn't sit for days.'

She crossed her eyes, sucked in her cheeks,
affected a shrug and we burst out laughing,

though mine came with a few tears, unwittingly.
I saw Venus afresh, noticed that under the slap

her features were drawn, her bright-red
lips were miserable when immobile.

'Wassup?' I ventured quietly.
Her staff were drifting in, sweeping the floor,

fetching water, lighting lanterns.
Outside the street was coated with black.

'Nuffink to speak of.'
Her face suddenly crumpled into her right hand.

'Show must go on an' all that.'
'No, really, tell me,' I insisted, realizing

for the first time that Venus was my alma mater,
but that I knew Sweet FA about the desires

beneath the glamorous alter ego of glitz and wit,
had never really cared before.

I sat up, astonished at the revelation
that this was probably My First Adult Thought.

She looked me straight in the eyes,
not one ounce of glitter. 'It's like this.'

She slumped forward on the table,
both hands now cradling her face, pushing

her chalky white flesh into high cheekbones.
'You're either a figure for fucking or a fucking freak.

Everyone needs a one-and-only after a while.
I'm twenty-two, Zuky-do. Middle aged!

A Venus must 'ave an Adonis.
Even if it's just for a while. Bronzed, rippling,

adoring, preferably, compliant, essentially.
Someone to come home to, to cook

a pease pudding for of a winter's night.
Look at the facts.

Thousands of bloody years ago
the Ægyptians believed in a sparring partner,

a Mr and Mrs scenario, I'll stand by you,
mi' amore, if you stand by me.

Why can't I have it too? I'll never have children.
No Cupid to match-make us mere humans.

You and Alba are my sprogs,
but I need a husband! Not a touch-your-toes-

and-it'll-be-ten-bucks-more number.
Flippen 'eck! I need a bona fide husband!

I need a C-O-N-I-U-N-X!
Whadoesthatspell? Husband!'

She jumped up from her seat, began shouting
at her staff, 'Get a move on, you bunch

of loafers, no-hopers, trollops and has-beens.
The punters'll be here soon. Get your glad rags,

falsies and wigs on. You look a state!
I'm going out for a bit and if this taverna

ain't spick and span by the time
I get back, you'll be joining the paupers

queuing for handouts outside the mansions
of Cheapside on the morrow!'

She turned back to me.
'Let me ball-of-chalk you home, darlin'.

You're a woman of means now.
Ain't no scamp no more.

Prime target for muggers and ne'er-do-wells.'
'Yeah, right,' I replied. 'What does Juvenal say?

44

Never go out to supper without
having first made your will.'

'My dee-yah! You'll be quoting Plato next!'
'Actually, I've been studying poetry

with my professor, Theodorous.
I'm going to become a great poet.

I'd love to be famous for something.
Felix wants me educated, so how can he object?'

I pulled my brown woollen shawl over my head,
'Good,' she said, putting an arm around me.

'Keep you out of trouble.
Just make sure you write witty ditties about me.

I wanna be immortalized, dontchaknowit,
and ain't no one never gonna write

about your life but you. Once you're dead,
you never existed, baby, so get to it.'

Two heads taller than me, she steered me past
the brothel at the corner, its owner a man

from Gaul with a wet donkey's tail
of a moustache, who used to call out:

'I 'ave a Woppy, a Chinky, a Honky, a Paki,
a Gingery, an Araby, now all I need is a Blackie.

'Ow's about it, leetle girlie?'
In the old days Venus slapped his face

if he propositioned me, though
tonight his jaw dropped when I passed by,

transformed into a real uptown chick, I was.
Venus and I chuckled as we navigated

the dockland streets, slipping
on the slimy contents of chamber pots

thrown from the tenements.
She had long been a fantastic sight

in our town, originally from Camulodunum
on the east coast, she had acquired

an affected mockney accent,
part of *me re-invention package, my dee-yah!*

Fair hair was dyed black, piled with curly
hairpieces, wooden pattens raised

her sandals an unheard-of three inches
off the ground, and her feet were as large

as any man's. In her off-the-shoulder gowns
and dolled-up face, hair showed

where breasts usually sprouted. She used
to be followed by hordes, pelted with stones,

but folks got used to her,
most didn't give a damn and those who

did found their faces re-structured,
for it was not wise to bring out the man

in Venus, née Rufus.
Mount Venus was a haven for her kind,

men who loaned themselves out for cabarets
or private parties for rich married men

who liked the best of both sexes, disappeared
into the back room for anonymous antics.

Others just liked to parade in chic gowns.
The sassiest called out to soldiers from the bar,

'Ditch the beard for the lipstick, bay-bee!
and life'll *never* be the same again!'

to hoots of laughter. Alba and me were their pets,
allowed to watch and giggle, promising

not to tell a soul when a famous lawyer
or butch centurion emerged

from the back room unsteady on his legs,
in a wig, torn gown and smudged lipstick.

The first time we met, me and Alba
had joined in with a crowd throwing stones

at her as she sashayed up Newgate Street,
cream veil swept over her shoulder,

and a shopping basket swinging at her side.
She chased and easily caught us,

and was about to land us one
when she clocked we were 'stinkin' little raggas'

and released us with an earful of expletives.
Fascinated, we followed her every time

we saw her after that, stood outside her club
until she invited us in on condition

we sat quietly in the corner.
She once confided to us that at our age

she loved to rub the soft fabrics
of her sister's dresses against her cheeks

and prance around in them to much laughter
from her parents; but many years later,

when they discovered her doing the same
and sneaking out to date a local shepherd boy

at night, they kicked her out.
She'd not seen them since, and felt brutally

severed from her past, blanking
it all out to survive.

She came to Londinium, aged fourteen,
feeling like an orphan who quickly

became an urchin, a rent boy in fact, working
in the shadows of Spitalfields Cemetery after hours.

But she'd inherited her father's ambition
and business acumen. The result?

Spank (saucy panties and nookie kit),
a shop for the lady with a prick and no tits,

but the clientele was pathetically small,
so after much market research Mount Venus

was created to fill the gap in the club market,
and was making a pile.

'The thing is,' she'd say, 'a life without a past
is a life without roots. As there's no one

holding on to me ankles I can fly anywhere,
I became the woman you see before you.'

We didn't understand much of it then,
but whatever Venus said was *memorabile*

and over the years her words sailed
back into mind and made sense.

\*     \*     \*

I was glad of the escort home.
Felt vulnerable, never had before,

when I was nil, when I was *one of us*.
Tranio was waiting at the porticus for me,

a veritable Vesuvius eruptus bursting
in his neat little grey tunic, black hair

coming out of nostrils, ears, neck
and so thick on his legs no skin showed.

A torch was shaking in his hairy hand.
He opened his gob: 'The master ordered me

to keep an eye on you, missy ma'am.
It is my duty to inform you –'

I swept past him, I was the *madam*, after all.
He was my *slave*, after all.

Venus rolled her eyes at me, I whispered
she'd get an invite to a private do chez moi

next time Felix exited-off on
one of his long-distance gallivants,

and I'd tested the boundaries
enough to do what I liked when he was gone.

I blew a kiss from the doorway, watched
her hobble back into the night, raising her skirts

over the open drains, exposing
discus-thrower's calves (thankfully waxed).

I would have more days out on the town.

# SISTERFAMILIAS
## (Relative Values)

A girl certainly knows
where she stands when a Grand Matron

of Rome-cum-Orgy Queen
comes a-visiting this *quaint little town*

or *dump*, depending on her alcohol
intake or stage of premenstrual tension.


The Divine Antistia
was Felix's younger sister, twice married,

twice widowed, stinking rich
and top of the A list of every feast

between the Palatine Hill
and palazzi of Neapolis.


Days before the dominatrix
was borne in on a gilded sedan,

PAs arrived, cooks were installed
in the kitchen, invites sent to VIPs,

and the guest room decked out
with chains, whips and a life-size crucifix.

'So! This is *Illa Bella Negreeta!*'
she purred, billowing towards me

in dazzling turquoise silks,
bright gemstones on every finger,

a face fashionably white with lead
and pouting ochre-red lips.


'Cute, yes. Young, even better.
Stupid, no doubt.' Her violet eyes

ran slowly over my flesh
and singed every invisible hair.

She brushed lightly past,
talking loudly down the hallway.


'Come, Felix, a hog on a spit
and flagons of wine await us,

though I'd prefer little wifey here,
hottie, plumpie and my sweet juices

dripping on to her wagging tongue.
You *lucky* boy.'


What Antistia wanted
Antistia got, but I was Felix's missus

and protected. She stayed
two weeks. Felix came to bed at dawn,

if at all, insisted I bolt the door
until he knocked.

I heard clowns, poets, castanets
and much guffawing in the atrium,

followed by screams deeper
into the night, which held no real pain,

strangely, and sometimes a child's,
which did.


'You will never be one of us.'
At fourteen I was no longer a novelty.

After eight courses, Antistia swooned,
her Medusa-style wig fell over her eyes,

a coma loomed if she did not finger
her throat to start again.


'A real Roman is born and bred,
I don't care what anyone says,

and that goes for the emperor too,
jumped-up *Leeebyan*. Felix will never

take you to Rome, Little Miss *Nooobia*,
he has his career to think of.'


My tongue became wood.
I could never speak in her presence

or to Felix's cronies, who spoke
as if they owned the world. Well,

I guess they did. My words revealed me,
their ornate diction was a mask.

Felix's father had been a governor,
they had dined with the emperor's children,

my father spoke pidgin-Latin,
we ate off our laps in the doorway,

splattered with mud. Yet I was Roman too.
Civis Romana sum. It was all I had.

## ZULEIKA AND HER GIRLS

Two ginger girls arrived, captured
up north, the freckled sort (typical

of Caledonians). Felix ordered them
before he left for Rome.

When approached, they clawed the air
with filthy talons, mucus ran in clotted rivers

from pinched little noses,
their eyes were splattered mosquitoes,

courtesy of Tranio, to shut them up.
Fascinating, so vile, yet something

just for me, id and ego. Pets.
I ordered Tranio to chain them

to the jasmine tree and went to bed.
But savages were in my peristylium,

sweet jasmine became the foulest dung,
I heard the pad of feet, my door flew open,

vulgar babble, quickly overcome,
my limbs were torn off like rabbit legs,

scalped, my brains scooped out
like lumps of congealed maggots,

dribbling from lascivious mouths,
my sex carved out, stuck on a spear

as a bloody trophy, before they escaped
out the window and climbed

on to the roof, howling. I awoke.
Cold to the marrow. Alone.

*Tranio! Shut those fucking cats up!*
First light, to Huggin Hill Baths

on a chain. Tranio flung them
into the hot water of the caldarium

(*such* a tantrum), then on to a marble slab;
oil and pumice was rubbed

into their ribby little bodies and rolls of dirt
scraped off with a strigil.

I was eating a sausage and I must say,
it almost made me nauseous.

Next, my hairdresser, dressmaker,
manicurist, until, as they are now,

little ladies: their red curls piled high
are charmed serpents, and white lead

thankfully subdues their flecking.
Valeria and Aemilia, I call them,

and I hope they will become –
my devotees.

## ANOTHER WORLD, NATALE SOLUM
### (Native Soil)


Extracting stones from dates,
a delicate task, to leave the flesh intact,

a rare treat to be allowed inside the culina –
only when Felix and Tranio were out

and Cook had gone to the market.
I could pretend – my very own kitchen:

brazier in a corner, hare strung up
by its legs, amphorae against the wall,

baskets of vegetables, bunches of herbs,
beef stew simmering, table in the middle,

us three around it. Aemilia –
her chest like a washboard, a timorous voice,

when she spoke, which was hardly ever.
I still struggled with their strange pidgin.

At my side, Valeria, of late the Voluptuaria,
always the more loquacious of the two.

This afternoon she was on a roll.
'Mammy an Faither were chieftens, ye ken.'

(Oh, really, where had I heard *that* before.)
'Oor hame was a big roon stone hoose.

De hail of oor village could feast inower it.
After wark, everyone gaithered for denner,

we'd sit cross-legged in a big raing,
an eat breid an stew out of wuiden bowlies.

Efterwards de Druids would tell stories
aboot de goads, oor granfaither

was chief Druid, he could confabble wi thaim.'
'Put the stones in the bin, Aemilia.

Now let's fill them with the pine kernels,
and a dash of pepper.'

Our hands worked slowly. Time was ours.
'Ye had to gae through a guarded gate

fir we were ayeways being attacked by tribus.
Mammy would leid de sodgers into battle,

hir lang heir flying behind like fire,
standing on hir chariot she was so ferox,

all in de scud, face pentit blue wi an owl
tattooed on it, horse on hir stomach,

lowping salmon on hir feet.
She's always thraw de firsten javelin,

then skedaddled, yellyhooin like daft.
We'd watch from de safety of de hill-heid.'

'Here's the salt.' I sprinkled some from a pot
on to a plate. 'Roll the dates in it.'

I went over to the hot brazier,
poured honey into a pan. 'Bring them over.'

What was this fantastic tale she told?
Was the world outside such a strange place?

'Is this story for real?' I challenged.
'Whit dae ye mean?' she shot back.

I let it go, tossed dates into sizzling honey,
a matter of minutes and they would

be succulent temptresses, ready
for his highness's dessert at dinner.

'How did you end up at York?'
'One tid we were attacked in de nicht,

no one expecked it wi de sey so roch,
Mam was killed ootricht,

hir heid taeken away on a spear.
Us girls an Faither were taeken as sclaves

down to York an when we got there
he was taeken by an agent to Gaul.

We were sold at auction an de rist,
as ye ken, is historia.'

'Yes, and you arrived like wailing beasts.'
'We were so afeared when we saw ye.

We'd niver seen a bleck afore.
Terrible things had happened to us.'

So, this was all about sympathy.
But how could I put balm on their wounds

when my own were still so raw?
Suffering? Join the club, girls.

'Madam, worse was to come . . . Tranio . . .'
'Enough!' I cut her off, surprising myself,

but this little bonding exercise had to stop.
Anger had surged up from my depths

before I could recognize it.
'You will have your manumission when I die.'

Where did that come from?
Their heads fell. Silence.

So this was really a bid for liberty.
'There's no way Felix will free you now.'

I heard a sniffle from Aemilia.
I wanted to order her to stop,

after all, my well was full, was it not?
I carefully spooned the glittering,

honey-soaked dates out of the pan.
'Aemilia, put them on a silver plate,

we three will eat them in the peristylium,
until all the sweetness is inside us.'

# PRIMUM DETERGE EAM
## (Wipe It First)

A mural on three walls: cloudy blue skies,
a pale green lake with water lilies,

a brown swan; water-nymphs bathe
under a weeping willow, sloping shoulders,

generous hips, chunky beige thighs
with cellulite, calves taper to ankles thin

as thumbs. Carved into the wooden door
a Cupid with thick curls, his arrow aims

straight at me. The floor has shocking-pink
love hearts inside yellow square tiles;

a glass window opens on to the peristylium.
The Mistress of the House

is left to muse alone each morning,
because the Master of the House installed

only one swirling-pink marble seat
with gold trimmings in this, his magnificum

Templum of Excrementum.
I feel the snakes breathe of the early sun,

sweat streaks down my arms
as I struggle to release yesterday's gourmet

cuisine, processed, mashed-up, trying
to burst forth into the aqueduct below.

I recall the camaraderie of the public latrinae.
Two dolphins leapt over the entrance,

the world of grown-ups: who was shagging
whom, the price of beef, which official

took bribes, the best way to make
your own beer. The concerted family effort –

Dad on one side, Mops on t'other,
me and Catoo in the middle, little brown

batties frozen numb in winter, sponge sticks
in buckets of water at the ready;

the crumbling, one-armed statue
of the Goddess Fortune presiding over

a semicircle of twelve ardent excreters,
her noseless smile blessing us

with health and happiness.
Dad's instructions:

'One, two, tree and puuuusssssh!'
And we did, regular as the water clock Felix

bought for the atrium as soon
as they became the latest *must have, darling*

of every upper-class domus Londinii.
How many years ago? I had lost count.

I am done.
Nostalgia is a most efficient enema.

I walk into the atrium, gaze up
at the square hole of sky. You see, our villa

is built in the fashionable style of the Med,
as Felix always boasts.

'Great for British winters,' I once replied,
as snow fell on to the frozen fountain,

its centrepiece a statue of a snarling Medusa
(a strange choice, but Felix believed

low-class intruders would fear
they'd be turned to stone, and backtrack).

Water poured out of her open mouth,
and her flying dreadlocks, which normally

produced fine sprays,
had grown icicle extensions.

I snapped one off and sucked.
Felix's face froze too, then a flame

of irritation swept up from lips to forehead,
not igniting into rage as expected

but metamorphosing strangely into desire.
A difficult one this, not wanting to arouse either.

He has grown more fond of me than expected.
He needs me to love him, methinks.

He wants to reach out to me,
but he can't reveal himself –

the son of a patrician is not taught how.
Sometimes he curls his arms around me

at night as if I am the most precious
thing in his world, as if I am his soul

and without me he would be empty.
*You make life real*, he'd often said.

*Instead of a list of goals achieved*.
That was as far as he could take it.

I search his grey eyes, notice the blue
film of old age beginning to show,

their whites are the colour of yolk; bones
which pushed out pale brown cheeks

are buried, puffy skin swings in pouches
from a jaw where it had stuck to it,

I imagine. He was young once, I think.
Husband, I know you not. Do I want to?

A smirk whispers on my lips,
but before he is sure it exists I flash

my cutesy *Little Miss Innocens Smile* –
he is a sucker for it.

'But of course we have central heating,'
I add.

# CAPISTRUM MARITALE
### (The Matrimonial Halter)

– JUVENAL

I

Ripples in your watery skin,
unseen beneath the volume

of groans. I hover
above the marital bed, the cat-gut

seams of our mattress split.
(3 courses, not 8, should suffice, mea delicia.)

II

Legs straight, you like me tight,
it is your size (and shame),

you tore me unformed,
drew blood before eggs ripened.

If I had a little girl . . .
I would call her . . . Claudia.

III

I have known only this, a shiver,
a million dreams expelled:

'Was I good?' *Magnifico!* I gasp,
floating down, swim

to the wash bowl, your dead sons
trickling down my legs.

# MODUS VIVENDI
## (A Way of Living)

'Good morning, madam.'
Ah! Tranio, Felix's bulldog, who lurks

behind columns as if spying in an ancient drama
on a demonic wife about to be caught

at adultery or infanticide or fratricide
or matricide or patricide.

He is short, less than five foot, and bulky,
walks as if bearing a sack of cabbages,

supervises the other subordinates
(I think we have fifty) with a gruff

street-seller's voice which reverberates
around the villa the entire day,

even when one is trying to siesta.
The legion of mice emerges noisily at dawn,

in plain regulation black tunicas and sandals.
They scurry up ladders to sponge

down pillars, wipe the gilded bronze statues
of the gods, clean oil lamps, draw water

from our well, empty the charcoal braziers,
dust the altar, weed the peristylium,

do the laundry. I sometimes think
that if we had fewer of them there'd be less

cleaning to do, is it not their dead skin
that creates most of the dust?

'How is madam today?'
He regards me with a subtle loathing,

I always feel it in my stomach, it does not
surface on to his face – so still

you sense he is a man of troubled passions.
I used to think the primary one was hate,

but today I am convinced the deeper one
is despair. His brows are stitched into a bushy

black line which splits his face into two parts.
It has always irked me. He *needs* a wife,

to set a pair of tweezers on them.
Tranio entered Blighty as Felix's manservant,

a ruthless sycophant, promotion
to Head Honcho was swift.

He surely takes the girls as he pleases,
a perk, but, as I stare him out

in this suspended moment, the clamour
of housework a faraway din, I realize

I have never seen him smile or joke.
He will die with no laughter lines.

'I'm as well as can be expected,' I reply softly,
conscious that my voice carries

a new awareness. I meant to say I was fine
in my usual dismissive manner

that barely conceals the sentiment:
As if *you* care.

'And how are you . . . Tranio?'
I ask, for the first time, ever.

*I* am supposed to run this household,
but he took all responsibility away

when I was newly-wed. I was a child,
sensed his resentment at my arrival,

at the attention I got from the master,
and he wanted a piece of me too,

the only woman in the house unattainable.
I would feel his hot breath on my neck

when I had not heard his footsteps precede it.
Would run and hide under a couch.

'As well as can be expected, madam.'
We do not look away.

'Yes,' I say. 'You need a wife,'
then rush past him before I see his eyes

spring out of their sockets and bounce
up and down on spongy tendons.

I add, 'I will persuade Felix,'
and I am off, with nothing to do,

but hot coals under my soles.

## DOESN'T TIME FLY WHEN YOU'RE HAVING FUN

My brain is dripping
through to the floor, my light

blue robe is the sky
and the sky seeps

into my skin, clings
to my damp bloated breasts, gathers

in a pool
at the top of my sodden thighs;

the appalling sweetness of honeysuckle
suffocates

my breathing, my ribcage
is crushing my lungs. I am dizzy.

I am cloying,
my flesh has sunk

into the lumpy straw stuffing
of my chaise longue,

my bones are welded to the frame,
I will melt into a pool

on the ground,
I will vaporize, a puff of steam,

and my lengthy epitaphium,
listing my great achievements:

*Zuleika Woz 'Ere.*

Valeria and Aemilia do not work
hard enough, the peacock fans I bought

last week barely flutter either side of me.
They complain of tiredness.

'Madam, oor arms ache so.'
I take a deep breath, though it will wear

me out, and tell them that dragging
boulders of granite in a convoy

of this nation's bipedal exports across
the midday deserts of Ægypt will help enrich

their understanding of the word *tired*.
At last the muted pad of a gong sounds,

my bath is ready, Cornelia my masseuse
awaits me, her fingers possess

the delicate touch of a flautist coupled
with the strength of an ironmonger.

If I am good to Felix, she comes every day,
if not, I do without. (*Such*

is the price of a blow job.)
The price of wealth is solitary bathing.

Valeria and Aemilia wait at the side,
legs dangling over high stools, calves

criss-crossed with thin leather straps.
I wish we could talk as girlfriends

but for some reason all they ever do
is agree with me. Spineless creatures!

My splashes echo around the walls
of this hollow room, pastel paintings

of scantily clad maidens by the lake
at Parnassus (my husband *is* obsessed).

I plunge down, hold my breath, ponder
the merits of never surfacing. Who will miss me?

After I have been oiled and scraped,
with all the finesse of a chef priming a skinned

pig for marinating, after I have been rubbed
and squeezed with all the finesse

of an expert baker and my body sizzles
like frying bacon, the girls dress me.

Later, Mops and Pops will dine with me.
When the patronus is at home

we have more salubrious visitors, such as

whoever he wants a favour from
whoever he wants to do business with
whoever he owes a favour to
whoever he has to bribe
whoever is a relative *and* well connected
whoever is handing out OREs that year.

Anyone not fulfilling the above criteria
don't get no invite. (Jove forbid

any of my pals should find themselves
sandwiched between a senator

and the governor in a reclining threesome
on a couch at a slap-up Chez Felix

when he is in residence.
Come to think of it, Venus would love it.

Alba too.) The wives of the Great and Good
talk over my shoulder – Antistia was spot on,

I will never be a Grand Dame
with a face of stale dough, cracks and all.

I am so used to eating alone, in company.
But a dusky maiden knows,

through their terrified glacier smiles
and the hungry eyes of their husbands

who will strip her naked and fling her
on the floor in the blinking nanosecond

of a Rapid Eye Movement,
that she is a knock-out objet d'art;

though it was a touch
disconcerting years ago, when she was eleven.

## AB ASINO IANAM
### (Wool from an Ass)

The Gracechurch Mob were late as usual.
I had been pacing the triclinium:

twenty-four strides in length, fourteen in width,
the mosaic pebble floor consisted

of six large concentric circles in a row,
grey on blue. The walls depicted

*The Rape of Persephone* in four gory stages –
all flailing limbs, flowing locks, a torn frock,

red streaks, screaming handmaidens,
a bearded Pluto, thunderous greys,

a pitchfork, wing'd babies. (Quite.)
An inscription on a wall read:

I    *Do not cast lustful glances at another man's wife.*
II   *Do not be coarse in your conversation.*
III  *Restrain from getting angry.*
IV   *If you cannot abide by these rules, go home.*

I wondered if my husband had thought
of telling his guests how to breathe, perhaps?

'Now, now, my good man, lead way.'
They had arrived. Dad was always pompous

with Tranio, hiding a multitude of nouveau riche
insecurities. It was another matter

with his son-in-law, grovelling so much
he might as well have walked

behind him on all fours, head nodding
like a mechanical wooden dog.

Under Felix's patronage, Dad's business
had expanded: he now owned six shops

spread throughout the city, had a staff
of fifteen, spent his days on inspection tours;

his gambling was also thankfully under control.
The door opened. Tranio entered.

'Madam, your father Anlamani, your mother
Qalhata, your brother Catullus.'

'Gratias, Tranio.' We had not met since morning.
We smiled at each other, for the first time,

ever. Mine swelled with gratitude
that perhaps we could be friends?

And only then did I realize that the sack
of cabbages had really been on my back,

he was not hunched at all, it was *I* who felt lighter.
He did need some dental care, I noticed,

when he smiled. I would see to an extraction.
Dad swaggered in as if he were the master

returning home and I the lowly visitor. Typical
behaviour when Felix was in absentia,

his swishy-swashy blue silk toga
over his swishy-swashy green silk tunica,

much too hip for a man his age, his wrinkled
brown left hand bearing gold rings studded

with huge ruby, garnet and plasma stones.
Mum slouched behind him in her black garb

as usual, head to toe, showing only hands
and face. She eyed the triclinium

as if she'd never seen it before, squinting
as if it were some dirty ghetto hovel.

My brother trailed behind in layers of trendy
yellows and oranges which illuminated

his gleaming blue-black skin like a torch.
He too had benefited from my husband's patronage,

the subsequent improvement in family diet –
had grown two heads taller than all of us,

yet still he possessed the soft, squidgy-lipped
face of the little boy I'd kick in the shins

when no one was looking.
We took our seats, Dad on the central couch,

Catullus on the right, me on the left, Mum
squatting on the floor in front of the table,

right in the path of the servers.
(You really couldn't take her anywhere.)

I bit into a sausage, scooped up a couple
of oysters, some salad, drank hot spiced wine

guaranteed to numb an agitated soul.
It was by official decree that only my family

could be trusted to dine with me
when His Highness was away. I dreamt

of the day I could hold my own parties.
Years ago I'd order in a singer, puppeteer or acrobat,

but I was a descendant of philistines,
who ignored them. Nuff said.

Today I derived my entertainment
from watching Little Bro eat,

quite fascinating, filling up his plate
in a panic if it were only three quarters full.

No self-control, you see, will eat
until he explodes, for his hunger is bottomless,

the result of having a great floppy tit
stuffed into his mouth whenever he cried,

yay! right up to the age of seven.
I have spent years pondering this lot,

it keeps the mind a-whirring.
'So! So! So!' Dad sang out. He slurped

an oyster from its shell, looked so awkward
eating lying down, never did back at Chez His.

'So! So! So!' he repeated, almost bald now,
his head a shiny walnut, tufts

of off-white cotton wool poking out
over his ears, his eyelids drooping with age,

two mud pools, heavy and impenetrable,
lurking underneath the hoods.

'I have importans news. Catullus is on up and up.'
He bit into a chicken leg, picked its threads

out of his teeth, made a sucking sound
with his tongue and lips, continued,

'My boy Catullus, my boy . . .'
'I know he's your son, Dad.'

'Don't be so impudens, girlie. I still your pater.
Show respect.'

Yeah, yeah, yeah, I thought, the father
who sold his daughter to the highest bidder.

Don't think I've forgotten or forgiven, buster.
'Tain't in my nature. I smiled affectionately.

'I know that too, Pops.'
We had never had a proper conversation,

whatever I said or however I said it
was always adjudged a big diss.

Sometimes I craved for the olden times
when he meant the world to me

(a time when my brain wasn't fully developed).
He waved an arm to his right,

'Catullus, sonny. Speak!'
But the Son of Sons was lost

in the Kingdom of Food, only a thump
on his back

while he sucked on a chicken leg
dangerously near his oesophagus

would jolt him out of it.
I snickered to myself, looked over at Mum,

but she'd stopped eating,
was thin as a liquorice stick, preferred

maize and bean stew to haute cuisine any day.
'So who's rude, Dad?' I nodded at the gannet.

'You too rude.' He looked askance at me,
stood up, adjusted his robes

at the shoulders, cleared his throat.
'This boy, this good Romanissimus boy,

of Nubian ancestors, whose parents sailed
single-handedly up Great River Nile;

this Catullus, my filius; Grandson of my Father;
Great Grandson of my Father's Father;

Father of my Future Grandchild; Grandfather
of my future Great Grandson; Uncle

to *your* Children (*ahem!*); Great Uncle
to their Children; Beloved Son of his Beloved

Mother, her Mother (his Grandmother)
and her Mother's Mother (his Great Grandmother).

So! This predecessor of those to come after;
this future ancestor and yet today, here

and now, last in line of all ancestors
going back to time beginning;

this ingeniosus boy has been accepta
at top public school for patricians in Roma.

Yes, to train to be officer in triumphant military.
I so proud.' Tears filled his eyes.

I looked around at the cheering millions.
'Fab!' I said, feeling the contents

of my meal churn in my stomach
like straw being mixed to make brick.

Such is the power of nepotism, my brother
the demi-god can barely string a sentence

together for all his educatio.
'Congratulations, brother dearest.

When are you going?'
He looked up absent-mindedly, blood

had been diverted on a desperate mission
from his brain to his intestines

to work his digestive juices.
'Eh? Eh? You thaid thomething?'

His balls had not yet dropped, he was still
the lisping pipsqueaker of yore. *Shame.*

'Congratulations,' I repeated.
'Oh, that,' and he went back to his True Love.

'How soon do thee depart?'
'Eh? Eh?' He looked up again. 'Oh . . . er, thoon.'

'Good,' I muttered, then said aloud,
'Good for you.'

I glanced over at the Virgin Mary.
She just sat there, her robes about her

like a black puddle, gazing at her one and only,
tears streaming down her cheeks.

'My boy,' she said softly, wiping her nose
with her right sleeve from cuff to shoulder.

'What a wonderful world we live in,'
I said aloud to no one in particular

and no one in particular was listening.
Dammit! Words were forming like rusty nails

in my mouth, coating my tongue,
scraping my gums. I spat them out at Dad:

'I've been writing poetry!'
But he'd over exerted himself, poor love,

his head propped up on one arm,
was nodding off.

'Poetry?' he replied eventually, an eye opening.
'Yes! I've been studying it with my professor,

Theodorous, in my Greek Lit. in Translation class.
He said it was absolutely imperative

that I speak Ancient Greek, but I said learning
one alphabet in a lifetime was enough, actually.

He made me read Homer's *Iliad*,
which I found bloody tedious, quite frankly.

All about the siege of Troy. I mean, who cares?
Just an intsy-wintsy bit old-fashioned?

Theodorous says I shouldn't write poetry
until I've studied the last thousand years

of the canon, learnt it off by heart
*and* can quote from it at random, *and* imitate it

before attempting my own stuff, and he says
it's imperative I start with hendecasyllables

à la Pliny Jr, but I retaliated, saying
I found the lot of it B-O-R-I-N-G,

to be honest, and then he really lost it,
said poetry's supposed to be difficult 'cos

it's high art, otherwise any Tom, Dick
or Hortensius would understand it, yeah!

Then he made me learn Virgil's *Aeneid*
off by heart for my Roman History class.

It's all about the founding of Rome. And it's,
oh, only twelve books long. Contemporary

'cos it's oh, only over two hundred years old.
You should hear him go on about Virgil,

*noster maximus poeta*, about how
the *Aeneid* will still be a classic text

in two millennia from now. As *if*.
Says all the notable poets were men, except

for some butch dyke who lived with a bunch
of lipstick lesbias on an island in Greece,

but she was really a minor poet and did
I know what asclepiad meant? Or trochee?

Or spondee? Or dactyl? Or cretic? No?
Oh, surprise, surprise! Well, when I did, then

I could give him backchat, and anyway
I'd never write good poetry because what did

I know about war, death, the gods
and the founding of countries?

But you see, Dad, what I really want to read
and hear is stuff about us, about now,

about Nubians in Londinium, about men
who dress up as women, about extramarital

peccadilloes, about girls getting married
to older men and on that note,

in the words of the great god Pliny,
*the one too early and the other too late* (ahem!).

And I don't care about the past
and I ain't writing for posterity –

he also says I should write for readers
five centuries hence.

Well, I'm a thoroughly modern miss
and who knows what life will be like then,

the Caledonians could rule the world for all we know.
So! So! So! I've started composing a few ditties.

At last I've found a way to express myself.
I know they're not brilliant yet, but you see,

if I keep at it . . . Watch . . . this . . . space!
Do you want to hear one?'

I was exhausted, my cheeks burnt,
my fists were clenched, my chest was tight,

I was frowning, I was frothing, I *would*
make contact with the aliens.

He-ll-oo-oo? Anyone ho-oo-me?
He was silent for a while, then just when

I thought he'd nodded off, he looked up,
made a sweeping pregnant-belly gesture.

'Tu,' he said, in a throaty, sleepy voice.
'What?' I replied.

'When you go make bambino?'
*Oh, sod off, you fucking wanker!*

nearly tumbled out of my mouth.
'Make soon, be a bona girl for your pater.'

Oblivious, Mum got up to leave, shook
the crumbs from her gown, went to sit

cross-legged on the portico, gazed
longingly at a star-filled night.

I ordered the servers to clear the table,
at which point Catullus's hearing

immediately improved and he quickly piled
as much as possible on to his plate,

and went into mastication overdrive, veins
popping up on his perspiring temples.

They left, eventually. The bloated
and boozed-out Boy Wonder was helped

into the carriage by three nightwatchmen.
The black ate them up. I looked up at the sky

Mum had been studying.
It was not one and the same.

IV

# IMPORTANT MATTERS OF STATE

A girl's gotten used to having six legs
instead of the common-or-garden two,

after all, one don't want one's glorious stola
trailing in the dirt no more, innit. Especially

when it's an orange and green damask
check with twisted gold thread, designed

by her favourite couturier Emporio Valentino.
My sedan awaits me and a train

of six slavelings – young boys, chosen
for their uniform height, curly hair

and handsome, big-nosed looks.
The sedan is custom-made,

pig and cow carvings adorn its wooden sides,
its maker's little joke no doubt.

Felix astonishes me, so lofty, yet no eye
for a workman's act of subversion.

My four bronzed sedan-bearers are waiting,
ex-charioteers fallen on hard times,

uniquely in this household, employees,
their bulging arms could crush a girl like me

(I do imagine it from time to time).
I get in, draw back the muslin drapes,

the sun is slithering down into the faraway
ocean, the air is beginning to tang,

my dear Alba awaits me.
I am borne into town where the workers

are on go-slow, we are not used
to these freak heat waves, but insipid

grey skies ten months of the year,
and insipid blue ones for two.

I take the path of the Walbrook Stream.
Alba's husband owns a small whitewashed villa

at Great Swan Alley, part of a new
development for the middle-class,

middle-income bracket.
Faeces float on the water,

I doubt you can drink from it these days,
and the verge is packed with the poor

out fishing, children skinny-dipping, the path
is clogged up with traffic, although bumpy,

it is more scenic than the road.
We reach the footbridge, turn left up

Copthall Avenue and we are almost there.
Alba's house has six rooms – she too married well,

but, whereas she stopped at four rungs,
I went straight to the top.

She is waiting in the doorway, calling out
to neighbours. Spotting my entourage

a long way off, she waves,
dying to tell me her latest goss.

She gathers her skirts and runs barefoot
through dried mud to meet me.

I feel a sharp contraction in my chest
for the carefree days of childhood.

Her once mousy, greasy crop, long grown out,
is swept into a glossy chignon,

her urchin's scrawny face fleshed out
with pink-flushed cheeks, her upturned nose

is chic rather than snub now,
her small soft mouth devoid of the sores

that plagued her childhood; taller than I,
she has gone from scruffy rag doll

to exquisite porcelain one.
She ushers me into the small lounge,

a low-ceilinged affair, stained
with the brown patches of lantern smoke.

'Come, let's take grape juice. Everyone's out.
Cato is off collaring tax-evaders at some

unpronounceable place in the bush
called Durovigutum, the nanny

has taken the grubs to the baths, the serfs
are out on errands. It is freedom time.'

I follow a ripe bruise at the nape
of her creamy neck, a little darker

than her lilac, low-cut, sleeveless tunica.
'So what's new and exciting?' I ask, knowing

that mundanity is anathema to her,
that she thrives on drama and subterfuge,

that I always followed her lead
when we were hoola-hooping brats,

getting into scrapes when other kids
taunted her with:

*Albaleta Skeleta!* or *Fester Features!*
'Guess what?' she replies, as usual, pausing,

forcing me into the ritual of:
'You know I can't guess, so cut out

the preamble and shoot from the hip, bay-bee!'
'Let's put it this way.' She reclines

in her wicker chair (a ladylike gesture),
then crosses her legs on its green linen cushion

into Lotus Position (a ragamuffin's one),
puts on a very received pronunciation accent:

'I have of late added to my list of amores.
Remember Sallust, the governor's secretary?'

'Or lackey, depending on your p.o.v.,' I replied.
She tutted but her pewter-goblet eyes

glistened with mischief.
'Here last night, late last night, in fact,

so late it was morning when he left.'
I tried to feign shock but this *was* predictable.

'Hence the lovebite, you slapper you!'
'A very adventurous lover, Zuleika,

reaching parts that a certain tax-collector
dare not explore. Let's just say

that my nickname for him is Donkey.'
'When the old man sees *that* . . .' I pointed

at the blossoming flower on her neck.
'Oh, he's away for five days and it'll be gone

by the time he comes waltzing in here
with his purse jangling with non-declarable

coins donated to Cato & Co.
by terrified victims who've been caught

fiddling their accounts.
Though I tell him that he and his gangster

colleagues had better watch it,
there might just be another Boudicca

out there ready to string 'em up and burn
the towns down.' She leant forward.

I was her only confidante in a town
where gossip spread like sewer rats.

'Horace!' she whispered triumphantly.
'You what?' I replied. I'd heard the first time.

'Horace! The actor. The *famous* actor.'
'You mean *the* Horace?' I teased.

'The one and only,' she replied.
'Wow! So you mean Horace the *actor*?'

She sighed impatiently.
'Not Horace the poet, then?'

She was about to hit me.
'Last Wednesday!'

I threw back my head and laughed.
I'd lost count of the ensuing break-up dramas:

*The bastard! The dog! The two-timing rat!*
*How could he do this to me? Never*
*trust a man with a moustache, a beard,*
*blue eyes, green eyes, black eyes, buck teeth,*
*gap teeth, small teeth, white teeth, brown teeth,*
*yellow teeth, pigeon toes, duck feet,*
*bandy legs, knock-knees, short legs,*
*long legs, fat legs, hairy legs, hairless legs,*
*oh, but I was so in love with him,*
*how dare he dump me when I could*
*have dumped him first! I'll never*
*ever get over him or him or him or him*
*or him (or occasionally her) or him or him*
*or him or him, that's it! No more lovers,*
*not in this lifetime or the next, nope,*
*nevernevernevernevernevernever* . . . . . . . .

'Do you mean never again?' I ventured,
wondering when she was going to learn

her lesson, that sex and love
were synonymous to her, so, for all her

'give it up girls' theorems, she couldn't get laid
without falling in love and getting hurt,

most of the fellas she went with only
wanted one thing, and those that didn't

she saw off. It was an addiction,
to the highs, to the lows, to the routes

towards both – but I kept my thoughts to myself.
I wasn't exactly an example of happily married bliss.

'Yes, I mean never again.'
'Oh, that's what I thought you meant.'

She'd give me a quizzical look,
too wrapped up in her one-act drama

to get my silly attempt at humour.
'Of course Hortensius is around,

but he'll bugger off soon, keeps pressurizing
me with *You Alba, Me Husband No. 2* rubbish.

As if I'd divorce Cato for a florist
and live in a tower block at Tower Hill.'

Alba caught Cato after fluttering her lashes
at his tailor-made cloaks every time

he came into the shop to buy a hamster
or squirrel for dinner. He wooed her parents

with gifts, flowers and an upwardly mobile
lifestyle for their daughter.

Now she was the mother of three baby girls:
twins and a solo act.

'Hope I'll give him a boy next time,
then I can stop breeding. What about you?'

Her tone was almost accusatory.
'When are you going extramarital?

You don't know what you're missing,
the whole town is at it.'

'Yes, but sex has always been an ordeal
for me, Alba. I'm used to it now,

but I can't say I really dig it.
I think I've got a libido, deep down.'

I'd wanted to talk about this for a long time.
It had been bothering me.

'You see, I discovered sex before desire.
At the age I married desire meant dreaming

about how to steal sweet cakes
without Mum catching me. Now, you married

a man you liked, therefore discovered sex
*with* desire. Big difference.'

Alba shook her head.
'My, my, we have been spending

a lot of time alone, haven't we?
Or reading too many books, I suspect.

Or are you on something?
Been eating those mushroom fritters again?

I don't know, give a girl an education
and life becomes much too complicated.

You're going too deep when the answer
is simple, YOU NEED A GOOD SHAG!'

She was on a roll – in future
I'd keep my thoughts to myself.

'You're every man's wet dream.
They'd be queuing up if a dusky bird

like you went on the extramarital market.
I could find you a man like that!'

She clicked her fingers.
'I know, I know,' I said curtly, looking

behind her at the wall which she'd crudely
painted with Bacchus and Ariadne.

Her perspective was all skew-whiff
and Ariadne appeared to have more bloody

body hair than Bacchus.
I could do better than that. Yet I sometimes

felt so inadequate with her,
so affronted by her ability to enrich

what could have been a humdrum existence.
Her exuberance showed me I'd lost mine.

I was supposed to have it all, not her.
I was the *It Girl*.

'Look at me!' She flung herself at my feet,
grabbed my ankles, stared up with a firey

intensity (*such* a drama queen).
Whenever I went introspective,

she got melodramatic, to put herself
at the centre again.

'Do you want a lover?'
'Why do you have to be so OTT?

Sit down and talk like a normal person.'
She glared at me. I ummed and ahhed,

twisting my neck like a horse straining
at the reins. She pinched my calves.

'I repeat, do . . . you . . . want . . . a . . . lover?'
Now her lips were over-articulating furiously

as if talking to someone deaf, dim or unable
to speak our lingo. I had to shut her up.

'Yes', I replied into my chin, almost inaudibly,
not sure that I did.

'Good! That's the first step.'
She let go of my legs, rolled over

on to her stomach, kicked her legs
into the air behind her, crossed them over,

and continued, obviously excited.
'Male, female, hermaphrodite, eunuch or beast?'

(We'd all heard stories about sheep-shaggers
in the nether regions of Britannia.)

'Male,' I said adamantly. 'Fully equipped.'
'Good! We'll work on it together. I mean

what does Felix expect?
You're still a teenager. Self-service? Bor-ing!

Yet he goes off to his German bints.
But I won't start on that one.

By the way, Zuleika, you're spreading
and you're not even pregnant.'

'I'll never fall pregnant for him, Alba.
I just know it, always have. I probably

can't anyway, he ruined me before I was ready.
He doesn't seem to care,

he's got her and all their blonde sproglets.'
'Fret not thyself over that one.

If I had a choice, I'd not have kids.
I should rename my twins Ball and Chain.

Now Zee, get a personal trainer,
lift some dumb-bells like everyone else,

or go to the gym. Your value's up
but you've got to maintain it. And by the way,

your frock's lovely, but haven't you heard?
Red is the new orange.

Now let me see to some grape juice.'
Rising in what appeared to be one movement

like a cat, she grabbed a chunk of flesh
from my waist.

'Gerrof!' I slapped her arm.
She glided towards the door. I shouted out,

'No! Felix isn't Cato, he'd never allow it.'
She affected a weary exasperation.

'Cato doesn't *like* it. He turns a blind eye.
So long as I fulfil my marital duties

in *every* department he lets it go,
otherwise he knows full well, I will go.'

'You would leave Cato?' This was new to me.
'If I had to.'

'How would you live?'
'What are parents for?'

'What about the girls, you'll lose them.'
'No one imprisons me. I'm not you.'

She swept out of the room.

* * *

I didn't want to go straight home.
I took the river path all the way to the docks,

picked up some scallops and oysters,
laid out on cabbage leaves,

from Thorsten's Fish Emporium.
Thorsten, a Saxon fishmonger, wore his pure

blond hair in a long ponytail, sported
a goatee, had always been good

to me years ago, with a wink and a discount,
even now when he knew I was loaded.

I looked into his kindly face, still ruddy
from years at sea. He was a bachelor too,

with no reputation for womanizing.
What would it be like to see him on top of me?

To have someone respect the *Handle with Care*
signs written all over my body, to look

into a sweating face that sought my pleasure
as much as it expressed its own. Thorsten?

'Is anyting ve matter, sveetard?' he asked,
in his strange, deep, sing-song accent.

Blood rushed to my cheeks, I hurried
back to my sedan without saying goodbye.

The city was smouldering, the docks
would stay busy until late.

I wanted its noise to drown out my own.
I had spent a lifetime avoiding

Alba's timely arrows of insight. Damn it,
she was so often right.

But was a lover really the answer?
It may be Alba's cure-all but I needed more,

I needed a raison d'être to make my mark.
I'd been working hard on my poetry,

I would work harder, yes, harder,
I would devote my every spare moment to it,

which meant most hours in any given day.
The storehouses and shops were packed.

London Bridge was a constant flow of oxen
pulling carts of farm produce from Southwark;

some soldiers rode in front of them, helmets
with red bristles, rectangular, red shields,

jackets glinting silver, their horses
visible through the crossed wooden

fencing, squashing everyone else to the sides;
trading ships were coming in, later fishing

boats would arrive, lanterns bobbing
on the waves; a store was selling glass

vases for flowers. I called out 'Quantum est?'
then stopped myself. What for?

I had bought a load, most of them unused.
Was I an idle-rich matrona after all?

A pathological comfort-buyer?
Barrels were being rolled off a barge

by burly stevedores in brown sacking
tunics and thick leather belts, or topless,

wearing skirts, every other word an expletive;
a pack of wild scabby dogs charged

on to the quay yelping at the thick legs
of sailors coming ashore in droves.

The Fisherman's Tavern was packed
with a drunken crowd of off-duty seamen,

displaying biceps with naked women tattoos:

*I Luv Mei Ling*
   *Zindiwe IV Me*
      *Yazmin, Mi Numero Uno Futuo*
         *Doris: Mi & Tu: IV Ever II Gether*

They were singing a raucous off-key
round of improvised sea shanties:

*Row, row, row your boat*
*gently down the stream,*

*merrily, merrily, merrily, merrily*
*life's no farkin' dream.*

The quay stank of fresh and rotten fish,
straw littered the ground. Four raggedy

slave rebels awaited exportation,
sitting against a warehouse wall overseen

by a spear-carrying guard, chained
at the neck and ankles, a sight in vulgar

trousers (unseen in any civilized town),
their legs drawn up towards sunken

bare chests. Builders were constructing
a ship at Blackfriars, a giant

white swan's neck rose before the mast
for good luck. Two fishermen ran along

the quay, carrying eight giant pike
strung on a pole slung across their naked,

scarred, sunburnt shoulders.
I had reached the wall; beyond lay

the River Fleet and beyond that the bush.
I about-turned, went back

down Lower Thames Street,
approached the Governor's Palace,

where I'd often dined with Felix at feasts
that lasted eight hours; attendants

kept busy sponging vomit off the floor
and furnishings, when the Right Honourables

stuck perfumed feathers
down their gullets, or, in the words of Juvenal,

*the guests soused the floor*
*with the washings of their insides.*

I took a left up the Walbrook, suddenly
ordered the men to stop.

It had been years, but I would walk
the rest of the way home.

# A QUIET BEDTIME VOICE

Her head
comes apart in two sections,

a fringe
with ringlets, plaited cone at the back, air

passes over newly naked
curls, moulded

to her face like a black
cooking pot, white

chalk is carefully wiped
off, dregs of vino, burnt

wood smeared
on to oily cloth, she

can see Zuleika now,
cormorant's wings sweep away

from wide cheekbones, jet
nostrils,

lips like bruised plums,
I am the deepest

of them all,
my amber necklace

is unclasped, gold
swan earrings slid out,

oval brooch
unpinned so my gown

slips off, delicate
fingers massage my head, skin rolls

away
from my mind, the day is over,

space, in between, tingles,
fingers uproot

the tangle
of vines in my shoulders, I

recline
into sighing breasts, Valeria

massages my fingers,
which ones are mine?

Aemilia
leans over from behind,

*Madam is sae blue*,
sotto voce in my ear,

*Madam is sae blue*,
her lips whisper-brush my neck,

I shoot wide open, my hands grab
the dressing table

to steady,
I am too often alone,

these wretched girls will play me
like a lyre.

## CUMULONIMBUS
### (or, It's That Time of the Month Again)

Wind, I feel you stir this blazing
summer night. This empty roof,
this sleeping town, this great stone wall
which circummures us.
I have never left its gates. What *is* out there?
Damn you, Jupiter. My womb is stuffed
with shifting cumulus, sky presses
down on my thoughts like the lid
of a lead coffin and I shrug my silken
nightie to the ground. Bring me
showers, make my red dye come,
wet these cupped offerings, swollen cones,
sore with ova, aroused with revolving thumbs. Let
the sky crack with silver. Let
me hear thunder. Let
me sleep this terrible, naked night.

V

# ZULEIKA GOES TO THE THEATRE

The emperor was in town
and some politicos were staging a show

to suck up to him. Valeria and Aemilia
adorned me beautifully and I wore

my favourite wig, which I'd bought
off an Arabian girl who was waiting tables

at a take-away caff in Bond Court.
It ran black and thick to her buttocks.

Aemilia cut if off there and then
and took it straight to my wig-maker

in Threadneedle Street. Now it's piled up
in intricate plaits and twists

with ivory combs and jangling hairpins
guaranteed to make ears prick up

upon my arrival anywhere. Felix left
three weeks ago. Dad sent me a theatre ticket –

he makes more of an effort now Catullus
is away at boarding school –

and I was carried through the riotous streets
to the Guildhall Theatre. Riff-raff

were fighting each other to get into the stalls,
the police were forming barricades, people

have been known to murder over seats.
My entourage followed with cushions,

chicken drumsticks, apples, bread,
sauces and an urnful of yellow wine.

The play began, a comoedia featuring
the fool Pappas and the greedy clown Madacus.

It was cheap entertainment for the masses,
it was tiresomely predictable, the audience

predictably boisterous, shouting,
laughing and cussing all around me.

I wasn't in the mood, my mind wandered
inside itself, where it was happiest.

Was this the highlight of my day?
My week? My month? Was this my life?

Then strangely I felt heat on my right cheek,
as if a flaming torch were being held too close.

The emperor was seated on a throne
some distance to my right, surrounded

by the excited hullaballoo of the male hoi polloi,
and I knew without looking

that his desert eyes were roaming over
my voluptuous corpus, my breasts

had become a sensitive second pair of eyes.
I glanced slyly over. I was right.

# OBSESSION

> His head is full of curls.
> He makes my mind a-whirl.
> He's big and power-full
> With the forearms of a bull.
> His eyes are burning coals
> That see into my soul.

It wasn't exactly my magnum opus,
but, as I'd never written a love poem

before, I forgave myself, and started again.
I couldn't get the most powerful man on earth

out of my mind. Nor could the town.
It was bursting with *emperana*: gossip-mongers

were pouring into the doctors with lock-jaw,
every social climber had their ladder out,

debutantes were *doing* new frocks and facials,
and every well-to-do matrona was assessing

the boobs and pubes of all eligible daughters
aged ten years upwards.

The town walked with a straight and proud back,
for not since Hadrian built the wall up north

had an emperor deigned to come west.
The city was no longer a minor

provincial backwater but could claim the label
*Urbanus, Heartland of Imperium.*

What's more, Severus was travelling single
(with only his guard of 2,000

brave and loyal men); the wife,
Julia Domna, aka Mother of the Camp,

had not come *with*, and his courtesan,
Camilla, an aristocrat of thoroughbred

pedigree from Lower Britannia, renowned
as his official camp-bed follower,

was now persona non grata.
Alas, she had passed her sell-by-date.

Poor old Camilla, wandering minstrels
roamed village and town singing cheap

and completely gratuitous ditties
to news-starved plebs about how Camilla

was really no Helen of Troy, tra la la, fiddle di do,
she rather resembled the Horse of Troy,

tra la la, fiddle di do, tra la la, fiddle di oom
pa pa, oom pa pa, that's how it goes,

oom pa pa oom pa pa, everyone knows
that she'd retired to her country estate

where she supervised the growth of parsnips,
trained horses for the equestrian games

and roamed incognito in the woods,
side-saddle on a pony.

# DUM VIVIMUS, VIVAMUS
### (While We Live, Let Us Live)
## OR, BABE TALK

'Whoooah, get *you*!' Venus sat
mock-open-mouthed as I recounted

*The Look* in great detail
and the passionate love affair that would ensue.

Alba fidgeted on her stool, impatient
to be centre stage again.

'Do you know how many men give me
*that look* in a single day?'

'I don't want your opinion, Alba, I just want
you to listen. I've never felt this before. It's fate.'

After all, Zuleika does mean 'The Magnificent One'.
'Yes darlin',' Venus cut in, 'you go for it. Wow,

I could be buddies with the future mistress
of Our Sev. Could end up Aunty V

to a bunch of emperitos.'
We were in Mount Venus. The bar was packed

and one of the worst bands in town, Nu Vox,
was playing the latest Latin jazz, badly:

Little Rex on antelope drums,
Prince Mahmood 111 on the lyre,

Puff Daddy Fabius on the tuba
and Madd Marcia on caterwauling vocals,

wriggling white triangles of flesh in a revealing
black stola made of fishermen's-net,

her dyed green hair spiked up with gluten,
lips smeared with charcoal.

She emitted glass-shattering vibratos
over a fusion of military marching horns,

the drum rolls of a mysterious Celtic cult
and the discordant twang of the harem harp.

Every so often a drunk punter would bash
his fist against his head, jerk shoulders, beat

his breast, stomp a foot and shout out,
*Groove on with it. Ah! Ah!*

Otherwise – they were completely ignored.
The Babe Triumvirate were in session,

huddled around a corner table, knocking it back.
Rocking her stool, Alba balanced

it on one leg precariously and folded her arms.
'Lissen-up, Zuleika, he'll be having a different

townie tart every night, so get real.'
'It's real to me. Sometimes you just know . . .'

'What's in a look?' she snapped back.
'If I'd've been there, he'd've looked at me too.'

'It wasn't just a *look*. It was like lightning
passing into my body and taking up residence.

This Über-babe is Über-charged, even now.
I'm buzzing. It's like my tits were my eyes,

they responded to *The Look* first.'
Alba sprang forwards, thumped her stool

on to its three legs, flung her arms open.
'He looked at you, for fuck's sake!

Do you think you're the only woman
he eyed up that afternoon?

Don't create an epic poem about it, Zee.'
'Girlfriend needs a doctor,' Venus joined in.

'Is there a doctor in the house?' she called out
into the room, all ultra-camp and sarky.

I mouthed, 'Watch . . . this . . . space.'
'Yes, dear,' Venus replied.

'You have 'im, then I'll have 'im, then Alba'll
have 'im, then the clap'll have 'im. What*ever*.'

Alba pinched her arm playfully,
but I wasn't laughing. Why was I the one

who never got her jollies, the side-kick
whose mantra was *No! You didn't!*

who went home to bed alone or to Felix,
same difference, for sex was tri-annual

these days, but, even as the thoughts surfaced,
I knew it really wasn't in me to screw

around willy-nilly like Alba,
to give myself piecemeal to the masses,

to lose something precious in the process.
'I will have him.'

My voice was quiet, steady.
Alba flung her head back, guffawing

hysterically or scornfully, I wasn't sure.
'He's too old for you!'

Faint spiders' webs were beginning to fan out
from her eyes. I smirked, imperceptively.

'Anyway, since when has age been a deterrent?
And haven't you heard about BDC?

Black Don't Crack. Just look at me and you.'
Venus looked from me to Alba, then vice versa.

'I think you've got some issues
to resolve here, kiddos?'

She beckoned to a barmaid. 'Some more vino
over here. Pronto! And make it *wet*!'

I drank the last of my honey wine, undiluted.
We were all silent and still for a few moments.

'Oh, Mama gets it. Alba's gone green-eyed
'cos Za Za's gone gooey-eyed.

You know what? Call me psychic,
but I think Zuleika's right. It's girlfriend's time.

What do the ancients say?
When the student is ready, the master will appear.

Give me five, Zuky-dot.' We slapped palms.
She turned to Alba, whose bottom lip

was pushed out into a six-year-old's sulk.
Lifting Alba's chin, Venus added softly,

'Get used to it, luv. The tables have turned.'
'Yeah, well, call me Cassandra.'

Then she turned on me:
'You'll be playing with fire.'

'I want to be on fire. I want to burn.
I want to be consumed. I've been dead

since my wedding night. I've been living
inside myself for years, I want to feel

extreme pain and extreme pleasure.
I want to risk death 'cos then I'll risk living,

I want to explode with desire,
I want to be drippy, drippy, happy, happy,

let it be sung from the rooftops,
Zuleika's gonna get some and cuuuuuuu . . . . . !'

I froze, for the room was suddenly silent,
not a cough, chink of goblet, sound of music,

from band, tarts, sailors, judges, firemen,
barmaids, refuse-collectors, stallholders,

accountants, ring-sellers, silk-manipulators,
soldiers, washermen, senators, policemen,

week-enders, part-timers, full-timers, old-timers,
new kids on the block – all had turned

to stare at me. Oh, sheeeeeet!
Coming to my rescue, Venus announced,

'Yes, folks, my girl here writes mighty fine poems
dontchafink. This is the latest.

Let's hear it for Zuleika the Nubian Poet!'
They clapped, unsure at first, then enthusiastically.

Alba grinned, squeezed my shoulder.
'Pax!' she said coquettishly. 'Pax,' I replied,

blowing a kiss from my palm to her.
Venus gave each of us a Herculean hug.

We were happy families again.
'Thanks, Venus,' I said. 'Quick-witted or what.'

'I have to be, it's a matter of survival.
Now you, Miss Self-Pity, have been protected

from the real world. You live
in clouds of comfort, talk to some of the folks

in here and you'll see how hard life is.
This is the underworld, baby.'

'Pain is always relative,' I replied.
Was *beat me up* tattooed on my forehead?

'Anyway! Change of subject.
Your Terence. How are you two getting on?'

Terence was Venus's long-time, big-time beau.
Last I heard it wasn't going well at all at all.

A married lawyer and father of six,
there was no way he was going to escort

Venus in her make-up and high heels
to any office dinners or political balls.

'Oh, he's around, my Tel.
He professes love but he won't act on it.

I remain his secret plaything,
and I'll not never be nuffink else.

Got to admit it. We've sailed the high seas
and now the ship's about to sink.

You know about the Emperor Hadrian, right?
Nearly a hundred years ago he cavorted

around the world with his pretty boy Antinous.
When said lad died prematurely, Hadrian

named a city in Africa after him, erected
over five hundred statues depicting

Cute Lips as various gods;
deified said lad, built a temple for his worship

(still going on today I might add) and so on
and so forthly and so rightly and what have you.

Now I've told Tel this little bit of history
a mille times. Precedent set many moons ago,

my man. Let's go public.
Just tell the trouble & strife

*Tuas res tibi habete*, in other words:
*Keep What's Yours for Yourself*

and she's divorced. She moves out, I move in.
But you know what? He's a coward. What is he?

I-G-N-A-V-U-S. Whadoesthatspell?
I won't go on with the charade no more.

Finis and next customer please. Whatever.'
She lifted her goblet, emptied it in one swig.

# MISSING PIECES: A PERFECT MATCH

Purple columbine, amaryllis,
lilac cyclamen, yellow chrysanthemum,

a single white orchid twisted with ivy,
all were wrapped in luxurious,

ultra-soft sheets of perfumed cream papyrus,
delivered at dawn courtesy

of the door-to-door service
of *Wild @ Heart*, the trendy 'flower boutique'

on Cannon Street, and, in bold italics,
a parchment note, each time, a word: *Anon*.

And on the fourteenth day,
a spray of three hundred exquisitae red rosae

(the girls and I counted each and every one),
it was pay-back time.

Oh, make me suffer!
Attached, the ancient Sappho poem:

> *If Jove would give the leafy bowers*
> *A queen for all this world of flowers,*
> *The rose would be the choice of Jove*
> *And blush the queen of every grove . . .*

It was simple enough to track me down,
one inquiry would quickly yield

the identity of the black chick
in understated chic sitting in the stalls

at the amphitheatre that afternoon.
Tranio arched a mischievous plucked eyebrow

as he handed over the bouquets
as if he and I were co-conspirators.

Wishful thinking, buster. This was *my* secret.
I'd convinced Felix years ago

that Tranio needed a wife, that as he wasn't exactly
mâitre d' of the Londinium Charm School,

he would live a happier, longer life,
everyone knew bachelors and widowers

did not last as long as their married
counterparts. I picked my moment.

Felix lay by my side, catching his breath,
oozing satisfaction, his sleepy member

curled up like a giant slug, still dribbling.
'Does he need one, do you think?'

he replied, the very idea clearly new to him.
'But of course,' I purred, wrapping

a firm warm leg around his flubbery waist,
and stroking his dazed, soggy gastropod.

'Everyone needs a one and only.'
I got the go-ahead, drew up a job description

and person spec, sent it to the Sales Manager
at the House of Venalicius plc –

the elite multinational slave-trading agency,
based in marble chambers at Poultry.

They replied by return of messenger
(the des res postcode of EC4 did not go amiss,

methinks), with a list of potential candidates
and quote for services rendered:

20% commission of the total cost of,
to be paid upon delivery. I made several trips

with Tranio to Queen's Wharf
to size up the latest consignments

from all over the empire, as well as native stock.
As they stood on the auction block,

I selected a short list. In no particular order,
my criteria: Beauty. Age. Dispositio.

Curriculum Vitae. References.
I marked them on a scale of one to ten and Mucia

won hands down with a score of 44 out of 50.

| Beauty | 8 |
|------------|-----|
| Age | 7 |
| Dispositio | 9 |
| CV | 10 |
| References | 10 |
| Total | 44 |

A robust, chubby all-rounder with a ready smile
and transferable skills, she had been a cook,

ornatrix and housekeeper with leading
patrician families in Noviomagus.

At twenty, she was pretty enough
to give a middle-aged man palpitations

when stripped to loincloth and brassiere
(Tranio perspired heavily), yet old enough

to handle the oft-displayed fascista tendencies
of our little enslaved dictator.

Stunted reproductions followed soon after:
a girl who still rolled about on her belly,

and a boy already strutting about the villa
on two short legs – rather like his father.

The mutually enamoured couple
could be heard after hours indulging

in horseplay in their whitewashed,
three-roomed bungalow which adjoined

the main house at the back,
built as a fabulous wedding present from –

Felix the Liberalis and I Want the World to See It.
Tranio would, of course,

henceforth be for ever in my debt.
It was collateral, should I ever need it.

# VENUS WINKS AT LOVERS' GAMES

Songbird Surprise
was my favourite dish,

and I knew it would be his.
From first sighting

I had imagined
being crushed into the imperiales

purple robes
of Emperor Septimius Severus,

his sword drawn
out of its gold and ruby

scabbard and plunged into me,
ruthlessly.

Oh, sweet death!
We were together,

finally,
in my triclinium,

a lyre-player
in the background,

as we reclined
on sofas, the low marble table

laid out with a little spread,
served in my floral red Samian

crockery: small songbirds
soaked

in asparagus sauce
with quails' eggs, dormice

cooked in honey
and poppy seed, salted fish

with oyster dressing,
my lord, milk-fed snails,

just for you,
fried jellyfish, bear cutlets,

sliced flamingo tongue
marinated in tumeric and clove oil, am

filling my hunger, par-
cooked

courgettes, boiled
whole, sautéed peacock

brains,
melt in my mouth,

you look across, am
stuffed

dates, torn between my teeth, sow's
udders,

lark's tongue in Gaul garlic, spiced
with perfumed peacock

feathers
and peppered

rose petals,
sweet wine cakes to follow, olives

with thyme,
is on our side, all drowned down

with finest African wine.
We were silent, letting

oils drip over lips
and chins, watching each other

lick it up with acrobatic tongues.
He was solid

like a gladiator,
my Libyan, my lover-to-be,

my libidinous warrior,
my belcher,

his black eyes
following the slope

of my shoulders, my shimmering
cerise gown, décolleté,

fastened with sapphire
clasps, set in gold, flattering

my shining bazookers,
the rise and fall,

with each excited breath.
He was in Britannia

waging war, he said, would leave
when the whole of Caledonia

had been taken,
from Hadrian's Wall

to the Antonine Wall
and way up to the North Sea.

His marriage was impossibile,
he said, his wife

had gone from swan
to donkey.

He knew Felix well,
had often dined with him

at his villa in Rome (news to me).
He called me to him,

nibbled my neck, his harsh
bristle scratching

my delicate skin, stuck
his tongue down my ear, making

me squeal, growled,
*Are you ready for war?*

## MY LEGIONARIUS

> I like you two ways
> either take off your crown of laurels
> drop your purple robes
> to the floor
> and come to me naked
> as a man
>
> or dress up.
>
> — ZULEIKA

Real soldiers wear tunics under armour,
my emperor does without.

Stands before me, metal bands
tied with leather straps

over a bull's chest, iron wings
protect shoulders from flying sabres.

I finger your second skin,
my lord, cold, polished, my reflection

cut into strips; your tawny trunks perfumed
with juniper oil,

hard with squeezing the damp flanks
of stallions, dagger gripped

for my forging.
Are you ready for war, soldier?

A centurion's crested helmet and visor,
curve of dramatic bristle.

Like an equus,
you roll your head, lightly brush

my inner thighs, leaving a trail of goose
bumps, and giggles,

then trace the tip of your sword
down the centre

of my torso. Dare I breathe?
Let your route

map a thin red line?
Silver goblets of burgundy vino by my bedside,

to toast the theatre of war.
*Close your eyes*, you command, a freezing

blade on my flamed cheek, hand around my neck.
I am your hostage.

I am dying. I am dying of your dulcet conquest.
You make my temples drip into my ears,

whisper obscenities,
plant blue and purple flowers

on my barren landscape;
here,

beseige me,
battery-ram my forted gateway,

you archer, stone-slinger, trumpeter,
give it to me, futuo me,

futuo me, my actor-emperor,
I hold

the pumping cheeks that rule the world,
I do. Ditch the empire

on your back,
Septimius,

it is crushing my carriage,
the weight of a soldier trained to march

thirty kilometres a day,
marching for centuries over roads

made with crushed skulls, legions
forming an impregnable walking

tortoiseshell,
on the battlefield, on

your back,
making the whole world Roman.

Vidi, Vici, Veni.
Take off your victory.

I am vanquished already, I can't fight you,
just stab me to death, again and again,

stab me to death, soldier.

# POST-COITAL CONSCIOUSNESS

suspended
on feathers we were
borne on wind windows framed azure sky far off silver
wicks flickering
embroidered silk throws
thrown to the ground were crushed indigo and crimson
anemones we did not stir soaked

anonymous limbs sprawled
a brutish arm sweetly

limp on my shoulder
deep breaths inflating his chest lifting
mine melded
chin into moist arc
of thick neck

mid-
summer mid-
night memory blaze

not since
the first months of life
had I felt another complete
myself

I knew
not
where I began

VI

# POST-COITAL COLLOQUIUM

'We exist only in the reflection of others.'
I was suddenly feeling very enlightened,

deep, and desperate to impress.
His lips puckered into a naturally

childish pout, reddish-brown, moist,
within kissable reach of mine,

and equally as fleshy. Long lashes, curly
as a newborn's, were at odds with a forehead

fronting a skull of smoothed rock;
two vertical thinking lines crossed

his frowning horizontal ones,
and if thoughts were things,

they would be storm'd waves, not outside
but crashing inside the cliff face.

I ran a finger down his bristly cheek.
This was as real as it got –

I'd just shagged the bleedin' emperor.
I wanted to scream out of the window,

do a frenzied dance in honour of Venus,
Glorious Queen of Love

(not the Glitzy Glamour Queen, but oh,
if *she* could see me now).

Venus, who sprang from the foam of the sea
(as you do), who was forced to marry Vulcan,

who had finally cast her spell on me.
After all these years, I had discovered

amore nihil mollius nihil violentius:
nothing is tamer or wilder than love.

'Aiwa, this is how we know ourselves,'
he replied, and I realized that each word

he offered the world was coated in certainty:
Yes or No was the language of my leader.

His voice possessed the rumble of a mortal
who will become a god when he dies,

I could already hear him booming down
from Mount Olympus, *I can see you-oo!*

I sat up. 'Who are you, Severus?'
I had discovered the miracle of love-making,

which dissolved the toughest carapace,
yesterday the question

would have been impertinent,
tonight it was simply – intimate.

He sighed. 'I am what I have to be.'
His breath suffused the room

with a sudden gust of melancholia.
'Who I really am is lost.

Was I that boy who went to the Temple of Apollo
and against music of night waves,

made secret offering to find out
if he would one day be imperator?

Whose father said, "Dream and it will manifest."
But when I replied, "Daddums, I *will* be emperor,"

he scoffed, "Are you mad? A Libyan? My son?"
Soon after I read fine words of Virgil,

who is noster maximus poet, of course.'
('Of course,' I echoed, a tad too quickly.)

'*They can because they think they can.*
I spent every night for years

visualizing myself wearing crown of laurels.
When at last time came to wear

what Picts call *Real McCoy*, it was simply
a case of what Gauls call déjà vu.

I had dream, Zuleika, that one day all peoples
on earth would be my subjects,

not just nine thousand k's of Europe,
North Africa and Middle Eastern territory,

but all those far-away tribes
of whom we know little or nothing.

Was I that boy who wrote poems in Punic
about homegrown gods Melqart and Shadrapa,

before he did similar in Greek and Latin?
Was I that boy who discovered that *colonia*

and *great ambition* spelt husband and wife,
but *colonia* and *fulfilled ambition* spelt divorce?

Who at seventeen sailed
down Wadi Leba on naval warship,

past crumbling boulevards, white colonnades,
past purple bougainvillea, and out into harbour,

past my waving familia, past the lighthouse,
past vision of salt caravans of camels

and nomads in the distant desert, traipsing
en route to hinterland to trade

with the kingdoms of the south,
while I headed north into great Mediterranean,

destined for HQ of think-tanks, spin doctors,
banks, commercial hubbub, intelligentsia,

and general razza-mattaza di Roma.'
He paused, arms folded

across his chest, black curls thinning
out as they trailed down to his belly button –

a lumpen warrior's knot.
I sat cross-legged, exposing myself,

what did I have to offer this giant among men
but my body?

He closed his eyes,
trying to recollect events of so long ago.

*I wanted to remake my town
with bright stones and glass!*

Oh, to fill his pause with my truth,
but Felix's refrain haunted me, still,

from the first days of our marriage –
silentium mulieri praestat ornatum,

silence is a woman's best adornment –
and I wasn't going to blow it tonight.

My own dream had been blown away,
as soon as my father heard it.

My girlish world was all colours and shapes,
a robe with fuschia stripes,

green cat's eyes blazing in a night alley,
the imperial beauty of the basilica.

Poems were meant to fulfil me instead,
but I failed to create pictures

with my words – or did I?
If he took me to Rome, to the desert . . . maybe . . .

His nomadic eyes settled on me,
so tenderly, as if my thoughts

had been spoken, and heard. I wanted to cry.
He stretched languorously, arched his back,

ribcage like the hull of a barge, protruding
through tautened skin.

He raised his muscled brown arms
to the ceiling – a messy old scar ran down

the inside of his left forearm,
like boiled goatskin. I wanted to stroke it.

He folded them behind his head,
cleared his throat. 'On road to omnipotence

I became centurion, senator,
magistratus, people's representative, tribune,

legate and finally governor.'
Pride and defiance infused every word.

'But I returned home often.
Lepcis is colonia, but prosperous one,

our vast olive groves produce world's finest.
That boy is the father of man before you,

who was ridiculed on arrival in Eternal City
because of his thick African accent.

Today he is icon to sixty million subjects
(give or take few hundred thousand),

yet he drinks potion of acidic nectar. Cheers!
To Managing Director of six hundred

squabbling, back-stabbing Board of Directors
running international Firm on Palatine Hill,

including other Africans who supported
that traitorous Tunisian dog, Clodius Albinus;

who became self-styled MD
while Governor of Britannia, committed

hari kari when hemmed in by my troops,
who removed his brain from his bollocks

and I, yes I, personally trampled
on his headless corpse with my stallion

until he was smashed chicken
(fitting end for coward).

Then I had him thrown into the Rhone,
to make nice chicken soup for amphibians.'

He chuckled as if recalling a humorous anecdote,
then his eyes swiftly shifted from ceiling to mine,

and speared me – all metal,
running cold down my spine, then melting,

molten liquid, flowing into the scoop of the bowl
between my hips. He took my hand

(if I could blush), a kitten's paw in a bear's,
rubbed my palm, suddenly dug a nail into it,

bloody hard. I held his gaze,
but flinched inside, flushed.

'Strong-arm tactics respected, worldwide.
Twenty-six senators executed for consulting

astrologer about *my* life expectancy,
five imperators killed year I took over Firm:

Commodus, Pertinax, Julianus, Niger
and Odious Clodius. *Septic Sev,*

they sneer behind my back. I ask you –
should leader be like lamb or lion?'

Somewhere over my left shoulder,
had appeared an audience. All the men

in my life did this, as if their words
were too important for my ears alone.

This was well rehearsed, over and over again
he had justified his position,

and now to me, though he need not.
He flung his arms in the air, shook his head.

'I am tired, Zuleika, tired of barbarians
clawing at my frontiers after good life,

tired of freedom-fighters, secessionists,
revolutionaries, seditious governors,

break-away factions, religious fantasists,
martyrs, spys, pirates and jumped-up

officers plotting to coup d'état me.
I am tired of hearing

*Sevva! Sevva! Sevva!     Out! Out! Out!*

*What do we want?     Freedom!*
*When do we want it? Now!*

*2, 4, 6, 8!*
*Who should we exterminate?*

This nonsense droning on in the distance
when I am trying to have my midday nap.

There are myriad descriptions
for these bastards, though I have just the one.'

He paused, twinkling, cueing me in.
'What's that?' I obliged.

'A pain in the bloody arse, my dear.
You see, I have simple motto:

*Give army pay rise and sod everyone else.*
Vanquished *will* protest, I do not blame them.

But may best man win.
I see him in my looking glass.

Enough! I am man of few words
and it has been long time

since I gave potted history to stranger.
It is like life flashing before my eyes.'

He closed his, for a second time,
I had ceased momentarily to exist. I rose,

threw on my silver nightgown, the marble
floor cooling my sweaty, sticky feet,

quietly opened the door. Two guards
were stationed outside it, invisible

yet omnipresent, my house
had been overrun by his Illyrian Guard.

I was a spectre, floating past, ostensibly
unnoticed, something yet nothing.

Be honest, Zeeks,
for all your pathetic poetic pretensions,

you're jus' a likkle housewife,
and to coin a phrase from Venus the Penis,

*you'll not never be nuffink else.*
I returned with a flagon of Dom Falernum

poured each of us a goblet.
'This,' he announced, alert again,

'is best sparkling vinum in the world.
Bubbles come from must pressed

from withered Ethiopian grapes, wine
is sealed in terracotta amphorae, stored

underground close to cold-water streams.
So you see, my dear, this is not plonk.

I bring only best gifts for such charming girl.'
'Cheers! Here's to longevity,' I toasted,

raising my goblet.
'Ah!' he exclaimed.

'Life and death. Who is winner?
Why can't Caledonians surrender?

I have only penetrated to Moray Firth,
morale is low, my soldiers hate the cold.

I *will* have Scotland. All ginger-heads
will come under my jurisdiction,

but they are bellicose buggers, have resisted
for two hundred years, are worse

than those bible-bashers in the east –
we are the chosen ones and thou shalt not

or you'll burn in hell unless you pray
to our three-for-the-price-of-one prophet.

You stamp out one lot, another pops up.
I am their ill wind. Only death will curtail me.'

He suddenly turned his back to me,
curled into a tight ball, a soft, maudlin voice

emerged, almost melodramatic:
'If I should die, think only this of me, Zuleika,

there's a corner somewhere deep
in Caledonia that is for ever Libya.'

Two toms hissed outside the window,
a barking pack of dogs raced

through the streets, way off I heard
the hypnotic drums of an all-night ritual,

the first cock crowed by the stream.
'What's the matter?' I asked, pressing

myself into his back.
'We believe in the stars in Africa,

and omens. Before I left for Britannia,
the stars said I will never return home.

Up north, an Ethiop with legion of Moors
at Hadrian's Wall waved garland

of cypress boughs at me.
It is terrible luck. He laughed in my face:

*You have overthrown all things, conquered
all things, now be a conquering god.*

Later I was in town to make offering
at Temple of Mithras, more Ethiops

were brought for sacrifice.
*Get them away*, I shouted. *Bad omen!*'

I slipped an arm around his hot midriff,
his body solid; I had never felt such quiet

physical power, unlike Felix,
who was like a sack of luke-warm water

that shifted to another spot
when pressure was applied.

'Am I not the deepest of them all?' I whispered.
He turned around, wrapped me

in his legs and arms like a warm bundle.
'You are pulcherrima babe.

You bring good luck.'
He rubbed his chin into the groove of my neck,

placed a hand on each of my breasts,
I felt my nipples heat up, grow slowly

erect in his palms. I looked beyond
the window, blue was gradually replacing

black, the stars had faded away, the full
moon was tinged with a translucent glow

that sent an eerie light into the room,
casting a shadow on us both.

'My beautiful anomaly, who are you?
Nubian, yet not. Woman, yet not?'

We lay listening to our breath as if still lying
on the banks of the Watling Stream

the night before, unable to sleep in the heat,
now oblivious to morning,

which emitted thin lines of brilliant light
through the shutters of the window

and on to the scenic walls of my cubiculum.
'I'm just me,' I replied, wishing

I had a great sob story to relate –
how I was abandoned as a child, ending up

marrying my old man, killing the old girl,
and was about to gouge out my eyes,

when the imperator charged up on a white stallion.
'I write poetry, that's all,' I half mumbled,

thinking, don't ask me to recite. No way.
'Julia too enjoys the finer arts!' he enthused.

Excuse me? Did I ask after the other half?
'She amuses herself with brat-pack

of luvvies for whom she is muse, favours
dishevelled boys in baggy tunicas,

who depict her nude in paintings and poems,
who graffiti *Vivat L'Revolution Y'All*

on the ghetto walls of Rome, then go home
to their parents' villas on Esquiline Hill,

with fifteen bathing chambers.
What can I do?

She will have her playthings and so do I.'
He leaned over, kissed my forehead,

traced my soft open lips with his,
leaving his morning breath mingling in mine.

'Is that all I am?' I asked, thinking,
there's nothing like a post-coital heart-to-heart

to put a girl in her place.
She was old, of that I could gloat,

she would be no match for youth and beauty.
The problem was, neither he nor she

knew there was a contest to be won.
'Perhaps not. I am rarely so candid

with all my women. Julia and I have good
understanding, she is my loyal companion,

but not my keeper, nor I hers.
I am what they call New Man, we follow

popular formula: *To Live Your Own Life.'*
*All* my women? Admit it, girl, you're one

of the many, not his one and only. Get real.
'But after first five years there are no surprises,

to second-guess opponent is essential,
but predictable wife? What can I do?

I am Sagittarius. She is Taurus.
I am swashbuckler, not couch turnip.

My sons are Aries and Scorpio.
Ah, my sons!' He shook his head.

Your wife is predictable? Then I will be zany,
exciting and spontaneous (for starters).

'Tell me about them.'
'They are alcoholic, despise each other,

abuse boys, embezzle funds, beat women,
hobnob with strippers and charioteers

and spend all day at the races.
What can you do when it is flesh and blood?

Can you feed them to cage of lions?
Can you pull out their fingernails one by one?

Geta is his mother's favourite,
Caracalla is mine, but he prances around

in blond wigs and Germania-style cloaks.
What can I do?

I am respectable, workaholic military man.
I keep them near me and under manners.'

How could your wife produce such wasters!
So it was Julia the Understanding One,

which meant I was just a charming new toy.
If she tried to rein him in, issued ultimatums,

he'd flee into my arms, wouldn't he?
What could I do?

His first wife, Paccia Mariana,
had died after ten years without issue.

'A local girl with intellectual catatonia.
She had no interest in machinations

of government and I none in beauty salons,
gossip and haute couture.'

('How terrible,' I had interjected.)
'You are too clever. I talk but you are silent.

What does life offer you, strange creature?'
When did anyone *ever* ask?

'I'm a nobody wanting to be a somebody.
I was born in this town, but I've never been outside.

I blame my parents, refugees from the Sudan.
This was the first place they felt safe,

so they never left.'
'What of Felix?'

We would of course come to that.
I sought the deceptively light tone that betrayed

the feeling I hoped to recognize: jealousy.
Instead it was casually dismissive,

this was a man who knew his place
in the order of things.

'What is there to say?'
There was too much to say,

but years ago I stopped reflecting
on my marriage, if I opened the lid

of that particular Pandora's box,
who knows what I might find.

'Like you, Felix is somewhat peripatetic,
though he never takes me *with*.

He wants this to be my world – little birdie
in a gilded cage, waiting for her master

to come home – and sing for him.
I have always been somewhat decorative.

Year ago he promised to take me
to his holiday villa in the Bay of Neapolis,

before the act of offering was replaced
with the belief that I was grateful for my lot.

My husband is a mind reader, of course.'
'Of course!' Severus laughed.

'My little minx is mistress of sarcasm!
What other surprises are in store for me?'

'Hang around and you'll find out, buster,'
slipped out of my mouth

before my mind shut its trapdoor.
'I intend to,' he replied, clearly delighted.

I could be cheeky with him, I realized, indeed
he even liked it. I was now on a roll.

'Anyway, that's where he summers
with his concubitch, blonde bratlets,

and other charming members
of the venerated House of Felix, or is it venereal?'

In truth it was I who felt like the concubine.
'Ursula.'

Now I knew her name. Finally.
'You know her?'

Once it became clear Felix would never speak
of her, or his children, I gave up all hope

of ever knowing my husband.
She was the shadow that trailed him.

He wanted my everything but only offered
bits of himself, the Londinium portion,

where he spends but three months a year.
'What is she like?'

After so many years, to finally know.
'Not like you.'

'You are too tactful. I want to know.'
'If you insist. Her face is scarred with smallpox pits,

she has black teeth, those that are left,
a moustache and she is completely bald, of course.'

'Very funny, big man,' I chuckled.
I pinched his side, releasing boyish giggles.

'No! You have found my Achilles heel.'
'Good!' I shouted, prodding mercilessly.

'If you insist! If you insist!
Ursula is beautiful in that aquiline

Northern way, so colourless her features
almost blur into each other.

She plays harp and trummel, she sings,
she describes herself as great tragedian,

though among thespians her histrionics
and high-pitched delivery are considered absurd.

She circles Felix at official functions
like white mountain lion, ready to attack

any woman who shows too much décolleté.
Do you want to hear more?'

I had heard enough.
I felt a tantrum coming on, it had been a while,

and not yet tested on my new lover.
'But you are much more astonishing find.

You are my sweet pulcherrima babe.'
'Of course! You big appeaser!'

'Do I need to lie? Have I chosen her or you?
On the other hand I have another motto:

Candida me capiet; capiet me flava puella.
I'm a sucker for a blonde – and a brunette!'

I slapped his arm playfully.
'What of her children?'

'Five boys.'
Now it was my turn to look away.

Why should I care? He showed me he did,
pulled me towards him, squeezed my face

between his hands, forcing me to look
straight into him, his voice strangely urgent.

'I will take you out of city, many times.
We will go down river to the amphitheatre

in Greenwich; we will follow River Westbourne
from Hyde Park to the jungle of Notting Hill,

camp out, have barbecue and if you are lucky'
– he winked at me – 'play slap and tickle.'

Then his voice sank, melancholic again,
he was the seasons rolled into minutes.

'We must savour every moment together.
Carpe diem, Zuleika.' Our cheeks touched.

'Carpe diem,' I added.
'Who knows what tomorrow will bring.'

# THE LANGUAGE OF LOVE (II)

After you have emptied yourself
of all the wars you have fought;
after you have shuddered and roared
and collapsed on top of me, sobbing,
your snores do not reverberate on my spine,
nor do you offer me your back, cold.

Always you ask who I am.
'What do you dream, carissima?'
your head heavy upon my breast.
'To be with you,' I quietly reply.
'To leave a whisper of myself in the world,
my ghost, a magna opera of words.'

I feel the sweep of your lash on my skin,
for my boy slips inside himself again,
to return to his core, his composure,
and I am left rowing with his legions inside,
a galley on a barren horizon,
when the battle is finally over.

# AMARI ALIQUID
## (Some Touch of Bitterness)


You come, you go,
some nights you stay

to shoot pearl drops into my navel
and marvel at childless skin.

I emerge from clouds,
sticky with fallen issue, to mute

spear-carrying guards,
and a house full of hushed slaves.

*Vale, Zuleika.* You stride away,
a palm-less wave, and I know

that to ask for more,
is to lose you.

VII

# ZULEIKA'S TRIP TO THE AMPHITHEATRE

> The Gorgeous Sev and I
> sailed down the Thames
>
> early one morning
> just as the sun rose o'er Londinium.
>
> It was our first hot date,
> we fed each other grapes,
>
> as we wafted south towards
> the forests of Greenwich.
>
> – ZULEIKA

A flotilla of barges left London Bridge
amidst much trumpeting fanfare, topped

and tailed by man-o'-wars and flanked
by cavalry outriders, who appeared

intermittently on the narrow paths
in between the foliage of the banks.

Severus sailed up ahead on the imperial barge,
long purple ribbons flapping

from the awning above
as he reclined on a couch and held court

with several senior sycophants
who sat fawning before him on the poop deck.

Going out with My Guy, I now realized,
meant there would be no splashy frolics

in our birthday suits, no bit-of-the-other
in the bushes, no stroll hand-in-hand

amongst the daisies while we gazed
into each other's dewy mi' amore eyes.

I would be nowhere near him, let alone
enjoy a good neck-twisting, jaw-aching,

lip-bruising, saliva-slurping snog.
Mistress Invisibilis had been assigned

a barge some distance behind,
with top-ranking wives who knew Felix well,

whose thinned raised eyebrows
and supercilious smirks begged the question:

How on earth did *Illa Bella Negreeta!*
manage to cadge a lift

with the imperial entourage
when the better half was off on an expeditio?

I was just working myself up to snap
at Valeria or Aemilia or to slap them, even,

when I clocked a young harpist sitting
in the V of the stern of his boat, wearing

a pastel-pink micro-mini
(usually the attire of ladies nocturnae,

*excuse me*) and exposing long shapely legs
right up to her crabby puny.

Her pale oval face, meanwhile, affected
the demure innocens of a Vestal Virgin,

while her thighs opened and closed
as rapidly as the flapping wings of a bird.

A fire ignited in my toes, soared
through my body, devoured my intestines,

heart and vocal cords, until it reached
my brain, where it stayed, roaring.

The plucking bitch! I closed my eyes.
I visualized. She stands. A squall arises.

She loses balance, topples into the river,
reveals a pastel-pink batty pitted

with festering sores, and the Thames
(magically metamorphosed into the Nile)

is alive with water buffalo, alligators, hippos
and an extended family of stingrays.

How *dare* she encroach. Bloody Harpy!
I *would* have words with him – a decision

that sensibly died as soon as it was born.
Was he attracted to her?

Was I just a flingette?
Was to love someone also to fear rejection?

A-M-O-R. It was tattooed on the fingers
of drunken machistos who loitered

outside bars and wolf-whistled at cute
young chicks, whilst grabbing their dicks,

pursing their lips and gyrating their hips;
it was what Alba went on about so much

that no one listened any more,
it was what my parents showed my brother,

what I'd never heard from the mouth of Felix,
and what Venus yearned for. A-M-O-R.

In the words of noster maximus poeta, yeah,
*Improbe amor, quid non mortalia pectora cogis?*

Oh, cruel love, to what extremes do you
not drive our human hearts?

I flung myself back on to clouds
of soft golden cushions, remembered

the nights crushed in his arms,
took a deep breath and calmed down.

The girls took it in turn to hold a peacock fan
over me, the sun, yet rising, could still

make my chalky face streak with charcoal.
We passed close to the riverbank, and

I stretched out my languid arms, brushed
weeping willow leaves through my fingers.

I saw the round mud huts
which I'd heard existed outside the city;

fields of cabbages, wheat, corn,
flocks of sheep grazing in fields,

wild horses galloping in the hills beyond.
I could breathe without fear of inhaling

human excrementum, or the acrid
clash of perfumes worn to annul it;

yet animal dung, I discovered,
was quite pleasant in its natural habitat.

We passed farmers in brown sacking tunics,
steering oxen and wooden ploughs;

they looked up, mouths agape, heads
slowly swivelled as our water-borne

paraphernalia passed musically downstream.
I floated and rocked, as if in a cradle,

to the music of a wind chime which a slavette
held up at the prow, my silver Valentino

robe with yellow flowery borders
spread lightly about me like air. I was pastoral,

I was a water nymph, I was in the land of the gods,
I was a maiden composed of pure ether,

I was so fucked up to have feared all this.
Ghetto girl or what?

Thanks, Mops. Thanks, Pops.
One of Venus's laconic gems popped

into my head. (She was *so* right.)
'Parents are to blame for everyfink.

*Every*fink, my dee-yah, *every*fink.'
Alba's voice jumped in too, ever the competitor:

'It's water. It's a barge. It's the sun. It's green.
Don't write an epic poem about it, Zee.'

I chuckled softly, wishing they were with.
We rounded a bend in the river, voices rose

in excitement, moving bodies shifted
weight. I opened my eyes,

everyone was standing. I rose, reluctantly,
looked dreamily to where they pointed,

squinting, the sun was now fierce,
and there it was – The Conqueror,

rising out of the tangled roof of forest,
a gargantuan spherical monument,

the likes of which the world west of Gaul
had not seen before. Surely it was one

of the wonders of the world, to stand
head and shoulders with the Parthenon

in Athens, the pyramids of ancient Nubia,
the Colosseum in Rome, embodying

the very ethos of empire: to conquer.
It was many storeys of stone high,

which had been quarried in deepest Kent
and transported upriver on barges; several

arched entrances circumnavigated its base,
blocked with people scrambling to get in.

Londinium was too small for such an edifice, so
the powers-that-be decided on Greenwich,

which would one day form
the southernmost boundary of the city,

from the River Fleet to the River Ravensbourne;
beyond that lay the marshy saltings

and impenetrable swamps of Thamesmead.
To its left lay several low-lying concrete

buildings, with a sign that announced
THE MITHRAS GLADIATORS TRAINING ACADEMIA.

A road cut through the forest from the north,
farmed land either side, carriages

and riders on horseback charged down it,
leaving clouds of dust and heat haze.

We moored to the sound of a heralding trumpet.
I was helped on to the banks,

lifted my skirts and was carried by sedan
over the mud. I had arrived.

## NULLI SECUNDUS

### (Second to None)

Severus strode towards the arched
triumphal entrance, his purple Armani toga

flowing behind him like wings,
his back straight, wide, unbreakable;

powerful thigh muscles flexed
over chunky scarred knees,

black lace-up booties crunched on gravel
and I thought, you, my darling arrogant

bastard, are just too damn sexy
for my face, *ta rah-tid!*

Nothing would ever get in his way, no one
could oppose him and survive.

He smashed a bottle of Dom Falernum
against the wall: this was his inaugural visit,

therefore the grand opening of The Conqueror.
He turned to the ecstatic crowds,

his be-ringed fist in a victory salute.
A castrato stepped forward, a slender

young man with earnest grey eyes
and lime-bleached curly-perm, thin legs

blending into his neat beige tunica;
he rubbed his hands nervously, clearly more

used to reaching a high C in the bushes
or singing for his supper in the baths

or for the Call-a-Castrato agency in Poultry,
which serviced private parties of dubious nature

and religious ceremonies of public ones.
He began to sing the Pater Patriae, fusing

the pure pitch of a pre-pubescent boy
with the emotional potency of a man

whose balls dropped long ago
and have since been well handled.

When he finished, there was reverent applause
as he bowed out, stumbling.

Stuffy formalities over, the crowd burst
into a jubilant round of *Vivat Emperor Sevva!*,

at which point The Severus, smiling indulgently,
raised his right hand to stop the salutations.

*Basta!* he bellowed,
and, swishing his toga like a toreador,

about-turned through the entrance.
His posse of the great, good and yours truly

followed behind in formal procession,
passing the lengthy stone plaques inscribing

for posterity a list of Britannia's
senior politicos at time of construction.

We entered the grand ceremonial hall,
its cavernous arched ceiling decorated

with vibrant reliefs of gladiator fights;
we moved through a damp-smelling corridor

lit by torches; climbed a stairway;
and, to a roar of fifteen thousand voices,

emerged out of a vomitorium
into the glare of sunlight and on to the podium

which housed the imperial box.
*He's with me!* I wanted to shout out

(just in case it's not obvious to y'all).
But Mistress Invisibilis was seated

with the other women in the dress circle
exactly ten rows behind The Severus.

I looked up at the clear blue sky above,
the tiers of seats which rose impressively

all around, packed with man, woman and child
in their bright, festive-best outfits;

vomitoria were built into the auditorium,
regurgitating scurrying latecomers;

each entrance had two tan-coloured,
wooden leopards fully stretched either side

on sloping buttresses, as if pouncing
on prey, heads down; the arena

was a giant pale-yellow oval of smooth,
unsullied sand. An orchestra

was positioned on a wooden platform
to my left, protected from the pit

by a bronze balustrade; they were dressed
in white tunicas with blue belts

and played a medley of ambient sounds
interspersed with rabble-rousing, jingoistic stuff

and hypnotic Celtic beats.
At one end, a man played the water organ;

at the other, women were giving it some
on the horn section; in between

were flutes, lutes, trummels, double-pipes,
pan pipes, harps, drums

and a quartet of ponytailed schoolboys
clacking away on castanets.

I found myself humming, shoulders jerking,
until my eyes, overwhelmed by the crowd,

roamed the restful beach of the arena,
registering for the first time the trap doors

around its circumference, the final
destination of our day's entertainment:

hapless beasts, both two-legged and four,
most of whom would exit prone. I shivered.

The Munera was our national sport.
I'd seen the banners, posters, tattoos,

I'd yawned through countless dinners
where the merits of prize fighters

were debated, I'd heard the soapbox eulogies,
the barroom bragging, and studiously

avoided the real thing.
This lot had looked forward to the big match

for weeks, had journeyed for miles,
some had camped outside for days

in goatskin tents or sheepskin sleeping bags,
street-vendors clambered over seats,

chucking up poppy-seed rolls or apples
or chicken drumsticks, catching

coins thrown down and putting
them into pouches whilst moving on.

A chant began to swell in the lower ranks.
*Why are we wai'ing! Why are we wai'ing!*

Until *Quiescete!* – shouted
by the coppers at the bottom of every tier,

spears at the ready – quickly shut them up.
I felt an overwhelming urge to take my rightful

place as official consort, slip my hand
unobtrusively under his clothes and work him,

watch him struggle to keep a straight face.
No. I would lift his skirts (and mine),

straddle him, send the masses into a frenzy
as I flashed my shiny, black, shimmering arse.

I'd sho nuff go down in history den,
sprawled all over the *Daily Looking Glass*:

ZULEIKA – THE WOMAN WHO SHOCKED A NATION.
It wasn't fair. We hadn't spoken all day.

I wanted recognition, I wanted commitment.
A tantrum stirred in my feet, but I checked myself.

It had only been one month, after all.
*Ave Imperator! Morituri te salutant.*

We who are about to die, salute thee.
Three hundred men were marched

into the arena by stewards, formed
into rows of thirty, came forward in groups

of ten to kneel before The Severus.
I had expected the famous Über-hunks

with pumped-up biceps and sex-packs,
the preening supertarts who were pursued

by every promiscuous debutante
who fancied a bit of wotless rough,

who were Guests of Honour at feasts,
intimate soirées and in-crowd orgy parties,

who were millionaires if free, and freed if not,
who lived in vulgares villae overstuffed

with Greek reproduction statues
and murals of themselves in heroic poses,

their penes super-enlarged and upstanding,
who were regulars in the news tablet *Ave!*

and were thus idolized by the lower classes,
analysed by the chattering classes

and satirized by the smug classes
in comic sketches at the theatre,

where they appeared as air-heads,
wot 'adn't mastered the lingua Latin proper,

wot didn't know their Horace
from their hors d'oeuvres, and who'd turn up

at the premier of a bowel movement
with their simpering, pretty-babe wives

wot came from the 'amlets of Essex.
But it was not to be.

Few of this merry bunch had diplomas
in Gladiator Moves from the Academia.

Most were from the ranks of old slaves, convicts,
Christians, prisoners of war and the poor

making a bid for solvency and stardom.
There were men whose cheeks

and bare chests had long ago caved in,
and boys who had not the years

to make solid the space between flesh
and bone with hardened muscle.

Tall, small, thin, infirm, it was only when
the ninth row came forward

that I saw that the back row was female,
beast-fodder, several noticeably pregnant.

*Ave Imperator! Morituri te salutant.*
Circus animals came on as warm-up acts.

Panthers drawing chariots raced
each other around the arena.

A tiger tenderly licked the hairy hand
of its owner. An elephant knelt

before the emperor and traced the word
*Yo!* in the sand with its trunk, another

carried an Indian boy in orange turban
and cream nappy, who did cartwheels

and handstands on its back. A bald man
put his head inside the mouth of a lion.

Then the real action began. Goaded
by armed stewards, buffaloes were pitted

against rhinos, lions tore apart the limbs
of jaguars, men were pitted against all.

A red cloth waved at a scabby bull,
a limping bear was pummelled with human fists,

a black cloak flung over the head
of a cross-eyed lion, pitchforks plunged

into mottled, striped or plain skin,
and pointed metal in the third eye

of any beast spelt death.
The crowd cheered as the victors

whooped around the arena,
doing silly walks, pulling funny faces.

These were the pros, the blood spilled
not human, pathetic quadrupeds

were worth less to a promoter than a star biped,
who'd entertain for years to come.

*Ave Imperator! Morituri te salutant.*
Five square iron cages on wheels carrying

five pacing lions were rolled noisily
across the sand by mules. There was a hush

as five naked women were led out of a trapdoor
on the left, chained at the wrists and ankles,

wild-eyed, scraggy-haired, gagged
with white cloth. Each was taken to a cage,

all were heavy with child. I felt a trickle
of moisture crawl over each vertebra

like a spider, I had been sipping some vino,
a mallet began a consistent tapping

against my temple. I recalled
that sometimes these women were smeared

with the semen of bulls and raped by them,
I'd heard it years ago and forgotten it

until now. The amphitheatre was a brazier,
it was too hot to look up at the sky,

the delirious crowds made me dizzy.
I wanted the band to play,

something loud, something heavy metal,
but they were quietly watching

as each woman was pushed into a cage.
I tried to put my eyes out of focus,

to witness and yet not,
as what had been human became chunks

for the butcher's block: raw tenderloin,
breast, brain, liver, heart,

were consumed until the lions, bloated,
vomiting what could not be digested,

surrounded by bloody meat on the bone,
clumps of hair sticking out of mouths,

stretched out on the floor, and slept.
The orchestra came alive, clashing symbols,

bashing drums, the crowd stood
and roared, and I with them,

*Encore! Encore!*
My tears subverted into blood vessels,

spilled out of ducts,
boiling red drops burnt small holes

into my cheeks, it was the girl
who so long ago had been stillborn

inside the woman, my throat was sore,
my eyes burnt, I screamed so hard

my stomach hurt, I rocked,
I hugged myself, the pitchfork entered

and turned, warm pee burst down my legs.
*Encore! Encore!* they cried as one.

Again and again and again and again
and each time I woke up,

it was my first night
in the Kingdom of the Dad, Dead, Father?

The music cut out.
Why did you forsake me?

The Grand Opening of The Conqueror
had turned into the Grand Opening

of my fucking Pandora's box –
and not since my wedding night,

had I cried.

# ABYSSUS ABYSSUM
## (One Depravity Leads to Another)


*Ave Imperator! Morituri te salutant.*
The living legend had been created

by a sculptor tapping away
for eons until he'd created cheekbones

worthy of the Olympian Atlas.
Instantly recognizable from graffiti art,

scrawled all over the slum walls of the city,
The Eradicator wore but a shoulder pad,

carried but a sword, its haft twinkling
with diamond sparks and topaz lights.

He was one of The Bad Boyz,
reigning champs of the World Wide Games,

the infamous band of glads who toured
the empire knocking out all oppo: Da Rock,

Undertaker, Sly and Son of Ty
(from whom women fled screaming).

To entertain his fans he did a war dance,
shaking his booty in frilly white undies

at the crowd, taunting the oppo, a little weed
whose see-through skin suggested

a hitherto extended stay in a Zero-Star dormitorium
at His Governor's Pleasure, his spindly

body lost in an oversized helmet,
thigh and shin greaves, metal sleeve

and round shield, as he tried to hold
a wooden, silver-tipped spear in one hand,

which suddenly lunged at the living legend,
an unsuccessful act of desperation

and no co-ordination, prompting
an expression of mock fear from our man,

who shouted, 'Ooh, I such a scaredy-cat!'
and then began to wave his sword

rapidly like a wand, entrapping
Little Weed in its dance,

following his shape but not touching,
up and down, over and around.

The orchestra improvised a slow drum roll
as counterpoint to his wizardry.

There would be no fight, I realized,
no mercy ah-beg-you, no thumbs-up

or thumbs-down, as he began to make incisions
on Little Weed's arms, chest, legs, nips

at first, red dots on white, longer strokes,
stripes, L-shaped cuts, shredding,

we knew what we wanted, hungered after it.
Now I understood it all, oh beautiful, terrible pain,

to witness you without my personal suffering,
let us know that we live, let us live!

Little Weed stood, so still, so life-like,
if he dared move, I held my breath,

how much longer, until the flow of life,
snuffed out, on the ground, now you

see him, que será, será, give it to us,
now, give us a little warm death

for the soul, until, spinning his sword
over his head, The Eradicator let out a war cry,

once more into the fray, we gasped,
dear friends, provincials, colonials, mob,

as he offered it to Little Weed's heart,
*such* a gift, who collapsed instantly,

with a weak cry, and 'twas Morte d'Weed,
alas poor fellow, his wound so deep,

such a sleep, he sleeps, we shouted
with sweet relief, we brought the fucking

house down, fucking brilliant, mate!
Who's the greatest! Who's the greatest!

we chanted, as the bad boy bowed
flamboyantly, ran around the arena brandishing

his excalibur like the Olympic torch,
while two stewards dragged Morte d' Weed

out by his legs, leaving a bloody ribbon
trailing in the sun-drenched sand.

None of us is guilty,
each of us took part, as limb
was severed from bleeding heart, I lost
my mind
was flung wide open,
found that demons danced inside,
you only know you truly live
when those before you –

of net and spear and sword and shield,
the clash of will
and skills, suspended breath
and disbelief, I was made numb
with the suspense of who will win and who
will – to each of them their fate
was in my thumb,
                    they live
inside me now all that was contained
has come undone.

VIII

# THUS ONE MAY GO TO THE STARS

 — VIRGIL

The Babe Three were lounging
on couches in my peristylium after a boozy

lunch of stuffed thrush and lentils.
We were limp goddesses, steeped

in lethargy, heady with the scent of jasmine.
This was our eternal summer, the first

for years when every day the gods
bestowed a ceiling of ravishing blue; the town

had shed its wintry self as if for ever,
as if summer's lease

required no yearly repayment.
Our clenched muscles released, our faces

opened, we smiled, no longer turning inward
because omnipresent clouds

pressed down to threaten rain, carriers
of a chill that seeped into our bones

and never left;
but, like the phoenix rising from the ashes

of deadened passions, we were reborn,
or so I thought.

Perhaps it was only I, covered in tingles,
as if his invisible fingers were always roaming

my flesh, his breath the very air around.
We lay as three muses,

so lovely, and so completely intemperate,
and now I had an imagination to inspire,

I would not fade.
Or did the sun shine too fierce upon my head

and create plants from seeds
that should have been left for dead?

How I craved to possess
he who cannot be possessed.

*A plaything!* A new refrain,
landing like an arrow on my temple

each time I remembered, more potent
than all his sweetest endearments.

All that I am not to him, I will become.
All that I need, he will provide.

Or should I stop drinking at lunch time?
Venus had been delighted by my news.

Alba said he just was using me.
'Come again?' I replied, to which she added,

'It's up to us to protect Zuleika.'
Venus snapped,

'Admit it, Alba, You're I-N-V-I-D-I-O-S-U-S.
You didn't snare the main man, innit.

I mean, omnipotent stallholders? *Excuse me!*'
Ooh, a bit below the purse-pouch, Veen.

But Alba could take on all comers.
'Venus, you're fake, every*fink*, my *dee-yah!*

about you is fake.' She began ticking
them off with her fingers. 'Clothes, voice, boobs . . .'

'Wrong! I'm true to what's inside me.
I allow the real Venus to float to the surface.

An' you sound just like me old man, Jeez!'
She began walking around the courtyard,

dragging her feet in leather flip-flops,
natural brown hair up in a ponytail.

I walked over to the rose bush,
picked off some crisped leaves.

'In case anyone's interested,' I called out, 'I'm

(a) happy
(b) having my assets plundered
(c) been to the countryside
(d) poems are pouring outa me like piss.'

'Glad to hear it.' Venus came up,
plucked a fuschia rose, put it behind her ear,

stamped her feet, clicked imaginary castanets.
'Fink I'll change me name to Carmen.

So when do I get to meet said hunk?'
Greatness would be hers by association.

I diverted: 'I want to be with him . . . for ever.'
Alba joined us, pale blue dress

clinging to ever expanding curves.
She fanned herself, wearily, like she'd lived

to a hundred and was giving us the benefit.
'For ever is a myth. For ever means

I hate you but hide it for the sake of the sprogs
and the security of your spondulicks.'

Like scales, she had to rise
so that I would sink.

The result? To weigh me down
or perhaps balance?

We muses always answered each other
as if in song; the words changed

but underneath the same old tune.
'Don't listen to her, Zuky-dot,' Venus enjoined,

'I believe in for ever. I believe in dreams.
I believe in finding my soul partner,

a life of domestic bliss, then sailing
off to Tranny Hades together.

Oh, to hear from my dearly beloved,
*quid nocte cenabimus, carissima,*

in other words,
what's for dinner tonight, darling.'

She began to sing, twirling her dress,
she grabbed my waist, we spun, we sung.

*There's a place for us,*
*somewhere a place for us . . .*

Alba mock-vomited. 'Slush queens!'
She crossed her arms, stood in a corner,

tapped a foot, aged eight again.
'Let's have a poetry party,' I sang out.

'Life is gloriosa! Zuleika est so felicissima!'
I stopped dancing. Venus flung herself

on to a couch, threw her legs up the back,
exposing three-day-old bristle.

'Tut! Tut!' I pointed at them.
'So?' she said. 'Who's gonna stroke

these Scotch eggs and say gruffly yet tenderly,
*Ouch! A little bit prickly tonight, luv.'*

'That's why we should have a poetry party.
You'll meet a different calibre of the male species.

I've been scribbling away for years now,
I want exposure. I want recognition.

I want a standing ovation!'
In truth I wanted Severus to hear of my work,

without the agony of seeing his judgement
flicker across a face I was learning to read;

to know of my talent through the acclaim
of an adoring public, to see

I was so much more than just a pretty babe.
'What say you, Albs?'

Alba turned away, not sure whether
to come out of her sulk, then chilling.

'Sorry, Veen, I love you the way you are.'
'Half-hearted apology accepta. What*ever*.'

Alba turned back to me.
'It's a brilliant idea, it's the in-thing,

I've been to loads and this manor is perfect.'
'I didn't mean here.'

'Felix is away, Tranio's your new best friend.
It's huge. It's luxuriosus. It'll be a gas.'

Venus nodded vigorously in agreement.
'Let's make it fancy dress too.

Guests can come as animal, vegetable . . .'
'Or mineral, perhaps?' I interjected. 'Bor-ing!

I was thinking of a recitatio-cum-orgy, actually.
I get to read my poems and the orgy

will pull in the crowds.
The tricky bit is getting poets to appear.'

'Sounds good to me,' Alba replied. 'Venus?'
'Sure, but no worries about an audience.

Everyone wants a laugh, 'specially if it's free.
As for poets, any old chance to show off.

I'll be MC, Master of Cunteries, darlinks.'
'Sorted,' I replied.

'Sorted,' Alba agreed.
'Now Zeeks, ring your ding-a-ling

and order some peppermint rosie lee
and some of that tasty carrot sexton blake,

we've got a happening to organize.'

# VERBOSA ORGIA

> Scarce a day has passed wherein we have not been
> entertained with the recital of some poems.
> – PLINY JR

Venus gushed over, all towering bouffant
and frou-frou orange gown.

'Ain't never MC'd a recitatio before, Zee,
only the Alternative Miss Londinium

at the Forum and drag nights at the club.
I'm so excited! Aren't you?'

My triclinium had been transformed into a packed
auditorium with rostrum, black drapes,

a sea of cushions and flagons of plonk
served up by Valeria and Aemilia, busy

pretending to avoid slappy-happy palms.
I'd gone for the literary sophisticate look:

floating black cape and three rings
on each hand, which I'd been told

was the least expected of all good poets.
Alba was flitting about in a backless

green frock, homing in on any young male
whose gems appeared genuine.

'Excited? If it means tap dancing teeth
and a cane for a spine – then yes.

I'll recite one poem and I'll go on last.'
I didn't mean to be terse,

but this new cocktail of hope and fear . . .
'Right you are, then, my little diva!'

Venus giggled. 'Now off into the fray!'
She pushed through the audience,

climbed clumsily on to the rostrum,
stood legs apart, arms akimbo.

'Right! Shut the fuck up, you fuckers!
We aim to turn you on wiv verse today,

but keep yer pricks in yer cotton knicks
till the end and poets, none-a-this

I'll bore you for five hours shit.
You've got ten mins each – max –

or I'll set Tranio on to yer an' you'll feel
his daisy roots right up yer kazi.

Say grrrr, Tranio.' 'Grrrr!' Tranio replied,
hitherto cross-armed at the door,

now beaming at the attention.
'Right! First up we have the magnificus!

The singularis! The splendiferous!
The fantasmagoricus Hrrathaghervood!

Give it up for the very real Authentic Pict!'
She jumped up, punched the air. 'Booyakah!'

Hrrathaghervood sprang barefoot
on to the rostrum, face dyed blue with woad,

snarling wolf tattooed on his forehead,
ginger dreadlocks down his back.

*There're only three groups of fowk I hate,*
*De Romans who're trying tae thief Scotland,*
*De Celts who've sold oot tae de Romans,*
*An de Christians who didnae wint nae bugger*
*tae enjoy thaimsels . . .*

He shook his locks, waved his arms about,
fingers bearing ten spoked rings,

as he strode up and down, shouting.
He finished to a standing ovation,

and comments on how beautifully
he shook his plait-things,

the exotic charm of his Pictish patois,
the symbolism of rings *as* knuckle-duster

and how brilliantly he *did* Anger.
Mesmerized by his voice, overwhelmed

by his stage presence, I had hardly
listened to his utterances, wondering

how I could possibly compete?
Venus clambered back on to the rostrum,

swigging en route and dribbling.
'Give it up one more time for that red-haired

barbarian Hrrathaghervood!'
She blew him a kiss, and winked.

'Come rant and rave at me, bay-bee, anytime!'
Next up was Pomponius Tarquin,

winner of the Governor's Award for poetry,
a stooped old man in a raven-black wig,

who swished his silk cloak disdainfully,
wore twenty rings, two to a finger.

'My new volumen,' he announced,
through Roman nose and pursed lips

(available at the back there for a discount),
'is called *Matter, A Moment*. This first poem

is called 'The Day My Cat Died'.
There are one hundred in the collection,

but I'll read only seventy-five of them now.'
There was a loud collective groan.

*Life exists, then life is gone. Such eternal*
*Questions, did my old predecessors, the great*
*Philosophers, pose. She was here, now she's not.*
*It was a grey day, the day my Posy died.*

Was I missing something?
I knew his sort, hadn't I married one?

To the patrician I was always less than,
as if my very birth were an aberration.

After the third rendition, the audience
began to talk, two plump middle-aged women

fondled each other's breasts in the front row,
an inebriated group was throwing

papyrus birds at Pomponius, until Venus,
hitherto fluttering her lashes at the Pict

(smiling surprisingly sweetly back at her),
finally noticed and bounced on to the stage.

'Awright, Pompy-baby, get off
or the bulldog'll 'ave yer!'

'But I have not yet finished!' he protested petulantly.
'Oh yes you have!' the audience chorused,

at which point he threw his volumen
at them and stormed out, muttering,

'Margaritas ante porcos! Yes, you heard!
Pearls before swine!'

Afternoon rolled gregariously into evening.
There was Calpurnius Tiro,

the 'mud, plough and sow' poet,
reported to be popular with sheep

and farmers nationwide, unfortunately
there were none in the audience;

Manumittio X, whose every poem began
*Take these chains from my heart*,

and finished with *I just wanna be free*.
Some told jokes in between their poems,

or just told jokes – they were popular,
as were those who sang and danced.

A gaunt, bald man announced
he was the great-great-great-great-great-great

grandson of God, donned a crown of thorns
and, as blood poured forth down his face, uttereth,

*Repent or the Lord will rain*
*Brimstone and fire,*
*Thrush and syphilis,*
*Herpes and gonorrhoea,*
*Divorce and unwanted pregnancies,*
*Vaginal warts and blindness*
*On Sodom . . .*

at which point Tranio had him dragged out.
I later heard he'd been duffed up

and left for dead in the street.
Verbosa Orgia had descended into an almighty

piss-up, feel-up and throw-up, the floor
was a pit of writhing flesh, grunts and gasps,

even Valeria and Aemilia were entangled
in a foursome at the back.

Had I given them permission?
I would have words on the morrow!

I felt as sober as a lictor,
the sensible one amidst mayhem,

yet I was supposed to be the Orgy Queen here.
I had sat quietly working myself up,

intimidated by the confidence of the poets
and the intolerance of the audience.

I looked for Venus, who had stopped policing
proceedings long ago, found her

on the Pict's lap, legs splayed either side,
hairy buttocks displayed for all to see.

(Honestly, I'd have to advise the girl.)
I dragged her off her new beau.

'Hello, Shooks, you shtill ere, luv.'
'Whatdyamean? I've not gone on yet!'

'Thash right. Shuch a brave shoul.
Isn't Hroshagurd luvverly. I call 'im Big P.

I fink ahve fallen in love.'
'Lissen-up, just introduce me will you.'

'Okey dokey, me old mate.'
She staggered over to the rostrum.

'Genlmen, the higlight of thish evening
is Zhleika, our very own Nubian princhess,

so SHURRUP AN' SHIT UP!'
She all but fell into the audience and all

but crawled back to Big P's lap.
I looked for Alba, who doubtless owned

some of the limbs sticking out
from the mass of worms in the corner.

My heart felt like it was gonna explode
and land messily on someone's lap.

I put my eyes out of focus, I felt faint, began,

*Identity Crisis: Who is she?*

*Am I the original Nubian princess*
*From Mother Africa?*
*Does the Nile run through my blood*
*In this materfutuo urban jungle*
*Called Londinium?*
*Do I feel a sense of lack*
*Because I am swarthy?*
*Or am I just a groovy chick*
*Living in the lap of luxury?*
*Am I a slave or a slave-owner?*
*Am I a Londinio or a Nubian?*
*Will my children be Roman or Nubinettes?*
*Were my parents vassals or pharaohs?*
*And who gives a damn!*

I found the courage to re-focus my eyes
and saw that the only person listening was Tranio

who nodded encouragingly at me,
in between uncontrollable yawns.

I left the room, for to strip and open
my legs was the only reason to remain.

## DUM SPIRO, SPERO
### *(While There's Life, There's Hope)*


'How dare you!' I screeched,
playing the Grand Dame of Londinium,

hands on hips, shoulders hunched, freezing
them in their footsteps as they entered

my cubiculum, sheepishly.
It was the morning after.

My pulsating brain was afloat in alcohol,
the result of six goblets of foul yellow vino

in the sleepless early-morning hours,
for after my show-stopping début,

my soul felt like a hollow bowl
that needed to be quickly filled up.

I had *not* been the star of the show. Factum.
The Authentic Pict clearly was. Factum.

Someone had to pay. Factum.
'Mistress non est very happy!'

'You have brought shame on me,
my husband, my parents, my ancestors.'

I was going to add, Yay!
You vixens will be responsible

for the Fall of the House of Felix,
but stopped myself just in time.

The room was still in subdued lamplight,
for I dared not allow daylight

to assault my tired, bloodshot eyes.
'Is it in your job description to have sex

with my guests? In case you have forgotten,
you are S-E-R-V-A-E. Whadoesthatspell?

Here to serve and obey, not get pissed,
cruise the joint, strip off and copulate

in flagrante delicto. I've a mind to send
you down to the docks to board

the first boat out to Gaul on the morrow,
wearing *lovely* iron necklaces.

By the way, I hear they do give girls regular
check-ups in the army's outposts of Syria.

What have you got to say for yourselves?'
I stared from one to the other.

Both hung their heads in shame (I hoped),
but sensed it could be fury, or perhaps fear?

It was so hard to read beneath the flecking.
Valeria, usually the braver of the two,

by far the plumper, prettier and brainier,
raised her head and started to speak,

but hesitated, closed her pale lips again.
'Well?' I said, as coldly as I could muster,

using Clarissa's RP classes to good effect.
(If I had known then how often

*How nunc brown vacca* would come in useful.)
Valeria looked to Aemilia for support,

but *she* looked close to tears.
'Madam is waiting,' I said, intoning

just like the late, gladly departed Antistia,
in fact sounding like every magniloqua

matrona I'd ever had the misfortune to meet,
with a little bit of Venus camposity

and the pompousness of Pops thrown in too.
What had I become? But a composite.

'We winted some dafferie, madam.'
'Fun? Is it not fun working for me?'

'Aye,' Valeria replied hastily,
'but nae that sorta dafferie. Tail-toddle, ye ken.'

'You mean you wanted sex?'
She chewed her bottom lip, nervously.

'Aye, there's naethin wrong wi it.'
The blighter, telling *me*.

'I thought you two serviced each other.
Sister to sister. *Such* are the times.'

'What we really wint is to git wed, madam.'
Shock did not register on my face.

'Why? Pray tell.'
''Cause it's what fowk do, isn't it?'

I glared at her. She stared me out.
'We wint to hiv bairns.'

Aemilia piped up at that.
'Aye, bairns. We hiv needs.'

They had never spoken of needs before.
What New Age thing was this?

Then the denarius dropped. Duur!
They'd observed me and my Sev,

and it was giving them silly ideas –
they'd never been inspired

by my sentence to the delectable Felix.
How could I let them marry?

I mean, the Vestal Virgins were just that.
Were they recruited from lustra?

No, they were pure, their devotion to Vesta
guaranteed to be absolute.

I'd have to find two new girls, tour the auctions,
it could take months to train them up.

What would I do without these two?
We'd virtually grown up together.

They kept me sane in this friggin' house.
'What about my needs?'

'You wouldna lose us, madam.
We'd still be yer personal servin' lasses.'

'Thanks for letting me know, Valeria.
My answer is, quite obviously – no.'

'Please, madam, think aboot it, at least.'
I went over to the dresser, sat down,

looked in the hand mirror, sighed.
'We could ax Felix.'

The girl was pushing me over the edge.
I did not turn around,

but watched them in the mirror.
'Felix will defer to me.'

'He'll dae oniething for ye, madam.
He'll even give us oor libertas if ye ax him.'

'From sex to marriage to manumissio –
all in three minutes. Quite remarkable.

Felix will do anything for me?
There is always a price to pay, ye ken.

You will have your libertas when I die,
as you are both well aware.'

They began to cry, hysterically.
'No!' I stood my ground.

'That's not a Y, or an A, but an N.'
'Please! Please!' they begged.

'We cannit gae on like this, we'd raither dee!
We're so non fortunatae.'

Here they were, chucking their pain at me,
as if I were a bloody sewage-collector,

as if I hadn't had a lifetime's worth myself.
They hadn't been thrown into the lion's den

with the likes of ille patronus, had they?
They'd lived the life of bloody O'Reilly

with a domina who'd never beaten them,
dressed them in exquisitus fabrics,

with nay an unkind word in all these years.
Other slaves were no more than sexual

chattels, or worked like mules,
or wore hand-me-downs – I'd dressed

these two in bloody Gucci, for Jove's sake!
Now I am responsible for their needs?

Tears began to fall down my cheeks.
I was supposed to be telling them off,

but they'd turned it round to their advantage.
I thought they were grateful.

They'd been such sweet, quiet girls,
floating around me, never a cross word.

Had I got them so wrong?
I realized I knew jack shit about them:

zilch, nil, nix, naught, niente, nulla.
There was that horror story years ago,

all about Boudicca reincarnate
and heads on spears,

but it was better to dismiss such things.
Life began for the girls when we met

and it had been good to them.
I needed to go and lie down, this day

should really pass by without me in it.
It was Aemilia's turn to make a pitch.

'We miss hame so much. Every nicht
we talk aboot it afore we go to dormio.

We picter everyone, hearken their vices.
We miss de air, de hulls . . .'

'Accept your fate like everyone else.
What we have is all we can hope for.'

Who was I kidding? I never stopped
plotting these days.

'My head feels a thousand times worse.
Bring me the hair of the dog, remove

my make-up, I'm going back to bed.'
'Will ye forethink yer answer, madam?'

'There's nothing to reconsider, Valeria,
and if you continue to pester me

you'll be back in those identity tags,
*Hold me lest I flee & return me to my master.*

You will remember the early days.
Now stop the bloody whingeing.'

They worked quietly, cleaning my face with oil
and cloth, hands gentle and assured,

as they'd always been, but what I now felt
was pure odium oozing out of every freckled pore

in their bodies. I was the person this world
had created me to be, and so were they,

though who I was becoming,
I was not so sure any more.

208

Our lives were in the hands of the gods,
though we could tinker with them, if lucky.

If lucky I will end up far away from here,
at my beloved's side, they can come with,

I will need them in a strange land; then
and only then can they marry.

Of this they will know, as and when.
One thing I knew for sure –

I had suddenly become
Public Enemy Numerus Primus. Factum.

'Za Za, you were da bomb.'
Venus landed two smackers on my cheeks.

'Star of the show, girlfriend!'
Alba gave me a body-popping hug.

'Thanks, but that's a bit rich considering
neither of you listened.'

'Oh, but we did,' they replied, looking as pleadingly
earnest as two liars could.

We were in the atrium, two days later.
I moved to the edge of the fountain,

where Medusa spat on my neck.
'No, you didn't.' I hastily wiped away an escaped

tear before others cottoned on and followed.
Venus put an arm around me.

'Sorry. Guilty as charged. I got drunk.'
'Me too,' Alba admitted. 'I was so excited

at being at my first orgy in months.'
'Surely there's more to life than sex?'

I raised a brow, cut an eye at her.
'Such as?'

'Listening to your best friend's first reading?'
She knew not where to look.

You were never going to sit and watch
me be a somebody, were you, Albs?

'Let's forget it. I went on too late.
No one cheered, said I was brilliant

or the Next Big Thing. Nothing.
I've had it with poetry. Finis.

My future lies with Severus, I've decided,
I'm going to make damn sure he marries me.'

Shock instantly replaced grovelling
on their pathetic, humbled mugs.

Venus jumped in: 'Zuleika, that's silly,
poetry's your lifeline, who cares if they don't clap,

it's not about that, it's about the art.'
Eager to change the subject, eh?

'It's about a standing ovation, Venus.
It's not fair, my whole life

has been one long trail of diarrhoea!'
'Are you premenstrual?' Here we go!

Alba's usual catty remark when conversations
got too deep and she wanted to shut me up.

'Oh, don't talk to me about periods,'
Venus exclaimed, shaking her head,

as if they were the bane of her life.
Alba and I, restraining our laughter, shouted

together, 'Shut up!', united again.
Venus took my chin in her hand, her motherly

gesture – she had several.
'A mistress has to be *strategic*, darling.

Ask for nothing, outright, anyway, never complain,
always give it up, take each day as it comes.'

She'd suddenly gone very RP.
'I'm with Veen,' Alba agreed.

'Be cautious. Be clever. Be calculating.'
'Point taken,' I said, thinking, yeah, right,

you two aren't exactly my role models.
I was my own best adviser on this one.

'So, Miss Venus, the Authentic Pict, eh?'
'To be honest, I'm very surprised at you,'

Alba butted in, frowning.
'I thought you wanted Normal.

I thought you wanted Stable.
I thought you wanted Respectable.'

Venus stretched her arms to the sky, the sun
nourishing her glowing face, devoid of slap.

'He's all those things, believe you me.
He's actually a very sweet young man

who wants to settle down.
We're both actors in one sense,

sensitive souls in this cruel, cruel world.
Do you know his real name is Robbie

and that he was born fifty miles south
of the Antonine Wall, so he's not a real Pict.'

It felt right, him and him.
'What's with the posh accent?' I asked.

'Ain't not never 'eard the like before, luv.'
'Actually, Alba was spot on, as usual,

it's time for the real me to come out of the trunk.
I've a skeleton under the bed, girlfriends.

Daddy was a leading senator in Rome,
he owns a massive estate in Camulodunum.

He also heads an important consortium
of loaded east-coast landowners.

I'd love to take Big P to meet the parents.
It's been fifteen years.

We'll hide in the bushes, jump out
when they go for their passata,

give the old bat and old bag heart seizure,
then the only son will inherit. I missed them

for years, you know, sent many an epistula
with the imperial postal service, each one

costing entry into the mysterious world
of my back passage, offering an olive branch

and my address, wherever it was in those days,
er . . . second tree from left outside the Forum

. . . er . . . third boat from bridge on the beach.
Did they reply? Even when I settled?

I'd love to turn their home-on-the-range
into an upmarket health farm,

call it The Steam Palazzo, for the RQN,
Retired Queen's Network, darlings.

I'm truly tiring of inner-city life,
These days I dream about running through fields,

the wind blowing through my wig,
and a buck-naked Big P panting after me

and flinging me down on a bed of buttercups.
Let's get some fresh air, come along.'

We went for a walk down to the river front,
linking arms, Venus in the middle,

our steps easily in rhythm with each other.
Singing loudly, we ignored

the bemused stares of those poor souls
on the docks who still lived in one room

with a bog hole in the corner
and a stove in the middle.

Life could be worse, I suppose.
*We are the three amicas!*

IX

# EVERY LOVER IS A SOLDIER
## (Militat Omnis Amans)

– OVID

We had left the city fortress at dawn,
crossing the small bridge over the River Fleet,

startling sleepy young sentries,
trembling hand-across-chest salutes,

our rattling open carriage which you drove,
whipping the rears of four furious stallions,

as you tore ferociously down the Strand,
profile fierce as Pluto, hungry for speed,

addicted to the pulse of battle.
Farmland spread up in hills to the right,

a ghostly, mist-filled Thames to the left,
three hundred armed guards galloping

on horseback, flashing red capes
up ahead, and behind; wagons with our provisions –

without the paraphernalia of state, this time,
the Great Danes and stuffed togas.

I thank you for that.
We climbed the winding path of Haymarket,

arms of trees forming an arbour, emerged
out of the cloud of mist into daylight.

I held on to my seat, as we raced
over the wild sloping grassland of Mayfair,

cut across the wheatfields of Hyde Park,
passed a sleeping hamlet of mud huts

by the Serpentine, followed the lumpen banks
of the River Westbourne, as our cavalcade

edged slowly into the humid jungle
at Bayswater, soldiers up ahead

cutting a path with axes. We entered afternoon,
sunlight began to filter through the trees.

I relaxed in my seat, surprised
by the noisy conversations of insects

and birds tree-hopping, frightened
small hoofs escaping into the undergrowth.

A large black spider,
suspended from a branch by a fragile thread,

almost brushed my face.
I inhaled the dew-soaked earth, damp bark,

wet fronds, a single
blade, wearing an opalescent earring,

at its tip. I offered
my naked, wind-beaten cheeks to the sun –

the humid breath of summer.
We crawled along a tributary, arrived at Notting Hill,

discovered an overgrown clearing
where the jungle swept down at Portobello,

quickly disentangled by our army of sickles.
A large Bedouin tent was erected,

a camp for the soldiers in the woods
who had been stationed at every stage

of our journey, you said, and beyond
to Kensington High and way out to Fulham.

*Yay! Such is the burden of omnipotens,
my dear.* I went exploring, wolves, bears,

savages were unwelcome visitors
in my mind. I flung them out,

I knew I was safe, here with you,
and three hundred soldiers.

I snapped the stems of forget-me-nots
from the base of a tree, found a raspberry bush,

picked a handful for you,
fed them on to your tongue, one by one.

We sat listlessly under an awning, ordered
flagons of beer, rustic-stylee,

a gong for room service, the air was heavy,
a wild hog roasted slowly on a spit,

basted with garlic and lovage oil,
mingling with the heady aroma of wood smoke.

I deepened my breaths,
you ripped its succulent hide apart

with your hands and proffered
with chunks of bread dipped in garum.

We tore at our feast, starving,
until we could not move,

you lay your lethargic head on my lap,
let the strain drain away.

'Why did you pick me?' I asked,
for I was in the mood for compliments.

'You were like desert girl in Londinium.
So beautiful. I will never see desert again.'

'Don't say that. Of course you will.'
'You cannot argue with science of stars.

Why did you like me?'
What, apart from the obvious, I thought.

Men with power et cetera.
Surely you can't be that naive, our Sev?

But in truth there was more to it.
'I knew you would make my world larger.

It was *so* small, inside and out,
I would discover more of myself through you.

Will you tell me about the Sahara?'
'We call it Bahr-bela-ma, sea without water.

Desert must be respected, it is ruthless.
Yes, worse than emperor, if it is possible.

Early Romans were afraid of desert,
it stopped empire going further south.

Like sky it can be all colours, reds, golds,
purples, black, silver, remarkable, like sky,

and like sky, you can see for ever.
It is colder at night than in Scotland. Yes!

In daytime is sun outside? No, sun is inside you,
and if you have no water, it erupts as blisters,

absorbs all your fluid, until you shrivel up and die.
Sometimes you are in middle of massif,

other times shifting dunes are everywhere,
for desert is always changing, it is rock

which billennia have crushed
into tiny particles of sand.

Sometimes you see salt caravans
of more than 30,000 camels,

stretching for miles.
Salt is sold ounce for ounce for gold.

It is like mirage, when you see something
that is not there. So wonderful.

Sometimes you will find oasis: palm trees,
pools, cash-and-carry shop,

but most of it is barren, a waste land,
then nomads wash in sand, not water.

You cannot imagine how beautiful it is, Zuleika.
Britannia is like pigs' ca ca in comparison.'

He waved a dismissive arm at the jungle,
took his goblet and clinked mine.

'Cheers! To Sahara!'
Then the blue sky quickly filled with thunderheads,

broke over us, lightning shot
out of the forefinger of Jupiter.

And then it rained, it rained et pluviam,
et pluviam et plurimam pluviam.

We ran inside the tent, you lay sprawled
on luxurious burgundy eastern rugs,

as a battalion of iron balls
descended through the leafy canopy

of old oak trees, battered the canvas roof
of our tent. A raven cawed

far off in the distance, a grunting
family of pigs scuttled past, charged

into the bushes,
our vista became splattering mud,

the phalanx of trees on the opposite bank
disappeared,

a hot bronze curtain met the river as vapour,
my fingers

penetrated your bushy hair,
pulled it up in tufts, squeezed the tension

out of your head,
to your quiet, grateful groans.

I untied the Gordian knots in your shoulders
with juniper oil,

pummelled your back
with my fists,

knuckle each vertebrae down to your coccyx,
knead your hard buttocks,

rub oil into your legs, bathe
your tired feet, squeeze

them until your tingles
shoot up my arm, I chew each toe

in turn until it is softened, bite
into your soles like a joint of pork,

you cannot help but giggle,
sir, I turn you over,

with my palms, rotate your temples, trace
the curves on your face, touching

yet not, three fingers inside your mouth, let you
suckle, baby,

from belly to breast, I massage
your chest

in concentric circles, pinch
your nipples, nibble gently, set my belly-dancer

tongue on to them, take your hands,
my love,

tie them above your head, with your belt,
I sit astride my steed,

take the reins, my flexible muscles
holding you in,

flexing like strong fists,
tighten and release,

teasing you, taming you, your eyes are shut,
you have died

and gone to Olympus, smiling,
I slap it off,

so hard my hand hurts,
your eyes shoot open like a dead man

dying,
I slap you again,

you feign amusement,
your eyes suggest *so this is slap and tickle*?

I take your riding crop, fold it,
lash your chest.

'Take that!' I hiss. 'How *dare* you humour me.
Who's the boss now?'

I ride you so hard I am becoming sore.
Forget

those stinking back-stabbers
in the senate in Rome, Severus,

those shit-stirrers, perfidious smilers,
has-beens, cunning

poisoners, ruthless young guns, arse-
lickers, mendacious gits,

wannabes – and your wife,
who won't play make-believe.

I know,
       Who?
       Who?
       Who?
       Who?

I demand with each merciless thrust.
'You *silly* girl,' you snicker, 'untie me now.'

I slap you again, but throw aside the whip,
for I have not the will, in truth,

to see you bleed.
'Outside!' I order, watch you struggle

to crawl
on your tied hands and knees, laughing

hysterically like a naughty child.
Is this so funny? I kick you hard in the ribs,

you collapse on your back,
when did anyone *ever* dare, my *imperator*?

I mount,
we are in mud, mud and more mud,

et caenum et caenum et plus caeni,
you are sprawled in it,

my legs have sunk
into it, my flattened hands

are imprinted on it,
rain pours down my back, over my head,

my nose, into my mouth, yours,
I gulp it in,

grab handfuls of mud, plaster your cheeks,
your chest,

in sludge,
you are helpless,

this is pure oestrus, sir,
we are mating

beasts,
with no history, no future

but my bloodline to continue.
I begin

riding my boy home.
'Who's the boss?'

He responds to my thrusts with such force
I almost fall off

him, he surges, he must surrender
before *I* break,

this friction will make me scream,
prematurely,

I stop, wait, letting his hardness
beg from inside, I act cold,

taunting.
'Don't stop now,' he panics.

'Who's the boss,' I repeat, folding my arms,
smirking.

'Please, Zuleika,'
'Say the magic words.'

'You are!'
'I am *what*?'

'You are –
my imperatrix, my canny dominatrix,

mistress of all you survey,'
he spews out,

a tad too arrogantly.
'Mmnn,' I reply,

'try saying it with more sincerity,
more humility, methinks.'

I move to get off him.
'No! You are boss,' he says urgently.

'Don't leave me now, come home
with me,

maman, take me home,'
he moans,

'take me home, maman,
I want to go home, home, home,'

please, Zuleika,
take me . . .'

I unbelt his hands,
his body spasms, he claws

my breasts with muddy fingers,
cries out, choking on a mouthful of rain,

he spumes
into me and we are all pulpa,

the swollen river
has become a torrent,

I hear it rushing past us,
*later we bathe in it, I dip*

your head
gently, rinse the mud from your curls,

rain showers us,
you clean my breasts

with wet hands,
make them shine again,

your weight holds out
against the current,

you hold me
so tight I do not fall,

we walk
back to the tent, me

leading you,
we dry each other off, gently,

with soft towels,
lie down together,

wrapped into ourselves,
our carriage is made of pure gold,

we sit on top of purple cushions,
this is our triumphal procession

into Rome.

Vivat Imperator Severus!
Vivat Imperator Severus!

Thousands are cheering
on the streets,

from windows, from the roofs of buildings,
hundreds of silver trumpets

are heralding your return,
after so long,

you have taken Scotland,
all the buildings and statues

are adorned,
with flowers and ribbons

wrapped around columns,
sandalwood burns in braziers,

the army is behind you,
dancers are ahead of you.

*Bellissima! Bellissima!*
they call out to your new bride.

We enter the Imperial Palace
on the Palatine Hill,

where we sleep
the sleep of newborns,

you hold me so tightly
I cannot move,

I am your life,
we will re-create each other,

we will call her
Claudia,

she will call you
Daddums.

I cannot hold out,
my body is erupting

like a volcano,
the sun inside me, lightning

striking me,
I am on fire,

I am riding a wave,
I grab the mud either side

to steady myself, but
it is slipping

through my fingers, I will
explode

into a billion fragments of sand,
into the rain, I throw

back my head
and howl.

X

# WHEN YOU LEAST EXPECT

Hands pressed down on my jugular.
I woke up, struggling to breathe, coughing,

the walls closed in, there was no air.
Wild-eyed, I quickly dressed, flung a veil

over my head, rushed outside, was sucked
towards the vortex of the town,

but the Temple was eerily silent.
Where was the drone of invocations?

Stalls were abandoned in the streets, braziers
left unchecked, goods hung unguarded

outside shops, doorways opened on to empty
workshops, ho hammers, no shouting,

yet the air hummed with activity, as if
they'd only just left. I hurriedly

turned into Lombard Street, hordes
were swaying towards the Forum, poured out

of alleys, swept into the swell of excited voices.
I tried to decipher the babble, no one would stop.

The bell of the Basilica began to resound
*Mortuus . . . in his sleep . . . Severus . . .*

The whirl of colour swam on without me –
shoals of fish around a rock.

# VALE, FAREWELL, MY LIBYAN

you
have
murdered me
you bastard

you have
died
at
York

# ALBATROSS

Requiescat in pace,
there is no more war, soldier.

I rock myself into night
which is day,
and day
which is night,

I rise,
the room is spinning and I am flying,

I have wings,
my span is great,
I take flight.

The sun is a gangrenous sore
oozing pus into the cesspit of the Thames;
when it has sunk
behind the mud flats of Southwark,
when I am indistinguishable from night,
I will swim to the ferryman,
sweet chariot of Charon,
coming for to carry me back
into oblivion,
to the waveless waters of my embryonic sac –
and as the waves make towards
the pebbled shore,
so will my minutes hasten towards my end,
leaving a crumpled pink frock,
and sling-backs.

## ANIMULA VAGULA
### (Little Soul Flitting Away)

*Please, I want to go to Hades.*
*Just put a coin in my mouth*
*and send me home to Daddy.*


My limbs rot inside my kid-leather curves,
dainty goatskin sandals lead me
across the cubiculum to my dresser,
my mind hobbles, my legs so light,
they defy gravity, almost.

A bone phoenix handle, a looking glass,
its wings hold up my silver polished world,
but I shift in and out of existence,
I cannot focus.

Hungry for air, my tissue absorbs my liquids.
Must breathe deeply
to survive; the stench of a decomposing corpse
is mine. My body accepts
the prison of bones, its decay.

I am only flesh and blood, Severus,
and you have staked my heart.

## DOMUM DULCE DOMUM
### (Home Sweet Home)

He sailed up the Thames, Felix the Great,
on a ship laden with amphorae of spices,

marble and fresh slaves from Palestine.
Severus had sent him to lead a trading

expedition to India, at the last minute,
he complained, RIP etc., but at his age

he was getting past all that gallivanting,
but wasn't he exsultatus to be home

with his so pulcherrima wife, especially
after all those beer-drinking Britannicos

on the east coast, stubbornly living
in mud huts and reeking of BO

as if they were still in the Bronze Age, I ask you.
'Londinium! You have grown on me,

as a child does on a parent,
after Roma, Neapolis, Alexandria,

Antioch, Carthage, Jerusalem –
you are the best city in the world!' he sang out,

flinging open the shutters on to the Walbrook
which passed to a sprinkle of rain below.

I noticed a full moon growing out
of his pudding-bowl haircut, and blue worms

wriggling in his even thinner calves.
He spun around: two more teeth had gone,

and the rest were a battered stone wall.
I *wanted* to smell juniper.

'Tonight we party!' He embraced me.
'Call Tranio! We will have jugglers,

acrobats, musicians, even poets, why not?
Invite the governor and all local notables

and right honourables, but first
to the baths in preparation for a feast

of culinary miracles and miraculous cunnilinctus.'
He winked, slapped my rump.

'My coming home present, mea delicia,'
then he disappeared outside

for a shit.

Valeria and Aemilia, my darling swine,
who could have predicted their betrayal?

You clothe and feed two stinking urchins
as if they were your own. You do *not* sell

them to a merchant from Europa
(for *plenty* baksheesh!). And your reward?

As soon as I left the house to go to Fish Street Hill
to select the choicest cod from the quay,

those evil-mongers poured poison into Felix's ears.
It was still morning when I returned, resolved

to put my desire on a boat and let it drown
in the infinite ocean surrounding our world.

As I walked in, those vixens rushed past me
without a glance or by-your-leave, ma'am.

And there stood Felix, facing Medusa, fisted
arms towards the sky as if in the denouement

of the ultima tragoedia.
'Husband?' I ventured, and he turned,

snarling like a rabid dog, and I realized
that on the perfumed bed of love

I had not cared about discovery
and in the torpor of my grief I had not thought

that my lover's protection would go with his life.
Felix asked no explanation, his mind

was as powerful as imperium and I
was some poor sod in a loincloth in Judaea.

'I, Felix Aurelius Lucius, created a lady
out of a sewer rat and your thanks?

I am the laughing stock of this town.
I trusted you and I have been *utterly* humiliated.'

I was banished to my cubiculum
and locked in.

# THE PRICE YOU PAY, MY BEAUTIFUL WIFE

Bread and cheese, baked eggs,
fish in spicy sauces; I pondered jumping

into the Walbrook, but where would I go?
Dad would as soon as kill me, I could

not involve the girls, for Felix would hunt
me down and make them pay, and to leave

the city wall was to risk unknown horrors.
Was my punishment to come?

A husband could do what he liked
and many an errant wife ended up

in an unmarked grave outside the city walls.
I did not scream, though, hammering

on the door for forgiveness,
but accepted what was due.

I had relished a death so sweet that nothing
would ever match it again;

nascentes morimur, from the moment
of being born, we die, after all.

I had lived my life.

# VADE IN PACE
## (Go in Peace)

When the door was unbolted,
my husband had gone, off to attend

the emperor's wake in York, Tranio said,
lowering his gaze. Had I paid my dues?

Those barbarian bitches had gone too.
This was ominous. Another week passed.

I was not allowed out of the house, I wandered
from room to room and only

when I was too weak to sit up did I find out
it was not despair sapping my energy

but arsenicum hidden in spicy sauces.
My home had become my mausoleum.

I asked for Alba and Venus: Tranio refused.
'I have my orders, miss.'

'Of course you owe *me* nothing. Not even a *wife*.
And by the way, it is madam to you.'

But I could not be angry with him, in truth.
Because he had not spilled the beans,

as he should have, he was implicated.
He had to survive. I was a goner anyway.

This time he followed Felix's instructions
as loyally as every good slave should.

What was it? So much each day, send word
when the little whore has snuffed it?

Another husband might have been proud
that the emperor had picked his wife

out of the millions queuing worldwide.
He will regret it, when he calms down,

after weeks, months, even years.
But he'll never be able to speak of it,

and it will rot like an incurable ulcer
festering inside his stomach.

It was the last days of summer, the sun
had become a faltering heart beat,

I lay down on a couch in the atrium,
I had lost the ability to walk.

I opened my eyes and saw Alba enter
through the main doorway. Alba.

Dear, dear Alba. She rushed over.
'Tranio sent for me. He's told me! The fuckwit!

I'll kill that grunting hog.
How long have you been like this?

No matter. Come, I'm taking you *with*.'
She tried to pull me up by my arms,

but I resisted. 'No, Alba. It's fate.'
'Oh, sod fucking fate, while we live, let us *live*!'

'No! It's too late now anyway.'
'I told you it would come to no good.

I will kill that grotesque bastard Felix. I *will*.'
Rage and sorrow competed to contort

the features on her face, neither winning.
'I'm dead anyway. Can't you see?

I was given life, then it was taken away,
the actual act of dying is mere procedure.

It's just breath now, a rain cloud on my chest,
and that's getting harder to push out.'

'Don't be so heroic, Zuleika. I can't stand it.'
'And don't be so dramatic, Alba.

This isn't a Greek tragoedia, though
it could be mistaken for one.'

'Life's so unfair, Zee.'
I was silent, then,

'Innit.'
'I can't imagine life without you.'

'Don't start whining. Just sit with me awhile,
and then go home, and remember me.'

It was all I allowed myself to think of now –
the first ten years, to remember

the married years, or the memory
of my euphoric summer of love,

felt like flinging myself atop a raging fire.
She sat down on the couch, held my hands,

tears flowing freely down cheeks brutalized
by bursting blood vessels.

'This shouldn't have happened, Zeeks.
This is unbearable, unbelievable, un –'

'You've been my *best* friend, Albs.'
'I know.'

'You're wonderful in spite of your faults.'
'I know.'

'What's going to become of you, eh?
You'll get VD one of these days. You can't

screw around for ever. You need to focus.'
'What, and end up like you?'

'Out of order, Albs. Bit below the purse-pouch.'
'Sorry, Zee! Sorry! Sorry! It's still sinking in.'

'There's no time for us to bicker. Answer me.'
'I'll be in search of more adventures, as usual.

I've me eye on someone, a lawyer this time.
I took V's hint. Omnipotent stallholders?'

She was completely beyond redemption, my Alba,
I hoped the gods would treat her gently.

'But this isn't about me, Zuleika, it's about you.'
'Which means it's about both of us.

Where is Venus the Penis?'
'Incommunicado. Can you believe it,

she's actually taken Big P to meet
her old boy and girl in deepest Camulodunum.

She'll be devastated. Absolutely gutted.'
'Tell her for me she's a silly old tart,

that I hope they're very happy together,
and have lots of hermaphrodite kiddies

with ginger dreadlocks and hendecasyllables
pouring out of their freckled little arses.'

'I will.' Her expression read – how can you
be funny at a time like this? How could I not?

I'd gone from my zenith to my nadir,
all in two short weeks. It was hysterical.

'Felix isn't a bad man, you know.
He's the person he was brought up to be,

like all of us, even Venus, except
he did it with less imagination than most.

The only original thing he did was to wed
below his class, even then he hid me away.

He never knew me, you know, never knew
the wild child who would want more,

never once asked, "What do *you* want?"'
'Zuleika, don't make excuses for that gargoyle.'

*There are drops of clarity,*
*Poison does that to you.*
*Imminent death allows the birth*
*Of new perspectives.*
*When there is nothing left to lose,*
*For everything is lost,*
*Truth is a most welcome friend.*

That's my swan song, I think
it's the only decent thing I've ever written.

I've called it "Mors Certa, Hora Incerta",
"Death Certain, Hour Uncertain".

Was I a plaything for Severus, do you think?'
It had been bugging me. The refrain.

'What? With all the attention he paid you?
Trips out, treats, quality time alone? *Hardly!*'

'You're right. I was of great comfort to him,
and vicky versa. Will you bury me, Alba?

You know Felix has no intention, nor The Pops.'
'Don't be so morbid.'

'I'm being pragmatic. Felix will chuck me out
as carrion, with a banner above my head:

*I curse Zuleika and her life and mind*
*and memory and liver and lungs mixed up*
*together; thus may she be condemned*
*to pouring water into bottomless jars for ever.*

Will you do it?'
'You know I will. 'Course I will.'

'Dress me in my violet damask dalmatica
with gold thread, it's laid out on my bed.

Severus sent for the material from the best
workshop in Syria, got a one-off made for me.

I wonder if they recognize designer labels
where I'm going? Get my hair

done in beautiful elaborate braids. Marcia'll do it,
she's head stylist at Kinky Girls on Cornhill.

I want a pillow of the sweetest smelling
bay leaves and a scallop-shell design

on the lid of my coffin so that my journey
is safe, oh, and don't forget my jet afro pick,

tweezers and especially my nail file –
I don't want to look a state when I arrive.

Can you imagine, gorgon's nails
and matted hair. Got that?'

'Right you are, ma'am,' she said, saluting.
'And I want to be buried at the cemetery

in Spitalfields, not some nondescript
out-of-town site for the plebs, get the money

off Cato or Venus. And last but not least,
a tombstone, with this inscription:

*To the spirits of the departed*
*And the memory of our pal Zuleika,*
*Who in her final summer*
*Lived a life fuller than any other.'*

We sat there. Words? What words?
'I wanted to be important, Albs.'

'You're important to me. We're sisters.'
'That's not the same, though, is it?

I wanted to be a great poet or mosaicist
or something. I'd have made a good empress.'

'The best!'
'It was all that bloody schooling that did it.

Theodorus going on about the greats for years
made me want to be a great myself.

Now it's too late. I'm still only eighteen.
It's my nineteenth birthday next week.

Light a candle for me. Now go home!
Your miserable face is making this worse.

*Go home.'*

EPILOGUE

# VIVAT ZULEIKA

It is you I have found to wear, Zuleika,
lying in a panel of summer,
your golden couch moved into the atrium
to feed your skin, for the last time.

I enter quietly from Watling Court,
the pounding bass and horns of the City's
square mile, suspended. Between
two columns, your couch faces a pool

fed by the aching stone mouth of Medusa.
A cloud chills you in its shadow
of passing – Zuleika moritura est.
Now is the time. I glide to where you lie,

look upon your pink robes, ruched,
décolleté, a mild stir with each tired breath,
pronounced mould of your face, obsidian
with light and sweat, so tranquilla

in your moment of leaving. I slip
into your skin, our chest stills, drains
to charcoal. You have expired, Zuleika,
and I will know you, from the inside.

# ACKNOWLEDGEMENTS

My heartfelt thanks to my editor Simon Prosser for his enthusiasm and meticulous editing, and to Donna Poppy, Keith Taylor, Amelia Fairney and the team at Penguin; my dynamic agent Hannah Griffiths at Curtis Brown; my tour manager Melanie Abrahams of Renaissance One; the Museum of London, especially Chandan Mahal and the Interpretation Unit, and the curator Jenny Hall; the Poetry Society for funding my residency at the museum; the Arts Council of England for my Writers Award 2000; the British Council Literature Department for opportunities to tour abroad; the following people for acts of support: Ruth Borthwick, Colin Channer, Kwame Dawes, Catriona Ferguson, Brendan Griggs, Mel Jennings, Helen Swords and Jacob Ross; and to Patricia St Hilaire and Victoria Evaristo for keeping me sane(r) with endless telephone conversations; and to the historian Peter Fryer, author of the truly groundbreaking book *Staying Power: The History of Black People in Britain*, where I first learnt that Africans had lived in Britain during the Roman occupation nearly eighteen hundred years ago.

## PENGUIN ESSENTIALS

SWALLOWING GEOGRAPHY/DEBORAH LEVY

Like her namesake Jack Kerouac, J.K. is always on the road, travelling Europe with her typewriter in a pillowcase. From J.K.'s irreverent, ironic perspective, Levy charts a new, dizzying, end-of-the-century world of shifting boundaries and displaced peoples.

'An exciting writer, sharp and shocking as the knives her characters wield' *Sunday Times*

THE BASTARD OF ISTANBUL/ELIF SHAFAK

*One rainy afternoon in Istanbul, a nineteen-year-old, unmarried woman walks into a doctor's surgery. 'I need to have an abortion,' she announces.*

Twenty years later, Asya Kazanci lives with her extended family in Istanbul. All the Kazanci men die in their early forties, victims of the mysterious family curse, so it is a house of women. Among them are Asya's beautiful, rebellious mother, her clairvoyant aunt, and their hopelessly hypochondriac sister. Into the midst for this madhouse comes Asya's feisty American cousin, and she's bringing long-hidden family secrets connected with Turkey's turbulent past in her wake. . .

'A beautiful book, the finest I've read' *Irish Times*

## PENGUIN ESSENTIALS

### THE ROTTERS' CLUB/JONATHAN COE

'*Sometimes I feel that I am destined always to be offstage whenever the main action occurs. That God has made me the victim of some cosmic practical joke, by assigning me little more than a walk-on part in my own life . . .*'

Coming of age in 1970s' Birmingham, teenager Benjamin Trotter is about to discover the agonies and ecstasies of growing up. Whether it is first love or last rites, IRA bombs or industrial strife, prog versus punk rock, expectations of bad poetry or an unexpected life-changing experience involving lost swimming trunks, *The Rotters' Club* is a heartfelt and hilarious portrait of a particular time and place featuring characters recognizable the world over . . .

'Very funny, a compulsive and gripping read' *The Times*

### THE PHOTOGRAPH/PENELOPE LIVELY

'*DO NOT OPEN - DESTROY.*'

The words on the envelope he has found are written in Kath's hand, but Glyn ignores his wife's instruction and breaks the seal. His life unwinds. For he finds a photograph showing Kath holding hands with another man. Unable to forget this long-ago act of betrayal he recklessly excavates the past, seeking out who knew what, tearing apart other lives as he tries to dig up the roots of his wife's infidelity. But what is the truth about Kath? What is the truth about their love? And can it survive this?

'Remarkable' *Sunday Telegraph*

## PENGUIN ESSENTIALS

## LIFE CLASS/PAT BARKER

'You were not allowed to talk in the life class . . .'

It is spring, 1914, and Paul Tarrant and Elinor Brooke are students at the Slade School of Art, gathering for life-drawing classes under the tutelage of Henry Tonks. Each finds this select new world difficult and they seek solace in one another. Yet just as they are beginning to admit their feelings towards each other war breaks out and Paul joins the Belgian Red Cross. At Ypres he experiences devastation so extraordinary that he wonders if he can ever convey it to another soul . . .

'Triumphant, shattering, inspiring' *The Times*

## BEAUTIFUL RUINS/JESS WALTER

'The actress arrived in his village the only way one could come directly . . .'

In spring 1962 American actress Dee Moray's boat motors into an Italian bay and the life of hotelier Pasquale Tursi. Dee - fleeing a film set, claiming to be dying and desperately awaiting her lover - throws herself on Pasquale's generous mercy. Fifty years later Pasquale lands in Hollywood, sporting a fedora and seeking a long-forgotten actress. Why he's come, what happened to Dee in Italy and, later, in LA, are questions that *Beautiful Ruins* answers in the most surprising and wonderfully entertaining manner.

'Exhilarating. Very, very funny' *The Times*